Analyzing
911
Homicide Calls

Practical Aspects and Applications

CRC SERIES IN
**PRACTICAL ASPECTS OF CRIMINAL
AND FORENSIC INVESTIGATIONS**

VERNON J. GEBERTH, BBA, MPS, FBINA *Series Editor*

Practical Homicide Investigation: Tactics, Procedures, and
Forensic Techniques, Fifth Edition
Vernon J. Geberth

Practical Homicide Investigation Checklist and Field Guide,
Second Edition
Vernon J. Geberth

Analyzing 911 Homicide Calls: Practical Aspects and Applications
Tracy Harpster and Susan H. Adams

Practical Aspects of Rape Investigation: A Multidisciplinary Approach,
Fifth Edition
Robert R. Hazelwood and Ann Wolbert Burgess

Munchausen by Proxy and Other Factitious Abuse: Practical and
Forensic Investigative Techniques
Robert R. Hazelwood and Ann Wolbert Burgess

Practical Analysis and Reconstruction of Shooting Incidents,
Second Edition
Edward E. Hueske

Gunshot Wounds: Practical Aspects of Firearms, Ballistics,
and Forensic Techniques, Third Edition
Vincent J. M. DiMaio

Informants, Cooperating Witnesses, and Undercover Investigations:
A Practical Guide to Law, Policy, and Procedure, Second Edition
Dennis G. Fitzgerald

Practical Military Ordnance Identification
Tom Gersbeck

Practical Cold Case Homicide Investigations Procedural Manual
Richard H. Walton

Autoerotic Deaths: Practical Forensic and Investigative Perspectives
Anny Sauvageau and Vernon J. Geberth

Practical Crime Scene Processing and Investigation, Second Edition
Ross M. Gardner

Practical Criminal Investigations in Correctional Facilities
William R. Bell

Practical Aspects of Interview and Interrogation, Second Edition
David E. Zulawski and Douglas E. Wicklander

Forensic Pathology, Second Edition
Dominick J. DiMaio and Vincent J. M. DiMaio

The Practical Methodology of Forensic Photography, Second Edition
David R. Redsicker

Quantitative-Qualitative Friction Ridge Analysis: An Introduction to Basic and Advanced Ridgeology
David R. Ashbaugh

Footwear Impression Evidence: Detection, Recovery, and Examination, Second Edition
William J. Bodziak

The Sexual Exploitation of Children: A Practical Guide to Assessment, Investigation, and Intervention, Second Edition
Seth L. Goldstein

Practical Aspects of Munchausen by Proxy and Munchausen Syndrome Investigation
Kathryn Artingstall

Practical Fire and Arson Investigation, Second Edition
David R. Redsicker and John J. O'Connor

Interpretation of Bloodstain Evidence at Crime Scenes, Second Edition
William G. Eckert and Stuart H. James

Investigating Computer Crime
Franklin Clark and Ken Diliberto

Practical Investigation Techniques
Kevin B. Kinnee

Friction Ridge Skin: Comparison and Identification of Fingerprints
James F. Cowger

Tire Imprint Evidence
Peter McDonald

Practical Gambling Investigation Techniques
Kevin B. Kinnee

Analyzing
911
Homicide Calls

Practical Aspects and Applications

Tracy Harpster | **Susan H. Adams**

CRC Press
Taylor & Francis Group
Boca Raton London New York

CRC Press is an imprint of the
Taylor & Francis Group, an **informa** business

CRC Press
Taylor & Francis Group
6000 Broken Sound Parkway NW, Suite 300
Boca Raton, FL 33487-2742

International Standard Book Number-13: 978-1-4987-3455-4 (Hardback)

Library of Congress Cataloging-in-Publication Data

Names: Harpster, Tracy, author. | Adams, Susan H., author.
Title: Analyzing 911 homicide calls : practical aspects and applications / by
Tracy Harpster and Susan H. Adams.
Description: 1 Edition. | Boca Raton : CRC Press, 2017. | Includes
bibliographical references and index.
Identifiers: LCCN 2016026647 | ISBN 9781498734554 (hardback : alk. paper) |
ISBN 9781315386508 (ebook)
Subjects: LCSH: Homicide investigation. | Telephone--Emergency reporting systems.
Classification: LCC HV8079.H6 H367 2016 | DDC 363.25/9523--dc23
LC record available at https://lccn.loc.gov/2016026647

Visit the Taylor & Francis Web site at
http://www.taylorandfrancis.com

and the CRC Press Web site at
http://www.crcpress.com

This book is dedicated to the victims of homicide and to their families.

It is written in the hope that law enforcement professionals will use our research to obtain justice for victims and peace for their families.

Contents

Section V
INDEPENDENT GUILTY INDICATORS

Section IX
CASE STUDIES

Editor's Note

This textbook is part of a series titled "Practical Aspects of Criminal and Forensic Investigation." This series was created by Vernon J. Geberth, a retired New York City Police Department lieutenant commander who is an author, educator, and consultant on homicide and forensic investigations.

This series has been designed to provide contemporary, comprehensive, and pragmatic information to the practitioner involved in criminal and forensic investigations by authors who are nationally recognized experts in their respective fields.

Forewords

Most homicide investigations begin with the same question, "911, what is your emergency?" What is said in the next few moments can have a profound impact on the course of the investigation. Could the person calling 911 actually be the killer you're looking for?

I first learned about the work of Deputy Chief Harpster and Dr. Adams while attending a course for homicide investigators. The instructor mentioned hearing about research that had been published on analyzing unique aspects of 911 calls. At the conclusion of the course, I immediately located and read the published work. I contacted the authors because I had an unresolved homicide with a 911 call made by the victim's wife. I sent the authors a recording and transcript of the 911 call with no other details of the case. They walked me through the call, pointing out critical clues that I had missed.

I've since learned about the indicators of guilt and innocence that exist within 911 calls. I've learned that innocent 911 callers convey information, while guilty callers may try to convince the dispatcher of their "story." Now when I'm called out for a homicide, I listen to the 911 call on the way to the scene before conducting any interviews.

If you are a homicide investigator reading this book, I can assure you that from now on you will analyze every 911 call reporting a death.

As for my unresolved case, the wife who called 911 has since been convicted of the very homicide she reported. She is serving life in prison.

Detective M. H.
Florida

I was called out to investigate a homicide death of a victim who had been repeatedly stabbed. I arrived at the victim's residence and met with the street officers who were questioning a male suspect. The suspect denied involvement in the crime; however, I was highly suspicious of him due to the fact that he had blood on his clothing, face, and hands and was in possession of a bloody knife. I noted that he had attempted to clean himself after he called 911 to report the crime, and he had attempted to hide his bloody clothes in his pickup truck. A quick background check revealed an extensive criminal history for meth distribution, and we immediately began to focus our investigation on this individual.

The suspect was transported to the police department for a formal interview while the crime scene was processed. Having attended Deputy Chief Harpster and Dr. Adams' 911 Homicide Analysis training in Cheyenne, Wyoming, one day earlier, I knew the importance of reviewing the 911 call in all death cases.

I quickly obtained an audio of the 911 call and examined it before I interviewed the caller, as I had just been taught. I noted that the caller had numerous innocent clues throughout the call. He immediately asked for help for the victim and focused on getting an ambulance to the scene. The caller had urgency in his voice and shared relevant information with the dispatcher. The caller had voice modulation and expressed fear for the safety of the victim and himself. I saw no guilty indicators in the suspect's call. I was confused by the innocent 911 call indicators because the information at the crime scene and the suspect's behavior clearly pointed to him as the suspect.

During the interview, the caller advised that he became covered in the victim's blood while giving him medical aid and CPR. He explained that the blood on his knife was due to the fact that he had armed himself, fearing for his own safety after he had attended to the victim.

At the beginning of the investigation, I was very skeptical of the suspect's account. However, after analyzing the 911 call and interviewing the suspect, I was confident the caller was not the killer. Later in the investigation, we recovered evidence that proved the caller's innocence. The real killer has since been arrested and has confessed to the murder.

Detective Sergeant Robert G. Terry
Wyoming

Authors' Note

To Our Readers,

The journey of studying 911 homicide calls has been filled with twists and turns. Homicides looked like accidents, and accidents looked like homicides. Gruesome scenes were actually medical events, and reported suicides were carefully staged murders. Children called 911 to save parents' lives, and parents called 911 after fatally shaking their children. Some spouses killed their mates, and other spouses tried desperately to save their mates.

The more we learned, the more we realized that every call is unique and worthy of study. Each call offered us additional tools to help uncover the truth. This book is the result of analyzing more than 1000 homicide calls over a 12-year period. The insight we offer in these chapters comes from cases with clear adjudications.

It is our hope that the material in this book will point readers toward the truth to help solve cases. With open minds, we can all continue the journey of learning what the 911 calls are telling us.

Acknowledgments

The authors would like to thank the following individuals who made major contributions to this book:

Detective Dole Burke, Dayton, Ohio Police Homicide/Warren County
    Coroner's Office
Captain Chris Fenerty, Retired, Exeter, New Hampshire Police
    Department
Vernon Geberth, NYPD, Retired P.H.I. Investigative Consultants, Inc.
Chief Deputy Coroner Sharon Green, Vernon Parish, Louisiana
    Coroner's Office
John Hess, Retired FBI Special Agent
Captain Kyle Marquart, Missouri State Patrol
Net Transcripts, Inc.
Aaron Vietor, City of Moraine, Ohio

We are also indebted to the many investigators who shared their cases and their insight with us and to our families who supported us.

Note: All 911 calls used to illustrate points throughout the book are from actual calls in death cases. The authors provided assistance in most of these cases and have changed the names to protect the identities of the victims and callers.

Introduction   I

The Critical Value
of 911 Call Analysis

1

"Truth will come to light. Murder cannot be hid long."
William Shakespeare

Homicide calls to 911 centers are unique. They originate from distressed callers confronted with urgent life-and-death situations. These initial phone contacts contain invaluable statements for they are (1) least edited by suspects' attempts to conceal the truth; (2) untainted, as later statements can be, by attorneys' coaching or counsel to remain silent; and (3) free of contamination from interviewers' verbal and nonverbal behavior. In fact, 911 calls are often the only pure statements of the entire investigation.

To ensure that the 911 call is as pristine as possible, skilled dispatchers go beyond the open-ended question, *"911, what is your emergency?"* and follow up with, *"What happened?"* The callers therefore choose where to begin the narrative and what to include in it without leading questions from dispatchers. This freedom of choice provides insight to the callers' focus.

The voluntariness of 911 calls increases their investigative value. Callers initiate the conversations, thus removing any questions regarding coercion. Callers under great emotional stress often give more information than intended. This spontaneous information can provide critical case leads by revealing details of events preceding the deaths, such as altercations or threats, and about the deaths themselves. The callers' voluntary words may reveal the true motive for the homicides.

A key advantage of 911 statements is that the dialogue is recorded, allowing investigators to analyze callers' voice tone, volume, pace, and pitch. The location and duration of pauses in the conversation provide further clues to the callers' focus.

A study of offenders in the state of Washington revealed that 19% of all homicide cases begin as 911 calls made by the offenders posing as innocent callers (Keppel, unpublished). It is likely that the actual number is much higher because the study only examined adjudicated homicide cases. Many homicides are not adjudicated because they are incorrectly declared to be suicides, missing persons cases, drug overdoses, or accidents, and these cases were not examined in the Washington study.

There are several reasons why homicide offenders call 911. If the murder occurred in the offender's home, the presence of the victim's body creates a problem. Because the phases of decomposition—temperature change, rigor, and lividity—begin immediately (Geberth, 2015), the offender must call 911 as soon as possible. Any delay would be obvious and something an innocent caller would not do. Consider the situation of a man babysitting his girl-friend's infant. The boyfriend would implicate himself if he delayed calling 911 long enough for the responding officers to find the baby in full rigor.

Another reason why guilty callers report their homicides, without confessing, is that many offenders had a relationship with their victims. These parents, spouses, and significant others would therefore be likely to notice the victims' deaths, and it would be unusual if they did not place the 911 calls. FBI crime reports reveal that in homicide cases when the rela-tionship between homicide offenders and victims was known, over 50% of the homicides were committed by family members or other acquaintances (FBI.gov, 2014). With this fact in mind, the value of analyzing 911 calls increases considerably.

Dispatchers, officers, and prosecutors trained in 911 analysis can gain vital insight about the callers. Trained dispatchers will be alert for clues of innocence and guilt, and they can send 911 calls to responding officers' mobile devices. With the knowledge gained from hearing both innocent callers and guilty callers, officers gain critical information to ensure officer safety at the scene and initiate thorough investigations. Officers trained in 911 analysis can identify investigative leads and relevant topics for productive interviews. Prosecutors skilled in the value of analyzing 911 calls can enlighten the jury in the opening and closing portions of the trial. If defendants take the stand, prosecutors can use the defendants' own words against them. If the callers are innocent, statements in their 911 calls can help exonerate them.

In many cases, the 911 call is the only statement an individual ever makes to law enforcement. An offender who calls 911 might demand an attorney or refuse to be interviewed. Too often, this essential evidence is overlooked dur-ing the course of the investigation and prosecution. A 911 call is similar to a crime scene; there is a unique opportunity at the outset to garner evidence about circumstances surrounding the homicide that might otherwise be lost.

Armed with insight from a structured approach to 911 analysis, dis-patchers, investigating officers, and prosecutors gain a clearer picture of the caller and the crime. The analysis of 911 calls offers a key for unlocking the truth in homicide cases.

The 911 Study

The authors analyzed 200 adjudicated death investigation 911 calls to examine indicators that might differentiate innocent from guilty callers. The current 911 study is expanded from previous research that examined a different data set of 100 adjudicated 911 homicide and death calls, with analysis by the same authors (Harpster, 2006; Adams and Harpster, 2008; Harpster et al., 2009).

In the current study, half of the callers were determined to be innocent of homicide and half were found by adjudication to be guilty. Innocent callers were defined as those who had no involvement in the crime. Guilty callers were those who either committed the homicide themselves or had a role in the crime or the cover-up. The authors listened to audio recordings of each call and reviewed all transcriptions for accuracy before examining the attributes of the calls. Ages of the callers ranged from 3 to over 70 years; victims ranged from newborns to individuals in their 80s. Callers and victims were male and female, and of African-American, Asian, Caucasian, and Latino descent.

The specific differences between innocent and guilty callers in the 911 study will be described throughout the following chapters and scored on a COPS Scale© (Considering Offender Probability in Statements), as seen in Figure 1.1. When analyzing 911 calls, all indicators that appear in the calls are scored with a check mark on the COPS Scale©. For any indicators that do not apply, "n/a" is circled on the COPS Scale©. No single indicator can determine innocence or guilt, but a majority of checks on the innocent or guilty side of the COPS Scale© inform investigators that the pattern of indicators is consistent with innocent or guilty calls in the 911 study.

911 COPS Scale ©

Considering Offender Probability in Statements

Place a check mark for any indicator that applies or circle n/a for not applicable

Innocent Indicators		Guilty Indicators

WHO is the call about?

Innocent	n/a	Guilty
Immediate Plea for Help for Victim ___	n/a	___ No Immediate Plea for Help for Victim
Immediate Assessment of Victim ___	n/a	___ No Immediate Assessment of Victim
Focus on Victim ___	n/a	___ Focus on Caller
No Acceptance of Victim's Death ___	n/a	___ Acceptance of Victim's Death
Aid Provided to Victim ___	n/a	___ No Aid Provided to Victim

WHAT is the call about?

Innocent	n/a	Guilty
Relevant Information ___	n/a	___ Extraneous Information
Sensory Details ___	n/a	___ Lack of Sensory Details
Prioritized Order ___	n/a	___ Inappropriate Order
Bleeding Comments ___	n/a	___ Blood/Brains Comments

HOW is the call made?

Innocent	n/a	Guilty
Urgency ___	n/a	___ No Urgency
Fear for Caller's Safety ___	n/a	___ No Fear for Caller's Safety
Proximity to Victim ___	n/a	___ No Proximity to Victim
Initial Sounds or Comments ___	n/a	___ Initial Delays

Aggressive Demands ___   n/a   Passive Defenses:

___ Defendant Mentality   ___ Ingratiating Remarks
___ Insults or Blames Victim ___ Mental Miscues
___ Minimizes

Cooperation with Dispatcher ___   n/a   Resistance to Dispatcher:

___ Dispatcher Confusion   ___ Diversion ___ Equivocation
___ Evasion ___ Hangs Up ___ Only Answers What's Asked
___ Pauses ___ Repetition ___ Self-Interruption
___ Short Answers   ___ Unintelligible Comments

Additional Guilty Indicators:

___ Attempts to Convince ___ Awkward Phrases   ___ Conflicting Facts ___ "Huh?" Factor ___ I Don't Know
___ Isolated "Please"   ___ Lack of Contractions ___ No Modulation   ___ Unexplained Knowledge

Deputy Chief Tracy Harpster (Tracy.Harpster@gmail.com) **and Susan H. Adams, Ph.D.**

Figure 1.1   COPS Scale©.

References

Adams, S., and Harpster, T. (2008), "911 Homicide Calls and Statement Analysis: Is the Caller the Killer?" *Law Enforcement Bulletin*.

FBI.gov (2014), Expanded Homicide Data Table 10. https://www.fbi.gov/about-us /cjis/ucr/crime-in-the-u.s/2014/crime-in-the-u.s.-2014/tables/expanded-homi cide-data/expanded_homicide_data_table_10_murder_circumstances_by _relationship_2014.xls

Geberth, V. J. (2015), *Practical Homicide Investigation: Tactics, Procedures and Forensic Techniques*, 5th Edition, CRC Press, Boca Raton, Florida.

Harpster, T. (2006), "The Nature of 911 Homicide Calls: Using 911 Homicide Calls to Identify Indicators of Innocence and Guilt," OhioLINK.

Harpster, T., Adams, S., and Jarvis, J. (2009), "Analyzing 911 Homicide Calls for Indicators of Guilt or Innocence: An Exploratory Analysis," *Homicide Studies*, 13: 69–93.

Keppel, R. Unpublished research study, Seattle University, Seattle, Washington.

Case Study: Mr. and Mrs. Hunt

2

It rang twice before Dispatcher Davis picked up the line and asked the same question she had asked a hundred times that day, *"911, what is your emergency?"*

A voice responded, *"I just got to my in-laws house, they didn't come to church this morning and my wife and I were worried...I found them in the—there's been a break-in, I think!"* The caller was talking so fast that the words ran together. The dispatcher couldn't even tell if the caller was a woman or a man because the voice was so high pitched.

"Slow down—I can't understand you," Dispatcher Davis responded.

The caller yelled into the phone, *"Somebody broke in and tore up their house. There is stuff everywhere. My wife's parents are dead!"*

Dispatcher Davis, stunned for a second, wasn't processing what she just heard. Her heart began to race as she stuttered, *"Did...did you say somebody is dead? Who is dead?"* she asked.

"Please, oh my God...please!" the caller sobbed. There was a short pause before the dispatcher regained her bearings. Her training and experience kicked in and she took control.

The caller screamed, *"Someone broke in!"*

"Give me your address," Dispatcher Davis barked. The call came in on a cell phone and she had no idea where to send the officers. As she typed the call information into her computer, Dispatcher Davis tried to focus. *"What happened to them, sir?"*

"Oh my God, oh my God, oh my God!" came the reply.

Dispatcher Davis knew from her training that if she lowered her voice and sounded composed, she could help calm down the caller. However, she was rattled herself and commanded, *"Sir, what is your address, give me your address right now, sir,"* much louder than she had intended.

Her words sounded more like a yell than a calming tactic, but they redirected the caller. *"It's East Kennedy Street...2322 East Kennedy Street."*

As Dispatcher Davis typed out the call to the street officers' cruiser computers, she instructed the caller, *"OK, hold on a second."* The caller stayed on the line, waiting until the street officers radioed that they were en route to the scene.

Turning her attention back to the caller, Dispatcher Davis asked, *"Sir, what's your name?"*

"My name is...Jake."

"Jake, are you sure it's too late? Do you want me to help you with CPR?"

This time there was no pause after her question as the caller immediately responded, *"There is blood everywhere...it's all over the floor."*

The thought of blood snapped Dispatcher Davis into rescue mode and she directed Jake to assess his in-laws' condition. *"Can you check for pulses?"*

Jake cried, *"I don't want to move them."*

Still concerned about the victims, Dispatcher Davis asked, *"Jake, was this an accident or did somebody hurt them?"*

Jake cried into the phone, *"This was not an accident!"*

Fighting a sudden wave of emotion, Dispatcher Davis redirected, *"Are you sure they're both gone, are they breathing...do they have pulses?"*

"Oh my God, oh my God, oh my God...what am I going to do?" Jake wailed. *"Help me."*

Dispatcher Davis again tried to calm Jake down. *"Take deep breaths, Jake. Help is on the way. Are you hurt?"*

"Huh?" he responded.

"Does it look like someone broke in?" Dispatcher Davis struggled to think clearly.

"I don't know what's going on here!" Jake cried.

Fearing for Jake's safety, Dispatcher Davis directed him to move away from the scene. *"Jake, go outside and wait there for the police."*

"I am outside. I'm in the driveway...there is blood all over the floor!"

Dispatcher Davis wished the officers could speed it up. It felt like it was taking forever for them to arrive, but she knew they were doing all they could to respond as quickly as possible. The ambulance was still a few minutes away when she heard the officer's sirens over Jake's phone. She knew they were getting close now. *"You're doing a great job, Jake. They're almost there."*

As the sirens grew louder, Jake responded, *"I can see them...here they are."*

"OK, Jake you can hang up now." Dispatcher Davis was acutely aware that Jake remained on the phone. She could hear the first officer on the scene yelling for Jake to get his hands up. Dispatcher Davis slowly clicked her computer screen, ending the call.

As she heard the radio traffic of other officers and medics arriving on scene, Dispatcher Davis realized that she did not know what happened to the victims. She wondered whether they had a bad accident, they committed suicide, or they were murdered. Something seemed wrong, yet, Jake did sound like a man in agony over the death of his wife's parents.

Just then the phone rang again and Dispatcher Davis answered, *"911, what is your emergency?"*

The caller yelled, *"Get over here NOW!! Some idiot just stole my kid's bike! It's a green 10-speed Schwinn and it's brand fucking new! HURRY!"*

* * *

Officer Latessa was the first to pull into the victim's complex. Dispatcher Davis had relayed that a screaming caller reported that two people were dead, but she didn't have much more information. One dead person could mean all sorts of things: a medical event, an overdose, an accident, a suicide, a homicide. But two dead people probably meant murder.

Officer Latessa's mind was racing as he parked his cruiser three houses from the victims' address. If this was a homicide, the killer could still be in the vicinity. His hand was on the grip of his Colt .45 as he stepped out of the car. He held back for just a second until he saw his backup pulling in around the corner. He recognized the officer in his backup's cruiser immediately—it was his best friend, Officer Hamilton. The two officers had worked together for years and were inseparable on and off duty.

Quickly scanning the scene, Officer Latessa saw a crying man standing on the front porch of the house. *"Get your hands up!"* he yelled, pointing his .45 toward the subject in the ready position.

The officers carefully approached Jake who was babbling incoherently. Officer Hamilton kept his gun in the ready position as Officer Latessa patted down Jake for weapons. The cops had no idea what had happened or who the suspects might be and they were taking no chances. They questioned Jake but could make no sense of his words through his sobbing. Officer Lewis arrived on scene next and since he only had a year on the force he was told to stay with Jake, try to get him to calm down, and get some sort of story from him. The young officer asked Jake what had happened, but all he could make out through the witness's sobbing was that he "had just come from church and found his in-laws dead inside" and that he immediately called his wife and 911.

After slowly approaching the open front door, the officers entered the house with their guns drawn. As they cautiously walked inside, they were both shocked when they saw an elderly female on the living room floor, in a pool of blood. She was lying on her back, approximately eight feet from the doorway. As they crept closer, their shoes started to stick to the floor. The carpet was so saturated with congealing blood that it was bonding to the bottoms of their shoes and it unnerved them both.

While he tried to process what his eyes were telling him, Officer Latessa saw something sticking out of the female's chest. He inched closer and saw that it was a three-inch, gold crucifix. It was protruding from her chest, but most of the blood was around her head and shoulders. Officer Latessa looked past her and saw her husband. He was about twenty feet beyond his wife, near the hallway, and he also had a crucifix sticking out of his chest. Although they were both experienced, tough cops, the officers were repulsed by the scene. It felt like they had stepped into a horror movie. Officer Hamilton smelled a strange metallic odor and he didn't like it. *"What's that damn smell?"* he whispered to his partner.

"It's the blood," his partner whispered back. For months, Officer Hamilton would talk about that horrific metallic smell from the iron in all that blood.

Immediately securing the house to make sure the killer was not still in the home, the officers scanned and searched each room as a team. Once they were certain that the house was cleared, they turned their attention to the victims.

The female's hair was matted with blood and covered most of her face. Officer Latessa holstered his gun and reached back to pull rubber gloves from his belt pocket. Pushing the hair and dried blood aside, he searched in vain for a carotid pulse. Leaning over with his ear to her mouth, he heard nothing and saw no rising chest movement.

The officers now focused on the male who was sprawled out on his back with blood crusted on his forehead and chin. They noticed little, yellow squares on the carpet but didn't recognize them as broken teeth until after they had stepped on them. Both officers were amazed at the cast off blood that tracked up the wall.

As he reached for the husband's pulse, Officer Hamilton felt something drop onto his shoulder. It was a clump of blood and tissue that had made it all the way to the ceiling. The officers looked up to see more tissue hanging precariously above them. Officer Hamilton almost vomited but completed his job, finding no pulse.

The officers began to examine the scene and take notes. The evidence technicians would be responsible for photographing, collecting evidence, and printing the scene, but it was the first responders' job to record the initial details of the scene. The officers knew that the bosses would eventually show up, and both of them had dreams of becoming detectives. Screwing up this scene could be costly. Officer Hamilton leaned over to examine the male more closely but looked up just in time to see another bloody clump about to drip down from the ceiling and thought better of it.

The medics arrived and assessed the victims, determined they were deceased, and left without disturbing the scene. As the evidence technicians and sergeants pulled up, Officer Lewis watched the commotion and wanted to peek inside. However, he remained outside with Jake not willing to get yelled at by the Sarge who was walking past him, into the house.

It was a Sunday, so it took the detectives longer than usual to get to the scene, as they were all home watching football. The first two detectives who arrived at the house were met by Officer Lewis, who introduced them to the still sobbing Jake. They spoke to Jake briefly and then met with the second detective team who had just pulled up to the scene. All of the detectives went into the home and met with the patrol officers. The senior detective, taking control of the crime scene, scanned the room and the victims, and asked, *"Officer Latessa, tell me about the killer, from what you see here."*

This was Officer Latessa's moment to impress those he hoped would be his future teammates. *"I think it's one of those cult murders…look at the crosses sticking out of their chests. I think the killers are Satan Worshipers."* Officer Latessa had attended a satanic cult seminar in Philadelphia last year, and he finally was able to use what he learned at the conference. As usual, Officer Hamilton was impressed with his buddy and nodded his head in agreement.

The detective was a seasoned investigator. He knew the victims were struck numerous times just by the cast-off marks on the wall. He knew they had been dead for at least four hours because of the rigor. He also knew they had not been moved because of the lividity, and he knew very well not to step on the teeth and the blood at the scene. Further, he knew that this was not a cult murder. However, what he did not know was who had committed the murder or why. No one from the three law enforcement groups (the dispatcher, the street officers, the investigators) understood the critical importance of analyzing the 911 call…and the case eventually went cold.

What If?

If Dispatcher Davis had recognized clues to the innocence and guilt of 911 callers, she would have immediately advised her supervisor to the possibility that Jake may have just committed two murders. The supervisor would have alerted the street officers. If Officers Latessa, Hamilton, and Lewis had known that the assailant was standing within inches of them, they would have taken greater precautions for their safety and been more alert to his comments, gestures, and demeanor. If the detectives had received training in analyzing 911 homicide calls before they interviewed Jake, they could have focused on the indicators of guilt and used them as tools to uncover the truth. Instead, the dispatcher, street officers, and investigators lacked understanding of the importance of 911 call analysis and thus missed crucial clues for solving the case.

Fortunately, recordings provide law enforcement with immediate and permanent access to 911 calls. Investigators who listen to these calls as they approach the crime scenes arrive armed with critical insight gained from the callers' words and tone of voice. For example, why might a 911 caller focus on a break-in instead of on the victims, unless the caller was involved in the crime? Conversely, an innocent caller might immediately demand help and yell into the phone to get the ambulance to speed up, in an effort to save a child's life.

Investigators recognize the difference between the voice of a caller desperately trying to save a life and the voice of a caller simply reporting a death. In death investigations, both innocent and guilty callers are under great stress, but for different reasons. Innocent callers are under stress due to concern for critically injured victims and the need to get immediate help. Guilty callers are under duress from killing another human being or aiding in the homicide (Grossman, 1996). The 911 call, replayed by investigators before stepping onto the crime scene, can reveal these differences and alert investigators to any discrepancies between the call and the scene. After leaving the crime scene, investigators can analyze the call and transcript in depth, to gain additional insight about the caller, develop investigative leads, and prepare interview strategies.

Reference

Grossman, D. (1996), *On Killing: The Psychological Cost of Learning to Kill in War and Society*, Back Bay Books, New York.

Who Is the Call About?

II

Does the Caller Demand Help?

3

"People must help one and other; it is nature's law."

Jean de le Fontaine

When citizens call 911, they can count on hearing a real person answering their call and asking about the emergency. In assault cases with victims in critical condition, callers are expected to immediately state the need to get help for the victims. Investigators can gain insight to the innocence or guilt of 911 callers by determining if a plea for help is made at the earliest logical opportunity in the 911 call. If dispatchers begin the call with, *"911, what is your emergency?"* an Immediate Plea for Help for victim should follow. If dispatchers instead ask, *"911, where is your emergency?"* it is reasonable that callers would provide the address of the emergency before stating their plea for help.

The following phrases are examples of Immediate Pleas for Help that appeared at the earliest logical points in the calls: *"Send an ambulance,"* *"We need help,"* and *"Get someone here."* Simply reporting an event or asking, *"Are they on the way?"* or *"Can you send someone over here?"* does not qualify as a plea for help.

Compare the following 911 calls regarding the critical condition of two babies:

Call #1
Dispatcher: *"911, what is your emergency?"*
Innocent Caller: *"My baby's not breathing—I need an ambulance* at 775 Maple!"*

Call #2
Dispatcher: *"911, what is your emergency?"*
Guilty Caller: *"I have an infant. He's not breathing."*

In Call #1, an innocent mother identified the emergency and made an immediate plea for help for her baby. In Call #2, a guilty father never asked for help throughout his rather lengthy call. The real purpose of the father's call

---

* Innocent indicators are enclosed in rectangles and guilty indicators are underlined.

was not to obtain help but to report the death of his four-month-old infant. The father had shaken the infant to death but did not admit to his actions until confronted with the infant's autopsy report. The report revealed multiple fractures at different stages of healing; the father was guilty of inflicting the injuries and was convicted of homicide.

Forty percent of the calls in the 911 study included an Immediate Plea for Help for Victims. As shown in Figure 3.1, over 3/4 of these immediate pleas were made by innocent callers (79%); guilty callers made 21%.

It is important to consider whether any extenuating circumstances affect the indicators of innocence or guilt. When examining an immediate plea for help for a victim, for example, note when dispatchers advised the callers that help was on the way. If dispatchers provided this information, or it was clear that help was already being dispatched, there would be no need for callers to specifically demand help, knowing that task had already been accomplished.

Callers who committed homicides and then staged the scenes called 911 to report the deaths, display the scenes, and have the bodies removed. In these situations, there was no emergency and no need to demand immediate help, unlike the situations with innocent callers. In fact, the victims of guilty callers may have been dead for hours while the offenders changed clothes and arranged the setting. The following example is from a caller who later pled guilty.

Dispatcher: *"911, what is your emergency?"*
Guilty Caller: *"I just got home and my wife is dead."*

There was no plea for help in this call because the caller's wife had been killed much earlier. The guilty caller was simply reporting the death rather than demanding any medical aid to save his wife's life. The husband was convicted of his wife's murder.

Investigators listening to 911 calls should listen carefully to determine not only if a plea was made but also for whom the plea was made. Innocent callers trying to save lives demanded help specifically for the victims. Guilty callers, however, often asked for help only for themselves. Innocent

Figure 3.1 Percentages of Innocent vs. Guilty Callers in "Immediate Plea for Help."

callers were characterized by their focus on getting help to the victims as quickly as possible. Guilty callers who realized the gravity of their crimes and the frightening consequences often focused solely on getting help for themselves.

Help was clearly demanded for the victim in the following call:

Dispatcher: *"Where is the injured person?"*
Innocent Caller: *"We have the guy here and* he needs help now!*"*

In another case, a convicted drug dealer contacted 911 after a subject was shot on his street:

Dispatcher: *"911, what is your emergency?"*
Innocent Caller: *"*I need an ambulance *at 55 Southside, hurry up please."*
Dispatcher: *"What's the phone number there sir?"*
Innocent Caller: *"She's shot in the head... I don't know...* JUST GET TO 55 SOUTHSIDE!*"*

The previous caller had a lengthy criminal history and had been to prison several times, thus making him an immediate suspect in the homicide. However, during his 911 call, he demanded help for the injured victim and he was found to be innocent of the crime.

Guilty callers who have committed the horrific crime of homicide may become frightened about their future and plead for help for themselves rather than for the victims. In such cases, the guilty callers' focus is clearly on their own needs rather than on the victims' needs. This was particularly relevant in murders that were not premeditated. Because the acts were rash, the call-ers regretted their actions, and their goals were for self-preservation.

In the next example, the caller never asked for help for his critically injured father. He only asked for help for himself.

Dispatcher: *"What happened to your father?"*
Guilty Caller: *"Say something to me. Help me!"*

The son was more concerned with his own situation than his father's condition. He was worried about what would happen to him in the future, rather than what had happened to his father. The son was later convicted of murdering his father.

Although callers may experience some degree of shock at a death scene, this is not a viable excuse to avoid seeking help for victims. The data and case histories collected in the 200 adjudicated cases in the 911 study showed that when loved ones were critically injured, innocent callers, even those in shock, were able to cooperate and focus on getting help for the victims.

In the following case, a husband witnessed his wife shoot herself in the head with a .45 caliber round:

Dispatcher:	*"What's the address sir?"*
Innocent Caller:	*"GET HERE NOW! SHE'S STILL BREATHING HURRY UP, GET THEM HERE NOW!"*

This husband, who saw the horrifying damage resulting from the large caliber bullet, was in extreme stress and shock. However, he did not hesitate to demand Immediate Help for the Victim.

In the following case, a three-year-old boy witnessed his father accidentally cut his radial and ulnar arteries with a wood chisel. The father began to bleed out and collapsed to the floor, unconscious, while a large pool of blood surrounded his body. The distraught child picked up the phone and dialed 911:

Dispatcher:	*"911, what is your emergency?"*
Innocent Caller:	*"Daddy needs help!"*
Dispatcher:	*"Do you need the ambulance?"*
Innocent Caller:	*"DADDY NEEDS HELP RIGHT AWAY!"*
Dispatcher:	*"Ok, they're on their-"*
Innocent Caller:	***"YOU HAVE TO COME. HE REALLY NEEDS HELP!"***

In this case, the traumatized child was still able to focus on the victim and demanded immediate help for his father. He was under extreme stress and shock; however, he still was able to focus on the victim and demand help for his father.

Lastly, a 60-year-old mentally challenged woman called 911 when she discovered her brother in critical condition. The brother, who lived in a trailer with 13 dogs, suffered from malnutrition, as did his starving dogs. A medical event caused him to collapse to the floor and as he lay dying, his dogs began to eat his exposed face and hand. Despite the gruesome scene, the shocked sister, with the mental capabilities of a five-year-old, immediately called 911. She focused on the victim and urgently demanded help for him.

All three of the previous subjects were in shock and under great stress when they called 911, including a three-year-old child and a mentally challenged adult. The 911 study revealed that innocent callers of varied ages, even when under extreme stress, were able to call 911 and state an Immediate Plea for Help for Victims.

MR. AND MRS. HUNT CASE

Returning to the unsolved case of Mr. and Mrs. Hunt...

A year after the death of Mr. and Mrs. Hunt, investigators reviewed Jake's call using the principles of 911 Homicide Call Analysis. They were stunned by the absence of an immediate plea for help for the victims, particularly since Jake was related to the victims. No wonder the dispatcher thought something seemed wrong with Jake's call. She knew for sure that something was wrong after comparing Jake's call with the next call that came into the dispatch center:

"Get over here NOW!! Some idiot just stole my kid's bike!"

In contrast to Jake's call, the bike call had an immediate plea for help...and no one was even injured.

The closest that Jake came to asking for help was near the end of the call:

"...what am I going to do? Help me."

In examining this plea, it is evident that Jake was not asking for help for the victims; he was asking for help for himself.

Innocent Indicators   **Guilty Indicators**

____ Immediate Plea for Help for Victim   n/a   _✓_ No Immediate Plea for Help for Victim

Does the Caller Provide an Immediate Assessment of the Victim?

4

"Power, today, comes from sharing information, not withholding it."

Keith Ferrazzi

All 911 callers make at least a cursory assessment of victims in order to know whether a 911 call is necessary. Most innocent callers in the 911 study made the initial evaluation, called 911, and then provided an immediate assessment of the victims' condition. This approach provides dispatchers with the information needed to determine the best way to aid the victim. Guilty callers, however, were less likely to volunteer an immediate assessment of the victim's condition, thus limiting the dispatchers' ability to provide help.

The following list provides specific assessments of victims that callers should immediately share with dispatchers:

1. Massive head or torso injuries
2. Obvious gun shot or stab wounds
3. Possible suicide implements at the scene, such as pill bottles, needles, hanging devices, razors, guns
4. Profuse bleeding from a wound
5. Unresponsiveness
6. Victim in full rigor
7. Victim submerged in water
8. Victim's skin color (pale, gray, ashen, blue) and signs of lividity
9. Vomit at the scene

Generally, innocent 911 callers continued to assess the victims' condition throughout the call, and they anxiously updated the dispatcher with any changes, both positive and negative. They also voluntarily assessed the crime scene and promptly shared the details with the dispatchers. The crime scene details included weapons at the scene and possible assailants, including their descriptions, actions, dialogue, weapons, and direction of exit.

In the 911 study, 67% of the callers provided the dispatcher with an immediate assessment of the victim. Innocent callers provided immediate

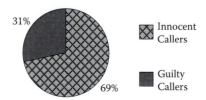

Figure 4.1 Percentages of Innocent vs. Guilty Callers in "Immediate Assessment of Victim."

assessments more than twice as often as guilty callers (69% vs. 31%) as illustrated in Figure 4.1. Ninety-three percent of all innocent callers offered immediate assessments of the victims, but only 41% of guilty callers did so.

In the following case, an innocent caller had touched the victim to assess the victim's condition:

Dispatcher:	*"911, what is your emergency?"*
Innocent Caller:	*"We need you to send someone down to the Sutton Apartments. We have a resident who's lying on the floor and he feels cold to the touch."*
Dispatcher:	*"What apartment is he in?"*
Innocent Caller:	*"18."*
Dispatcher:	*"Did you say you touched him to see if he had like a pulse, or was warm or cold?"*
Innocent Caller:	*"Well, I touched his face. His face is ice cold."*

The caller made an initial evaluation, determined that the event merited a call to 911, and provided an immediate assessment of the victim to the dispatcher. The investigation revealed that the victim died from a heart attack; the 911 caller was not involved in any crime.

In the next case, a man called 911 regarding a friend's suicide.

Innocent Caller:	*"MIKE!"*
Dispatcher:	*"911, what is your emergency?"*
Innocent Caller:	*"MIKE! Hey I need an ambulance like really quick. I'm at my buddy's house at 222 Norris and he shot himself."*
Dispatcher:	*"Ok, I'm sending them out, is he breathing?"*
Innocent Caller:	*"No, he shot himself in the head, he's bleeding bad from the side of his head. There's a gun laying here. Oh no Mike...."*
Dispatcher:	*"Does he still feel warm?"*
Innocent Caller:	*"Yes! He does, he still feels warm!"*

The innocent caller quickly assessed the victim and the scene and then called 911 to get help. The caller volunteered his initial assessment to the dispatcher and continued to evaluate the victim throughout the call. He shared the following assessment: the injury originated from a gunshot, the wound was to the victim's head, the victim was bleeding profusely, a gun was present at the scene, and the victim was still warm. This initial and continuing assessment painted a clear picture for the dispatcher and expedited aid to the victim. The investigation revealed that the victim had been treated for posttraumatic stress disorder, had threatened suicide in the past, and had endured a recent breakup with his girlfriend. No foul play was suspected.

In contrast to innocent callers, many guilty 911 callers failed to volunteer immediate assessments of victims and the crime scenes, and acted as if they had not assessed the victims. Yet, if they had not assessed the victims at all, they would have no reason to call 911. Dispatchers were forced to extract information from these callers in order to understand the full nature of the event. The dispatchers were often stunned to learn midway through the 911 calls that the victims were in critical conditions.

In the following case, the dispatcher did not learn the severity of the event until late in the call:

Dispatcher: *"911, what is your emergency?"*
Guilty Caller: *"Please send somebody."*
Dispatcher: *"What's the problem, Ma'am?"*
Guilty Caller: *"My baby!"*
Dispatcher: *"Give me your address."*
Guilty Caller: *"Oh my God!"*
Dispatcher: *"Give me your address."*
Guilty Caller: *"556 Globe Drive..."*
Dispatcher: *"Ok, tell me what's wrong with the baby."*
Guilty Caller: *"Oh my God, oh my God!"*
Dispatcher: *"Ma'am, is your baby ok?"*
Guilty Caller: *"NO!"*
Dispatcher: *"Ma'am...is the baby breathing?"*
Guilty Caller: *"Nooo..."*
Dispatcher: *"...is there a pulse?"*
Guilty Caller: *"Nooo, she's stiff."*

The mother failed to share her assessment with the dispatcher and only provided it after repeated questioning. She eventually confessed that she had smothered her baby while on drugs. The mother was convicted of the offense.

In another case, a wife called 911 concerning her husband and did not provide a complete assessment until she was specifically asked.

Dispatcher:	*"911, what is your emergency?"*
Guilty Caller:	*"Help me!"*
Dispatcher:	*"Ok, Ma'am, slow down and tell me what's going on."*
Guilty Caller:	*"My husband is dead!"*
Dispatcher:	*"What's your address?"*
Guilty Caller:	*"73 Wilmott Street, please hurry!"*
Dispatcher:	*"Ok, slow down, tell me what happened."*
Guilty Caller:	*"My husband is dead! Oh my God."*
Dispatcher:	*"Has he been sick lately?"*
Guilty Caller:	*"No, he's been shot. A guy came in and shot him."*

The wife allegedly possessed knowledge of an intruder entering her home and shooting her husband; however, she failed to immediately divulge these details. Her failure to share the vital information led the dispatcher to assume that the victim had suffered a medical event. The wife never advised where the victim was shot and provided no description of an offender. The investigation revealed that the wife convinced her boyfriend to kill her husband, and she then fabricated the intruder story. Both the wife and her boyfriend were convicted of murder.

MR. AND MRS. HUNT CASE

Jake told the dispatcher that his wife's parents were dead and, *"There is blood everywhere."* Yet, he claimed not to know if they were breathing or if they had pulses.

Dispatcher: *"Are you sure they're both gone, are they breathing...do they have pulses?"*

Jake: *"I don't know. Oh my God, oh my God, oh my God...what am I going to do? Help me."*

Jake failed to provide a full and immediate assessment of the victims.

Innocent Indicators

_____ Immediate Assessment of Victims   n/a

Guilty Indicators

__✓__ No Immediate Assessment of Victims

Who Is the Caller's Focus?

5

"There is not a man of us who does not at times need a helping hand to be stretched out to him, and then shame upon him who will not stretch out the helping hand to his brother."

Theodore Roosevelt

The purpose of calling 911 during a critical event is to get medical help to victims as quickly as possible. Therefore, most innocent callers in the 911 study focused on the victims throughout the 911 calls, demanding help for them, offering relevant details to the dispatchers, and aiding the victims with CPR and other medical assistance. The guilty callers were often more focused on their own problems than on the victims' conditions. Some guilty callers repeatedly mentioned open doors or disheveled rooms, thus focusing on false intruders rather than on the needs of the victims.

The focus of the callers was usually apparent within the first few seconds of the 911 call. Innocent callers in the 911 study were more likely than guilty callers to identify the victims, describe their injuries, and demand help for them. Innocent callers provided updates on victims' conditions and attempted to aid them; they rarely focused on themselves.

The Focus on Victim indicator was present in 45% of the calls in the 911 study. Eight times as many innocent callers focused on the victims (89%) than did guilty callers (11%). This was one of the strongest indicators of innocence in the 911 study. See Figure 5.1.

In the following case, a woman called 911. Her focus remained on the victim, her neighbor.

Dispatcher: *"911, State your emergency."*

Innocent Caller: *"I'm in Sandy Marcos's apartment in Glendale. I need 911 down here right away. She's in a chair, blood running out of her mouth and it don't look like she's breathing so I need somebody here. Hurry, please hurry."*

The caller's focus was on her neighbor's condition and on efforts to save her neighbor's life. The neighbor subsequently died, and the caller was not involved in the death.

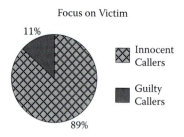

Figure 5.1 Percentages of Innocent vs. Guilty Callers in "Focus on Victim."

A man called 911 regarding an unresponsive woman. This caller also focused on the victim, and he volunteered updates on the victim's condition as the ending of this call illustrates:

Innocent Caller: *"Do you have an ambulance?"*
Dispatcher: *"Sir, they are already on the way, OK?"*
Innocent Caller: *"Okay, cause she's bleeding from the side of her head."*
Dispatcher: *"They're almost there…"*

The subsequent investigation revealed that the victim had fallen while intoxicated, and she died from the accident.

Unlike the majority of innocent callers, some guilty callers focused primarily on themselves and rarely mentioned the victims unless specifically asked about them. The Focus on Caller indicator was characterized by the callers' frequent use of the personal pronoun "I." These callers talked about their own problems, including minor physical or emotional problems. These personal problems paled in comparison with the severity of the situations, in which other people lost their lives.

Thirteen percent of the calls in the 911 study revealed a Focus on Caller indicator. It is noteworthy that no innocent callers used this indicator, as illustrated in Figure 5.2.

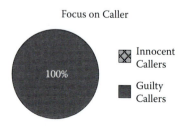

Figure 5.2 Percentages of Innocent vs. Guilty Callers in "Focus on Caller."

In an arson/homicide case, a mother ran to a neighbor's trailer home and begged to use the phone in the middle of the night. Once she had the phone, she called 911 for help and explained:

Guilty Caller: *"Ya'll better hurry up, my youngin's are in there."*
Dispatcher: *"Your kids are in there, I understand that."*
Guilty Caller: *"I lost my cell phone, I can't find my house phone, I burned my foot trying to get my kids."*

Instead of keeping her focus on her dying children, this mother shifted her focus to her lost phones and her slightly burned foot. An innocent mother would be so desperate to save her children that she would have ignored her own minor problems. This mother was found guilty of murdering her children and setting the fire to conceal her crime.

Many guilty 911 callers focused on their own physical well-being even when they had not sustained any injuries during an event. For example, a man called 911 to report that his wife had drowned in the river and he had pulled her out. As the dispatcher was giving him CPR instructions, he complained about his discomfort:

Dispatcher: *"OK, sir, you are doing a good job, tell me if she is breathing at all."*
Guilty Caller: *"I am so cold, I don't know if she is, I am so cold, are they coming?"*

The caller, who focused more on himself than on his wife, was eventually convicted of his wife's homicide.

In another case, a 911 caller refused to approach her injured husband. She would not assess his condition or provide aid to him, as he lay dying. When the dispatcher directed the caller to help her husband, the caller resisted by focusing on herself:

Guilty Caller: *"I just, I can't be here with the blood. I'm sorry, I can't do it. I just can't. I get panicked at the sight of blood When are they gonna be here? Do you know?"*

The investigation revealed that the wife was responsible for her husband's death, and she was convicted of homicide.

In a similar call, a husband was advised that medical aid was on the way to help his gravely injured wife. Even though the husband was uninjured, he wanted help for himself:

Dispatcher: *"OK, an ambulance is on the way..."*
Guilty Caller: *"I just don't know what I'm going to do. Where will I go from here? I need some help. I feel sick."*

Instead of focusing on his wife and her critical condition, the husband focused on himself. The wife died, and the husband was found guilty of her death.

A wife called 911 and told the dispatcher that her husband had committed suicide. As the dispatcher was asking questions in an effort to get the medics to the scene as quickly as possible, the wife calmly stated:

Guilty Caller: *"Not a good time for him to do this to me."*

Instead of focusing on her husband, the wife focused on her own problem as if the timing of his alleged suicide inconvenienced her. The wife was later found guilty of her husband's murder.

Some callers told the dispatchers about more than one problem. The following caller stated that he returned home to find his wife on the floor in a pool of blood. When the dispatcher advised the caller about sending help, the caller responded as follows:

Dispatcher: *"I'm sending them sir."*
Guilty Caller: *"No wait, I got another problem...my son is an EMT...he's gonna hear the call."*

The caller was so concerned that his son might respond to the scene that he told the dispatcher to wait. Advising that he had "another problem" revealed that the caller viewed his wife's situation as his first problem. The caller's focus was on his own problems rather than on his wife's survival. Months later, the caller was convicted of his wife's murder; thus, she did turn out to be a "problem" for him.

The callers' focus can also be revealed by analyzing the specific words used when seeking aid. Innocent callers typically demanded "help" or an "ambulance," but guilty callers frequently asked for "police." The word "ambulance" connotes emergency medical aid for the victims and reveals that the callers are focused on the victims' survival. However, depending on the context, the word "police" may suggest a crime. An active shooting case would require police presence, but an accidental child bathtub drowning would not. In true accidental death cases, innocent callers typically demanded an ambulance for medical aid.

In the 911 study, callers who focused on themselves repeatedly used the pronoun "I" as they described their own problems. Unlike in general criminal suspect statements in which the use of "I" adds personal conviction and is associated with truthfulness, overuse of the pronoun "I" in 911 calls reveals the callers' misplaced focus. The purpose of 911 calls is to get help for victims. Unless the callers are also victims, there is no need for the callers to be the focus of attention.

Considerations

Callers who were in immediate danger from offenders focused on both the victims' safety and their own. If offenders were still in the vicinity, it would be expected that the callers would be concerned with their own survival; therefore, this would not be considered a guilty indicator.

MR. AND MRS. HUNT CASE

When the dispatcher asked Jake to check his dying in-laws, he focused instead on himself:

Dispatcher: *"Are you sure they're both gone, are they breathing...do they have pulses?"*

Caller: *"I don't know. Oh my God, oh my God, oh my God...what am I going to do? Help me."*

Innocent Indicators		**Guilty Indicators**
____ Focus on the Victim	n/a	_✓_ Focus on the Caller

Does the Caller Accept the Victim's Death?

6

> *"When you have lost hope, you have lost everything.*
> *And when you think all is lost, when all is dire and bleak, there is*
> *always hope."*
>
> Pittacus Lore

Innocent 911 callers cling to hope—hope that they can keep their loved one alive while the medics are en route, hope that the medics will get there in time to save their loved one, and, in many cases, hope for a miracle. Some guilty callers, particularly in premeditated murder cases, reveal their Acceptance of Death of the victim because the death comes as no surprise.

Many innocent callers in the 911 study found it difficult to mentally process the circumstances of sudden deaths. They instinctively refused to accept the deaths, particularly the deaths of relatives or friends. Even when it was obvious that the victims had been deceased for some time, some innocent callers were unable to verbalize the word "dead."

In the book *Unbroken*, Laura Hillenbrand tells the story of Louie Zamperini's ordeal of being shot down over the Pacific Ocean and drifting in a rubber raft for 47 days. Louie was then captured and tortured in a Japanese prisoner-of-war camp for more than two years. His family only knew that he was shot down with his crew; the plane's debris and survivors were never located. A year and a half later, the U.S. government sent the Zamperini family a letter declaring Louie Zamperini officially dead. Louie's sister, Sylvie, responded by saying (Hillenbrand, 2010):

"None of us believed it. None of us. Never once. Not underneath even."

Despite overwhelming odds and logic, the Zamperini family refused to accept the death of Louie and never gave up hope. In their one-in-a-million case, the miracle happened and Louie Zamperini came home to them, alive.

In a recent case, the father of a depressed son was told by officers that his son had committed suicide by jumping off a bridge. The father refused to accept his son's death and told the officers, *"I don't believe it!"* He ran to his son's room, got on the boy's computer, and read his Facebook entry stating that he was going to jump off the George Washington Bridge. The father still could not believe that his son was dead, and he refused to believe that his son had killed himself. He told the officers that someone must have kidnapped his son and also written the Facebook message posing as his son. The father clung to hope and yelled at the detectives in defiance. The detectives finally took him to the coroner's office where he saw his son. The father later stated

"...when I saw his body at the morgue I was forced to accept the fact that he was (three-second pause) that he was (three-second pause) dead."

The reality was heart-wrenching for the father. Even after time had passed, the father could barely utter the word "dead."

In a recent case, a mother thought it unusual that her teenage daughter was sleeping so late and went upstairs to the girl's room to wake her. The mother, an experienced ER nurse, tugged on her daughter's leg and realized that the girl was cold. She threw back the blankets and started CPR despite the fact that the victim was stiff and in full rigor with lividity present. She continued CPR until the medics arrived and forced her to stop. When she was later asked why she initiated CPR on her daughter, who appeared to be deceased, the mother stated

"I work in a hospital everyday where there are machines that can perform miracles and bring people back to life. I hoped my daughter would get that miracle."

In fact, the medical literature is replete with cases of victims who have survived gunshot wounds to the brain and multiple knife stabs to the heart. Children submerged under water for more than 66 minutes have been resuscitated (Hughes et al., 2002). Innocent people cling to the hope that their loved ones will survive.

An innocent wife was so focused on her husband's survival that she continually coached him throughout the 911 call, with remarks such as the following:

Innocent Caller: "The ambulance is on the way! You hear me? You hear this? Fight!"

The wife refused to give up hope and believed that her husband would survive.

Individuals pass through stages of grief (Kübler-Ross and Kessler, 2005) to process the reality that their loved one is actually dead, as illustrated in Figure 6.1. While the Acceptance of Death timeline varies for each person and circumstance, few individuals can immediately accept the news of an unexpected death without processing through stages to reach acceptance. The same stages of grief apply to innocent callers who contact 911 to seek help for their dying loved ones.

Figure 6.1 Stages of Grief.

Callers who readily accepted the death of victims were often directly guilty or complicit in the offense. The Acceptance of Death indicator was present when callers asserted that the victims were dead when the actual condition (i.e., living or dead) would not necessarily be known by the callers. Therefore, if 911 callers do not know the actual physiological condition of the victims, they should not declare the victims' demise to the dispatchers. In contrast to the examples of innocent callers who cling to hope, many guilty callers immediately accepted the victims' deaths, even if the victims were friends or family members.

Over a third of the calls in the 911 study (36%) contained Acceptance of Death. Almost twice as many guilty callers expressed Acceptance of Death (66%) as did innocent callers (34%). See Figure 6.2.

As an example of Acceptance of Death, a husband contacted 911 and made the following statement regarding his wife:

Dispatcher: *"911, what is your emergency?"*
Guilty Caller: *"I just got home from work and <u>my wife is lying in bed dead</u>!"*

In this communication, it was obvious that the caller had no difficulty accepting the death of his wife. Unlike the previous innocent examples, this caller was not in a denial stage when learning of the passing of his wife, but already in the acceptance stage. The subsequent investigation revealed that the caller had killed his wife with premeditation well before calling 911, and he was convicted of the crime.

In another case, a 32-year-old male called 911 and stated as follows:

Dispatcher: *"911, what is your emergency?"*
Guilty Caller: *"<u>My Dad got killed…</u>"*

Acceptance of Death

Figure 6.2 Percentages of Innocent vs. Guilty Callers in "Acceptance of Death."

The caller chose the word "killed," indicating his Acceptance of Death of his father. In fact, the father was still alive and suffering from a fractured skull when the medics responded to the scene. He died en route to the hospital. The son accepted the death of his father and gave up hope *before* his father died. He also used passive language, "got killed," to avoid identifying the offender. The son was later convicted of the homicide.

As a variation on the Acceptance of Death indicator, some callers made comments about victims in the process of dying. A call from a 37-year-old male illustrates this variation:

Dispatcher: *"What's wrong with your Dad?"*
Guilty Caller: *"He's dyyyyyiiinng..."*

This son also accepted the death of his father while his father was still living. The father later died as a result of injuries inflicted by the son who was later convicted of homicide.

Innocent 911 callers did not refer to their loved ones in terms of death or dying. Instead, they focused on survival, and their determination was heard in their urgent voices. In contrast, many guilty callers had resignation in their voices as they accepted the victims' death. The offenders were certain of the deaths because, having committed the murders, they knew how and when they took place. Some offenders killed the victims and then left the premises to return hours later, "discover" the homicide, and call it in. These types of 911 callers could accept the victims' deaths because the concept of death was not new to them.

In cases in which callers had nothing to hide, they typically believed their loved ones could be saved. If the victims were deceased, callers hoped they could be resuscitated. When a pronouncement of death was made, this was so difficult to process that innocent callers expressed disbelief and distress. If callers instead express a sense of resignation and Acceptance of Death, especially with a lack of emotion, the death of the victim may not be a surprise.

Considerations

Even if callers equivocally state, *"I think my wife's dead,"* this qualifies as Acceptance of Death because their focus is inappropriately on death instead of survival. However, when 911 callers discover victims who are clearly dead, the Acceptance of Death Indicator does not apply. For example, in cases in which the victim has been decapitated, burned beyond identification, or starting to decompose, this indicator is not applicable. It is reasonable that these callers would have to accept their loved one's death if found in these conditions.

MR. AND MRS. HUNT CASE
Jake immediately accepted the deaths of his in-laws and did not focus on their survival. He told the dispatcher, *"...my wife's parents are dead!"*

Innocent Indicators		Guilty Indicators
___ No Acceptance of Victim's Death	n/a	_✓_ Acceptance of Victim's Death

References

Hillenbrand, L. (2010), *Unbroken: A World War II Story of Survival, Resilience, and Redemption*, Random House, New York.

Hughes, S.K., Nilsson, D.E., Boyer, R.S., Bolte, R.G., Hoffman, R.O., Lewine, J.D., and Bigler, E.D. (2002), "Neurodevelopmental Outcome for Extended Cold Water Drowning: A Longitudinal Case Study," *Journal of the International Neuropsychological Society*, 8: 588–595.

Kübler-Ross, E., and Kessler, D. (2005), *On Grief and Grieving: Finding the Meaning of Grief through the Five Stages of Loss*, Scribner, New York.

Does the Caller Provide Aid to the Victim as Directed?

7

"Always help someone. You might be the only one who does."

Anonymous

Most 911 dispatchers are trained in CPR and first aid, and they are experienced in directing callers to assist critically injured victims. In some dispatch centers, CPR and first aid instructions are printed on laminated cards so dispatchers can accurately provide directions to the callers, even when under stress. Innocent callers typically followed the dispatchers' directions to Provide Aid to Victims, especially if the callers and victims had a close relationship. These callers were eager to help their loved ones, and they cooperated with dispatchers when directed to check for breathing and pulse. They willingly placed direct pressure on open wounds, removed objects from the victims' mouths, and initiated CPR. The primary goal for innocent callers was to get medical aid to the victims as quickly as possible and to provide basic aid until the professionals arrived.

In the following case, note the cooperation and efforts made by the innocent 911 caller:

Dispatcher: *"I want you to do a finger sweep of her mouth and make sure there are no obstructions."*

Innocent Caller: *"I did it, there's nothing in there."*

Dispatcher: *"Ok, put her flat on her back and tilt her head back." "Put your hand in the center of her chest and push down about two inches. Do it 30 times. Pump hard and fast. Count out loud for me."*

Innocent Caller: *"One...two...three...four...five-"*

Dispatcher: *"Do it faster."*

Innocent Caller: *"One and two and three and four and five and six-"*

Dispatcher: *"No, do it faster!"*

Innocent Caller: *"One, two, three, four, five, six, seven, eight, nine, ten, eleven, twelve, thirteen, fourteen, fifteen, sixteen, seventeen, eighteen, nineteen, twenty, twenty-one, twenty-two, twenty-three, twenty-four, twenty-five, twenty-six, twenty-seven, twenty-eight, twenty-nine, thirty. Where are you guys? Tell them to hurry!"*

Numerous innocent 911 callers attempted to stop the victims' bleeding by applying direct pressure or initiating CPR without any prompting by the dispatchers. The focus of these callers was clearly on saving the lives of the victims.

In contrast, some of the callers who committed homicides were reluctant to render any type of aid to the victims, even when they had a close relationship with the injured persons. Guilty 911 callers who intentionally shot, stabbed, or choked a person may not want the victim to survive. Additionally, they may refuse to resuscitate the victim for fear of saving the only witness who could incriminate them.

Most (94%) of the 911 study callers who revealed No Aid Provided to Victim were guilty. Only 6% of these callers were innocent, as shown in Figure 7.1. This indicator was present in 9% of the calls in the 911 study.

In some cases, the victims may have been dead for hours, and guilty callers knew that any attempts at medical aid were futile. Because of this, they often resisted even basic tasks like checking for breathing or a pulse, actions that innocent callers were likely to perform. Some guilty 911 callers killed their victims and then left the area to establish alibis. Returning hours or days later, they called 911 to report they had "*found*" the victims. These offenders knew, without a doubt, that the victims were dead, and these guilty callers did not want to go through the unpleasant motions of attempting CPR on a corpse.

In the following case, a husband called 911 after his wife allegedly overdosed on her medications:

Dispatcher:	"*911, what is your emergency?*"
Guilty Caller:	"*My wife overdosed on her meds!*"
Dispatcher:	"*Ok, does she have a pulse?*"
Guilty Caller:	"*I don't know, she's on the bed.*"
Dispatcher:	"*Ok, check and see if she's breathing?*"
Guilty Caller:	"*I don't think she is!*"
Dispatcher:	"*Get her off the bed, put her on the floor. I'm going to help you with CPR.*"

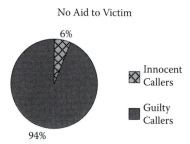

Figure 7.1   Percentages of Innocent vs. Guilty Callers in "No Aid to Victim."

Guilty Caller: *"I don't think I can, she's real heavy-set."*
Dispatcher: *"Pull her onto the floor!"*
Guilty Caller: *"I don't want to hurt her."*

The husband resisted aiding the victim by pulling her onto the floor to initiate CPR, with the feeble excuse *"...she's real heavy-set."* When ordered by the dispatcher to put the victim on the floor, the husband again resisted, adding the illogical comment *"I don't want to hurt her."* An innocent husband should not hesitate to pull his dying wife off the bed to initiate lifesaving measures. The husband eventually confessed that he intentionally overdosed his wife by mixing medications into her food. He was convicted of her murder.

In the following case, a 911 caller reported that his girlfriend had fallen down the stairs:

Dispatcher: *"Where is she hurt at?"*
Guilty Caller: *"I think the back of her head."*
Dispatcher: *"Can you get a clean towel and put pressure on the back of her head?"*
Guilty Caller: *"No, I can't, her head is all bloody and I'm not trying to be mean, but no can do, I can't look at it."*

The caller refused to render simple, basic aid to the victim. He later confessed to assaulting his girlfriend with a hammer and was convicted of her murder.

Some guilty callers resisted assessing the victims or providing aid, because they already knew the manner and time of death. These offenders, however, were sometimes forced to reply to dispatchers who asked why the callers refused to assist the victims, as illustrated in the following two examples:

Example 1:

Dispatcher: *"Ok, I'm going to tell you how to do CPR, will you try it?"*
Guilty Caller: *"No, no I don't want to."*
Dispatcher: *"Why not?"*
Guilty Caller: *"I just don't think I'd be very good at it."*

Example 2:

Dispatcher: *"Pull your wife out of the water."*
Guilty Caller: *"Ok, she's out."*
Dispatcher: *"All right, lay her flat, we are going to do CPR."*
Guilty Caller: *"I can't!"*
Dispatcher: *"Why not?"*
Guilty Caller: *"My CPR card is expired."*

In the previous examples, the callers were responsible for the deaths of the victims. They had no intention of administering CPR, and they were both convicted of their crimes. If callers reporting critical incidents involving loved ones refused to aid the victims, the dispatchers' simple question *"Why not?"* can prove to be insightful. Innocent callers in the 911 study provided logical explanations, while guilty callers offered illogical excuses.

There is a significant but less obvious reason why numerous guilty callers resisted giving basic medical aid to victims. Offenders who killed in their homes may stage crime scenes to divert attention away from themselves. It takes a great deal of effort to stage a crime scene correctly and offenders want to ensure that the setting is viewed *"as is."* First responders will observe the scene, photograph the area, and articulate their observations in a police report. This evidence could potentially be used at trial, and it benefits the guilty 911 callers to preserve the scene. Innocent callers prioritized aiding the victims, and they did not care if they disturbed the setting by moving the victim or objects.

In the following case, a husband called 911 to report that his wife had committed suicide:

Dispatcher:	*"911, what is your emergency?"*
Guilty Caller:	*"My wife just committed suicide."*
Dispatcher:	*"Is she breathing?"*
Guilty Caller:	*"I don't think she is breathing."*
Dispatcher:	*"How did she do it?"*
Guilty Caller:	*"She shot herself."*
Dispatcher:	*"Where did she shoot herself at?"*
Guilty Caller:	*"In the bed."*
Dispatcher:	*"No, where did she shoot herself? In the head?"*
Guilty Caller:	*"Yes, in the head."*
Dispatcher:	*"Ok, pull her to the floor and we will start CPR."*
Guilty Caller:	*"I can't, I can't.... I'm panicking...when they will get here?"*

When the first responders arrived, they saw the deceased victim lying in bed with a pistol in her hand. They photographed the scene and articulated the circumstances in their police reports. As the investigation developed, the husband's story unraveled. The detectives learned that he had a girlfriend who later provided evidence against him. The husband was eventually convicted of murdering of his wife. He did not want to pull his wife off the bed onto the floor because the gun would have slipped from her hand, thus disturbing his carefully created scene.

In contrast to guilty callers, most innocent callers who refused to cooperate in administering CPR offered logical explanations. In the following case, an innocent husband called 911 after witnessing his wife shoot herself:

Dispatcher: *"Ok, lay her flat on her back and tilt her head back."*
Innocent Caller: *"Oh nooooo."*
Dispatcher: *"I want you to give her two quick breaths and pump her chest thirty times very quickly."*
Innocent Caller: *"I can't."*
Dispatcher: *"Give her the breaths!"*
Innocent Caller: *"I just can't."*
Dispatcher: *"Why not?"*
Innocent Caller: *"Her face.........is gone."*

The innocent husband assessed his wife's wounds, but her injuries made it physically impossible to initiate CPR. It was very difficult for him to utter the words, *"Her face.........is gone."* He had to be forced to deliver that horrific statement.

In the 911 research, four different levels of Providing Medical Aid were evident.

1. 911 Callers Who Initiated Medical Aid without Prompting
   Callers who had already assessed the victim and were providing medical aid without being directed to do so by the dispatcher were usually innocent of the offense. These callers wanted the victims to survive and did not wait for the dispatchers' directions or for the professionals to arrive. Even if the callers or others might be administering CPR incorrectly, the fact that they were attempting the lifesaving measures indicated genuine concern for the victims.

2. 911 Callers Who Agreed to Provide Medical Aid after Prompting
   Callers who agreed to administer medical aid after prompting by dispatchers were also usually innocent of the offense. Whether they were the persons giving aid or whether the task fell to others at the scene, their cooperation in the lifesaving event was noteworthy.

3. 911 Callers Who Were Reluctant to Provide Medical Aid
   Callers who offered weak excuses when directed to cooperate in lifesaving measures confused the dispatchers, who tried desperately to assist in providing aid to victims. These callers revealed a lack of compassion and were often guilty of the offense.

4. 911 Callers Who Refused to Attempt Medical Aid
   Callers who categorically refused the dispatchers' directives to attempt medical aid without valid reasons were the most suspect of all the subsets. Some of these callers simply ignored the dispatchers'

repeated commands to help the victims, while others, without explanation, explicitly stated that they would not comply. These callers were usually guilty of the offense.

Offenders may attempt to fake the act of performing medical aid. Some guilty callers pretended to give CPR to appease the dispatchers or to appear innocent. In one case, a husband seemed to be following the dispatcher's instructions for CPR as he counted out loud while allegedly administering chest compressions to his wife. After 15 compressions, he made loud blowing sounds as if he were breathing into her mouth. However, when the medics arrived on scene, the caller's wife, a *"drowning victim,"* was still submerged in the bathtub. The husband, who had faked the CPR, was convicted of homicide. During actual administration of CPR, those who provide aid are out of breath and unable to talk normally on the phone; prolonged CPR efforts are exhausting.*

In another case, a husband and wife were allegedly involved in an all-terrain vehicle accident that catapulted them both into a pond. The husband said he swam to shore before calling 911. The dispatcher directed him to pull his wife out of the water and initiate CPR. The caller complied by counting out numbers for compressions and making blowing sounds at the appropriate times during the process. When challenged on his account, the husband admitted that his efforts to perform CPR were feigned, and he was later convicted of murdering his wife.

A husband called 911 and advised that he just returned from a trip out of state to find a suicide note on the door and his wife lying on the bathroom floor in a pool of blood:

Dispatcher:	*"Are you able or willing to go in there?"*
Guilty Caller:	*"Oh my God! What?"*
Dispatcher:	*"Are you able or willing to get in there?"*
Guilty Caller:	*"I, I can try but her feet are on the floor, she's blocking the door and, there's blood everywhere. Oh my God. Oh my God, oh my God, oh my God. Oh my God."*
Dispatcher:	*"Can you see a gun or anything?"*
Guilty Caller:	*"No. There's scissors or something, it looks like she cut herself or just stabbed herself in the neck or something, there's just, Oh my God."*
Dispatcher:	*"Okay. Are you able to get in there with her?"*
Guilty Caller:	*"What?"*
Dispatcher:	*"Can you tell where she cut herself?"*

* Zafares, Angela.

Guilty Caller: *"I can't. It looks like there's blood all over her neck or something."*

Dispatcher: *"Can you get in there with her?"*

Guilty Caller: *"What? I'm in the … I'm downstairs, I'm not upstairs, there's an upstairs bathroom."*

Dispatcher: *"Okay."*

Guilty Caller: *"Oh my God, oh my God, oh my God."*

Dispatcher: *"Are you able or willing to try to get in the door?"*

Guilty Caller: *"No, I can't deal with it. I just, oh my God. Please just send somebody."*

The dispatcher asked the caller five times to go in the room with his wife. The husband repeatedly resisted the dispatcher's attempts to assist him in providing medical aid to his wife. The investigation revealed that the husband was the offender, and he was subsequently convicted of homicide.

MR. AND MRS. HUNT CASE

Jake resisted the dispatcher's attempt to help him provide medical aid to the victims:

Dispatcher: *"Jake, are you sure it's too late? Do you want me to help you with CPR?"*

Caller: *"There is blood everywhere..it's all over the floor."*

Dispatcher: *"Can you check for pulses?"*

Caller: *"I don't want to move them."*

Innocent Indicators		**Guilty Indicators**
___ Aid Provided to Victim	n/a	✔ No Aid Provided to Victim

What Is the Call About?

III

Is the Information Relevant?

"It does not require many words to speak the truth."

Chief Joseph of the Nez Perce

The callers who contacted 911 in an effort to save a life were under great stress; some of them cried or wailed during the calls. Yet even in their highly emotional state, most innocent callers realized the need to provide enough relevant information to dispatchers to enable them to direct medics to the correct location.

Communication expectations are explained by four basic maxims of communication: manner, quantity, quality, and relation (Grice, 1989). The *manner maxim* states that dialogue should be explicit, without ambiguous or confusing expressions. Speakers should strive to make their words clearly understood by listeners. The *quantity maxim* asserts that conversation should be as succinct as possible. Discourse is meant to include neither more nor less information than is necessary. The *quality maxim* requires that cooperative speakers provide information they believe to be true. A speaker who chooses to provide inaccurate information such as exaggeration is expected to make this exception to the maxim clear to the listeners. Finally, the *relation maxim* declares that effective conversation is relevant. Discourse should relate to the topic and avoid irrelevant information. In summary, the communication maxims mean that cooperative speakers are clear, brief, true, and relevant. If any of these basic rules of communication are intentionally violated, the speaker may not intend to convey complete and accurate information. A 911 caller who violates the communication maxims may not want the dispatcher to know the whole truth.

Innocent callers typically needed no prompting to answer the questions, "Who?" and "What?" Some callers also answered the "Where?" "When?" and "How?" questions before they were asked. In the following case, the caller provided Relevant Information about what was happening and who was in danger:

Dispatcher: *"911, what is your emergency?"*
Innocent Caller: *"This lady's trailer's on fire and her baby's in there—we need help."*

In the following exchange, the caller provided answers to the questions "Where?" "Who?" and "What?"

Dispatcher: *"911, what is your emergency?"*
Innocent Caller: *"Hey! I'm up here on ahh, I think it's Hudson or something. Somebody ran up on this boy and shot him six times."*

The dispatcher immediately knew where the location was, who the victim was, and what happened to him. Details regarding the number of shots heard were also included, without being asked.

In the following call, the dispatcher first asked the "Where?" question, to which the caller promptly provided the location of the emergency and a demand for help. The dispatcher then asked the "What?" question and without hesitation, the caller answered the question and voluntarily provided additional information about the victim's condition.

Dispatcher: *"Fire and EMS, where is your emergency?"*
Innocent Caller: *"I need an ambulance at 401 Nassau, at Lincoln Elementary."*
Dispatcher: *"OK, what's going on there?"*
Innocent Caller: *"A kid fell down the steps. He's bleeding real bad."*

The innocent caller provided relevant information to expedite help for the victim.

In the following case, parents could not make phone contact with their 21-year-old daughter who was attending college three hours away. The parents drove to their daughter's apartment and entered the residence, where the mother immediately called 911:

Dispatcher: *"911, what is your emergency?"*
Innocent Caller: *"(crying) SEND THE AMBULANCE TO APARTMENT 19 SENECA, MY DAUGHTER'S HURT SHE'S NOT BREATHING SHE'S BLEEDING!"*
Dispatcher: *"Where is she bleeding at?"*
Innocent Caller: *"(sobbing) All over, all over, hurry, hurry!"*
Dispatcher: *"Does she have a pulse?"*
Innocent Caller: *"NO! (sobbing) My husband is doing CPR, please hurry!"*
Dispatcher: *"Is she in her bedroom?"*
Innocent Caller: *"NO! She was in the bathtub and we pulled her out and she's on the floor. My husband is trying to breathe for her. WHERE ARE YOU, WHERE IS THE AMBULANCE?"*

Dispatcher:	*"You said she's on the floor?"*
Innocent Caller:	*"YES! She was in the tub, she's got her clothes on and some-body has hurt her. She's bruised and bloody, please help (sobbing)."*
Dispatcher:	*"Did she fall or something?"*
Innocent Caller:	*"(sobbing) NO! FIND HER BOYFRIEND, HE DID THIS TO HER! FIND PEYTON HAWKINS, HE DID THIS. SHE BROKE UP WITH HIM OH MY GOD! WHERE IS THE AMBULANCE?"*

The mother provided relevant information, so the dispatcher would understand the severity of the event. The subsequent investigation revealed that the victim's boyfriend had beaten her to death after she ended their relationship. Further inquiry disclosed that the suspect had also murdered an old girlfriend from a different town. He was eventually convicted of both murders.

In contrast to 911 calls filled with relevant information to get help as quickly as possible, some calls contained Extraneous Information. Information that does not appear to be relevant to the victim's situation is considered extraneous. Such comments do not contribute to aiding the victims and may delay help.

In the 911 study, 22% of all calls contained Extraneous Information. Most of these calls (93%) were made by guilty callers; only 7% were from innocent callers, as shown in Figure 8.1. This was one of the strongest indicators of guilt in the 911 study, as more than 13 times as many guilty callers used Extraneous Information as did innocent callers.

There are two major reasons why guilty callers provided Extraneous Information. One reason was to deflect blame away from the callers to other persons or events. If callers can divert the dispatchers' attention away from themselves, they may be able to avoid the dispatchers' probing questions

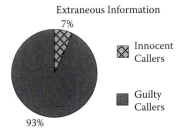

Figure 8.1 Percentages of Innocent vs. Guilty Callers in "Extraneous Information."

about their actions. A second reason guilty callers included Extraneous Information was because they had an overwhelming need to express it. It was information so vital to them that they could not omit it.

As an example of using Extraneous Information to deflect blame, a mother called 911 and explained that her son was having difficulty breathing. The dispatcher asked about the son:

Dispatcher: *"How old is your son?"*
Guilty Caller: *"He's only six, he's like eaten an apple and he's burpin' it up, he's not, not, it's like a seizure type, type. We got in a, yeah, we got in a car wreck about two months ago."*

The mother did not explain any connection between her son's critical breathing condition and a previous car wreck. She hoped the dispatcher would assume that the car wreck was the reason for the boy's distress. The investigation revealed that the mother's boyfriend severely beat the six-year-old boy in the mother's presence, and the car wreck was unrelated to the boy's injuries. The boy died before the medics arrived at the scene, and the autopsy revealed fractures to the victims' skull, ribs, wrists, and fingers. The boyfriend was convicted of homicide.

Regarding the second reason why guilty callers included Extraneous Information, key information that is foremost in one's mind is hard to conceal. Although the information may appear to be unrelated, the callers had such an overwhelming need to express it that they did not realize it might incriminate them. Guilty callers have unknowingly disclosed why they felt they had to commit the homicide. The Extraneous Information can provide investigators with keen insight to events that preceded the 911 call. Close scrutiny of Extraneous Information can reveal what is on the callers' minds.

To illustrate the value of examining Extraneous Information, consider the case of a stepfather who called 911 to report that his four-year-old stepdaughter was having a seizure.

Dispatcher: *"Does it look like she's having a seizure, can you, I mean, are her hands shaking? What's going on?"*
Guilty Caller: *"No, she's not shaking, she's almost like comatose… She complained of a headache about 20 minutes ago… She's been screaming really, really loud. She threw up water."*

The phrase "she threw up water" is quite different from "she threw up." The later phrase appears to be sufficient; therefore, the inclusion of the word "water" indicates that the stepfather was thinking about water. The word "water" may seem extraneous, but the stepfather had a need to include this word; in his mind, it was relevant. In fact, during the phone call, the father mentioned water three times. Investigators pondered the use of this word and surmised that water was somehow related to the girls' death. Drowning was one of the possibilities considered. Although the victim's body was not wet, the investigators kept an open mind and focused on water when they interviewed the stepfather.

The investigation revealed that the father had given his stepdaughter and his biological daughter glasses of water. The four-year-old stepdaughter knocked her glass over, spilling her water in the kitchen, and the agitated father yelled that she could not have any more. While the father was cleaning the spill, the stepdaughter took a drink from her sister's water glass. Now enraged, the father tied his stepdaughter to a chair, filled an empty two-liter Coke bottle with water and forced his stepdaughter to drink all of it. This caused hyponatremia, a condition that occurs when water is consumed too rapidly for the body to process it, resulting in an imbalance of sodium and other electrolytes in the bloodstream.* The excess water in the blood can be fatal and in this case it was. The father was convicted of homicide.

In addition to recognizing the presence of Extraneous Information, it is also important to note its location within the call. When extraneous comments appeared in the first few seconds of the 911 calls, it distracted from the victims' emergency, confused the dispatchers, and delayed aid. Some guilty callers began their calls by offering alibis. Callers who prioritized this type of Extraneous Information over germane details regarding critically injured victims were often guilty of the offense.

MR. AND MRS. HUNT CASE

Jake's call revealed a lack of relevant information about his in-laws' injuries and no extraneous information; thus, these indicators remain unchecked.

Innocent Indicators		**Guilty Indicators**
____ Relevant Information	n/a	____ Extraneous Information

Reference

Grice, P. (1989), *Studies in the Way of Words*, Harvard University, Cambridge, Massachusetts.

---

* Mayo Clinic, Rochester, Minnesota; http://www.mayoclinic.org/diseases-conditions /hyponatremia/basics/definition/con-20031445

How Does the Caller Describe the Situation?

"The truth of the story lies in the details."

Paul Auster

Innocent 911 callers seeking medical help communicated Sensory Details about the victims' conditions to ensure that appropriate aid would be dispatched. Through descriptions of sight, sound, smell, and touch (taste was not described in any of the 911 study calls), callers painted verbal pictures so dispatchers could clearly comprehend the nature of the emergency. Descriptions with Sensory Details also enabled dispatchers to aid the callers in stabilizing victims until help arrived. In contrast, many guilty callers equivocated instead of providing details. They offered vague comments that confused dispatchers and delayed proper medical response.

Credibility researchers cite unique sensory details as strong indicators of truthfulness in individuals' verbal statements (Adams and Jarvis, 2006). The most specific details in the 911 study created the sharpest images of the emergency situation. Innocent callers used Sensory Details to convey accurate information to obtain optimal medical aid.

In the 911 study, 27% of calls contained Sensory Details. Almost five times as many innocent callers (83%) included Sensory Details than did guilty callers (17%). See Figure 9.1.

A young woman called 911 to get help for her brother. She provided sensory details about her brother's condition without being prompted by the dispatcher:

Dispatcher: *"911, what is your emergency?"*
Innocent Caller: *"I need help. My brother's overdosing right now. Please get here. I'm at 4770 Roundhouse Court. He's gurgling and he's blue. He's not breathing. He's still got the needle in his hand. Please hurry."*

At the caller's first chance to speak, she provided Sensory Details of the sound of gurgling, the color of skin, and the sight of a needle in her brother's arm. The dispatcher was able to immediately assess the problem and dispatch help without delay. Despite the sister's clear descriptions and a prompt emergency response, the brother did not survive.

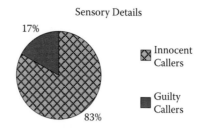

Figure 9.1 Percentages of Innocent vs. Guilty Callers in "Sensory Details."

In another case, a woman called 911 after hearing a gunshot.

Dispatcher: *"911, what is your address?"*
Innocent Caller: *"Bakersville Lane."*
Dispatcher: *"And what's going on there?"*
Innocent Caller: *"I just heard a loud noise, like a gun noise and I can't wake my husband up."*
Dispatcher: *"You heard a gun noise and what?*
Innocent Caller: *"I turned on the lights to wake up my husband and it's really, really bad."*
Dispatcher: *"What's really bad?"*
Innocent Caller: *"My husband. I was sleeping right next to him and I heard this loud noise and something hit me in the head. I thought he had gotten sick. I smelled gunpowder and I got up and turned on the lights and I saw all this blood right next to me."*

The wife's narrative was filled with details describing what she heard, felt, smelled, and saw. As she recounted the event, she placed herself back in the situation, reliving the sensory stimuli. The investigation revealed that the husband's ex-wife and boyfriend entered the house in the dark, shot the husband in the head, and left without being seen. The caller was innocent.

In striking contrast to innocent callers who spontaneously shared Sensory Details, some guilty callers in the 911 study were remarkable for their Lack of Sensory Details. After reporting their emergencies, these callers were reluctant to add additional information.

In the following case, a boyfriend called 911 regarding his girlfriend's baby:

Dispatcher: *"911."*
Guilty Caller: *"355 Trinity. I've got a 10-month-old baby. He's not breathing."*
Dispatcher: *"What's the address?"*
Guilty Caller: *"355 Trinity."*

Dispatcher: *"What's going on? Tell me exactly what happened. "*
Guilty Caller: *"He got—he threw up and he—he stopped breathing."*

After proving an initial assessment of the baby's condition, the caller stopped talking. The dispatcher had to ask specific questions to gain more information:

Dispatcher: *"What color are his lips?"*
Guilty Caller: *"They're purple."*
Dispatcher: *"What- what's his eyes doing?"*
Guilty Caller: *"His eyes are closed."*
Dispatcher: *"Okay. Are his eyes rolled back or..."*
Guilty Caller: *"No. His pupils are just fixed."*

This tedious method of obtaining information delayed the dispatcher's instructions for providing aid to the baby. The investigation revealed that the caller had shaken the baby, resulting in the baby's death.

In another example of Lack of Sensory Details, a man called 911 to report his mother's condition:

Dispatcher: *"911, what's your emergency?"*
Guilty Caller: *"Uh, my mom's dead on the kitchen floor."*
Dispatcher: *"You said your mom passed away?"*
Guilty Caller: *"Yes." (pause)*
Dispatcher: *"Ok let me get help started. I need to ask you a few questions. What do you think happened to her?"*
Guilty Caller: *"I don't know. I think I last talked to her Thursday." (pause)*
Dispatcher: *"So do you think she's been there since Thursday?"*
Guilty Caller: *"I don't know." (pause)*

The dispatcher did not know if the mom had a heart attack, had committed suicide, had fallen, or had been murdered. More details were needed to provide optimal assistance:

Dispatcher: *"Ok tell me exactly what's going on."*
Guilty Caller: *"She's just laying flat on her back on the kitchen floor and there's blood everywhere."*

The caller wasted time by withholding details about the victim. Although the caller volunteered a general assessment, the dispatcher needed Sensory Details to fully assess the situation. The caller was convicted of homicide.

MR. AND MRS. HUNT CASE
Jake provided a Lack of Sensory Details. Although he said that there was *"blood all over the floor,"* he failed to provide additional details such as where the blood was coming from, whether both of his in-laws were bleeding or just one, descriptions of the injuries, and additional specific conditions of the victims.

Innocent Indicators		**Guilty Indicators**
____Sensory Details	n/a	✔ Lack of Sensory Details

Reference

Adams, S., and Jarvis, J. (2006), "Indicators of Veracity and Deception: An Analysis of Written Statements Made to Police," *The International Journal of Speech, Language and the Law*, 13 (1), 1–22.

How Does the Caller Prioritize the Information?

10

"How, when, and where you say something can actually be more important then the message itself."

Anne Bruce and James S. Pepitone

In life-and-death situations, innocent 911 callers typically Prioritized the Order of their information by its importance to the victims. The most prioritized details were as follows: who was the victim, what happened to the victim, and where the victim was located. Some guilty callers, however, had different priorities. They furnished information in an Inappropriate Order by prioritizing their needs above the victims' needs.

Most 911 calls are of limited duration, and time is critical. The callers may have only a few seconds to communicate key details, as the calls may be interrupted or terminated. Dispatchers could be called away to handle radio traffic, callers may need to assist victims, interference on the line might cause inaudible dialogue, or the calls may become disconnected. Additionally, because time is of the essence in medical emergencies, wasted chatter could cost lives. Prioritization of Information is vital.

Innocent callers focused on victims first because the victims were the reason for the 911 calls. Once the details about victims were communicated to dispatchers, most innocent callers in the 911 study shifted to details about the event and the scene. Lastly, callers volunteered available clues regarding suspects to ensure safety and assist with the investigation. Rarely did innocent callers offer irrelevant information or focus on their own problems.

In the following example, a mother called 911 to demand help for her child:

Innocent Caller: *"NOOOOOO!"*
Dispatcher: *"911, what is your emergency?"*
Innocent Caller: *"Get an ambulance to 43 Arlow Street—my baby's choking—she's ain't breathin'—HURRY HURRY COME ON!"*
Dispatcher: *"What happened?"*
Innocent Caller: *"SHE'S CHOKING! The bread's laying out, she must have ate it and she's choking, come on!"*

59

The mother explained the event by prioritizing the need for an ambulance, and then providing her location, identifying the victim and the victim's condition, and describing the scene. The investigation revealed that the baby died because bread lodged in her esophagus had blocked her airway.

Conversely, many guilty 911 callers initially shared information that was of priority importance to them rather than furnishing information that was most important for the well-being of the victims. Alibi information and exculpatory information were often the first topics addressed with the dispatchers, revealing their importance to the guilty callers.

In the 911 study, 24% of callers used Inappropriate Order. Eighty-seven percent of these callers were guilty and 13% were innocent, as illustrated in Figure 10.1.

In the following example, a mother called 911 to report that intruders entered her home and attacked her two young sons and herself:

Dispatcher:	*"911, what is your emergency?"*
Guilty Caller:	*"Somebody came in...they broke in."*
Dispatcher:	*"Ma'am?"*
Guilty Caller:	*"They just stabbed me and my children."*
Dispatcher:	*"What?"*
Guilty Caller:	*"They just stabbed me and my kids...my little boys."*

In this case, the mother prioritized the offender (*"Somebody came in"*), then commented on the event (*"...they broke in."*) and focused on her own injury (*"They just stabbed me..."*). These topics were so important to the caller that she addressed them immediately. After those matters were shared, the mother added that her children were also victims in the assault. The investigation revealed that the mother's wounds were minor compared to her children's injuries that were fatal. Experts informed the court that the mother's wounds were self-inflicted, and she was convicted of killing her sons.

In the following case, a husband called 911 to report that his wife had been assaulted:

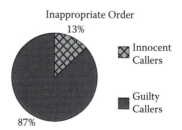

Figure 10.1 Percentages of Innocent vs. Guilty Callers in "Inappropriate Order."

Dispatcher:	*"911, what is your emergency?"*
Guilty Caller:	<u>*"I, uh, just got home, I've been workin' out of state."*</u>
Dispatcher:	*"Uh huh..."*
Guilty Caller:	<u>*"My kids are sleepin', they're in their rooms, they been sleep-*</u> <u>*ing all mornin'. I just got home and the place is a wreck. The*</u> <u>*whole house is tore up, everything.*</u> *And my wife, my wife is dead...it looks like she's been shot or something."*

The husband opened the 911 call by establishing an alibi, the most important issue to him: *"I, uh, just got home, I've been workin' out of state."* Next, he focused on his children, who were uninjured, by commenting, *"My kids are sleepin', they're in their room, they been sleeping all morning."* After discussing the children, the caller advised that he *"just got home...."* The next most important factor for the caller was to present an *"intruder"* theme by announcing that *"the place is a wreck. The whole house is tore up, everything."* Finally, he followed up by adding that his wife was *"dead"* and she *"had been shot or something."* Instead of using Inappropriate Order, the husband should have prioritized his wife's condition and her need for immediate aid. Only after establishing that the dispatcher understood the emergency and had dispatched help should the caller have offered details about himself and the unharmed children. The husband eventually confessed that he shot and killed his wife after she told him that she was seeking a divorce.

MR. AND MRS. HUNT CASE

Jake told the dispatcher that his in-laws *"didn't come to church this morning and my wife and I were worried."*

Next, he advised that there had been a burglary at the residence.

"...I found them in the...there's been a break-in, I think!"

Jake repeated the burglary theme by adding,

"Somebody broke in and tore up their house. There is stuff everywhere."

Finally, Jake shared the information that should have been the priority,

"My wife's parents are dead!"

This was Inappropriate Order for a scene with two critically injured individuals.

Innocent Indicators		**Guilty Indicators**
___ Prioritized Order	n/a	✔ Inappropriate Order

How Does the Caller Describe the Conditions?

11

"In films, murders are always very clean. I show how difficult it is and what a messy thing it is to kill a man."

Alfred Hitchcock

Innocent callers, focused on the victims' survival, spontaneously described the Condition of the Victims, such as their breathing, pulse, and bleeding. This differs from describing the Condition of the Scene, such as soiled carpets and stained furniture. Instead of addressing the victims' injuries, some guilty callers described blood on the floor or the couch.

In the 911 study, innocent callers provided details about the victims' bleeding and the location of the bleeding. The following exchange occurred after a man with an assault conviction called 911 and demanded an ambulance for his friend. The dispatcher assured the caller that help was en route.

Dispatcher: *"Sir, help is already on the way."*
Innocent Caller: *"Hurry, because* he's bleeding from the side of his head.*"*

In this case, the caller focused on the victim's condition. He volunteered information that his friend was bleeding, and he identified the site of the bleeding. Nowhere in the 911 call did the caller mention blood on the couch or the floor. Nevertheless, the caller was a person of interest because of his prior conviction. The friend died of his head injury, and the subsequent investigation revealed that the caller was innocent.

Inexperienced police officers and medics are often shocked at the amount of blood at crime scenes and accidents. The human body is composed of approximately 1.5 gallons of blood, and the average individual can *"bleed out"* within seconds if a major blood vessel leading from the heart is severed (Gutierrez et al., 2004). Most homicides involving firearms, knives, or other weapons are characterized by significant amounts of blood on the victim and at the crime scene. Callers to 911 lines, like inexperienced police officers and medics, are also shocked at the amount of blood at homicide scenes. Some 911 callers made spontaneous remarks about the amount of blood at the scene rather than focusing on the victim's bleeding.

Ten percent of the callers in the 911 study remarked on the Blood and Brains at the scene. Over five times as many guilty callers (84%) mentioned Blood and Brains as did innocent callers (16%), as illustrated in Figure 11.1.

The following exchange occurred between a dispatcher and a wife, who called 911 regarding her husband:

Dispatcher: *"Ok do you want to start CPR?"*
Guilty Caller: *"He's got blood all over the rug..."*

This wife was clearly more focused on the scene than on her husband. She eventually confessed that she had convinced her boyfriend to commit the homicide, and both were convicted of the murder.

A parallel reference to blood at the scene is brains at the scene. Examine the words of a husband who called 911 to report that his wife had committed suicide by shooting herself in the head with a handgun:

Dispatcher: *"Help is on the way, Rick."*
Guilty Caller: *"Her brains are on the back of the couch! Oh my God!"*

The husband failed to describe his wife's condition—severe bleeding. Instead, he remarked on the condition of the couch, and his focus was not on his wife and her injuries. The investigation revealed that the husband shot his wife, and he was later convicted of her murder.

In a similar case, when the 911 dispatcher asked a husband about the condition of his wife, he calmly stated

Guilty Caller: *"She's handcuffed and it looks like someone blew her brains out."*

The investigators in this case had prior training in 911 Homicide Call Analysis and noted the Blood and Brains indicator when reviewing the 911

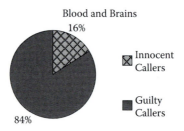

Figure 11.1 Percentages of Innocent vs. Guilty Callers in "Blood and Brains."

call. They interviewed the husband with the insight from the analysis and he confessed to the murder.

No innocent callers in the 911 study commented about victims' brains on the floor or on the wall. The question of why innocent callers do not mention brains at the scene has been the topic of ongoing discussion by investigators. Detective Mark Allison, after observing many homicide scenes, asserted that it is insensitive and disrespectful to share that a loved one's brains are "lying on the floor."* His theory is supported by a case in which a young boy's head was crushed as his mother backed her car out of the driveway. The scene was horrific and the child's brains were splattered on the car's tire. Several 911 calls were made by frantic neighbors; however, not one caller mentioned the child's brains on the tire or at the scene. To do so would have been considered disrespectful to the child.

Comments about vomit at the scenes are different from comments about Blood and Brains. Remarks about vomit can provide diagnostic information about the victims' condition. The following case illustrates this point:

Dispatcher: *"Does she have a pulse?*
Innocent Caller: *"I don't think so and I don't think she's breathing...she's thrown up all over the place!"*

The scene resembled a gruesome homicide; however, the autopsy report revealed that the wife had died from a drug overdose and the husband was innocent.

Considerations
Some victims of homicide do not bleed from their injuries. For example, victims of strangulation, suffocation, poisoning, and drowning rarely bleed. Therefore, the Bleeding indicator and the Blood and Brains indicator would not be relevant in these types of homicides.

* Detective Mark Allison, West Carrollton Police Department, Dayton, Ohio.

MR. AND MRS. HUNT CASE

Jake did not inform the dispatcher that his in-laws were bleeding. Instead, he remarked about blood at the scene.

Dispatcher: *"Jake, are you sure it's too late? Do you want me to help you with CPR?"*

Jake: *"There is blood everywhere…it's all over the floor."*

Later in the call, the dispatcher feared for Jake's safety and directed him to wait outside for the police. Jake advised

   "I am outside, I'm in the driveway…there is blood all over the floor!"

Innocent Indicators		**Guilty Indicators**
____ Bleeding Comments	n/a	✓ Blood and Brains Comments

Reference

Gutierrez, G., Reines, H.D., and Wulf-Gutierrez, M.E. (2004), "Clinical Review: Hemorrhagic Shock." *Journal of Critical Care.*

How Is the Call Made?   IV

Does the Caller Express Urgency or No Urgency?

12

"There must be a sense of urgency in a true emergency."

Anonymous

Like football players in competition, many callers "lined up on their side of the field," in either offensive or defensive roles. The offensive players took the initiative and charged forward, while the defensive players waited to react. Offensive, innocent callers in the 911 study yelled at dispatchers to speed up the emergency response. These callers were focused on getting medical aid to seriously injured victims as quickly as possible, and their calls revealed their sense of Urgency. Guilty callers often expressed No Urgency.

A British study examined fire emergency calls in London in an effort to determine which calls were reporting genuine fires and which were hoax calls. Urgency was identified as the most important characteristic in identifying authentic fire emergencies (Olsson, 2004). True emergencies—fires and medical crises—demanded urgent responses to save property and lives.

A sense of Urgency was evident in the following 911 call made by a father of a six-month-old son:

Dispatcher: *"911, what is your emergency?"*
Innocent Caller: *"I need an ambulance* | *RIGHT HERE AND RIGHT NOW!"* |

The caller's son was in respiratory distress due to excessive bedding covering his nose and mouth. The innocent father urgently tried to save his son's life, but the child died from suffocation. The manner of death was accidental.

Another innocent caller pleaded with the dispatcher to send help right away. When help was delayed, he enlisted the help of a neighbor and called 911 again to speed up the response:

Dispatch: *"911, what's your emergency?"*
Innocent Caller: *"I called earlier about a guy—we can't revive him! We're trying to get him help* | *right now!* | *I have a neighbor sitting at the entrance…"*
Dispatch: *"You're off of Blackthorn Drive?"*
Innocent Caller: *"Yes—yes I have a guy sitting out there in the truck to bring you guys down to this house. He's waiting on you*

69

guys. It's been like 10 minutes and | *I hear no sirens going off or nothing! COME ON!"*

The victim died despite the innocent caller's urgent pleas for help.

Thirty-nine percent of the calls in the 911 study contained Urgency. Of these calls, 79% were made by innocent callers and only 21% by guilty callers (see Figure 12.1).

Despite the life-and-death situations, some callers expressed No Urgency during their 911 calls. As an example of No Urgency, a wife called 911 regarding her husband:

Dispatcher: *"911, what is your emergency?"*
Guilty Caller: *"It's not really an emergency, but my husband committed suicide."*
Dispatcher: *"Just now?"*
Guilty Caller: *"Yeah, well, last night."*

The wife inadvertently revealed that she was aware her husband had committed suicide the previous night. However, she did not call 911 until the next day. Her delayed call and her lack of urgency revealed that her focus was not on her husband's survival. She was later found guilty of her husband's death.

In the next case, a caller reported that his wife had committed suicide. Consider the caller's instructions to the dispatcher:

Dispatcher: *"Help is on the way, they will be there in a minute..."*
Guilty Caller: *"Tell them not to use lights and siren, I don't want to disturb the neighborhood."*

As incredulous as it seems, the husband's concern for the neighborhood's tranquility was greater than his concern for his wife's survival. The lack of any urgency made this caller highly suspect. The results of the subsequent investigation confirmed the husband's guilt in the homicide.

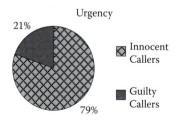

Figure 12.1 Percentages of Innocent vs. Guilty Callers in "Urgency."

When the 911 system is used to seek help in a potential fatality, especially when a personal relationship exists between the caller and the victim, the lack of Urgency is concerning. Some guilty callers failed to seek immediate aid for victims because they had no intention of saving the victims. These callers might have committed the murders well before placing the 911 calls and therefore knew that the victims were already deceased, rendering aid futile. The offenders might also need time to plan how to best stage the scene to mislead authorities.

It is important to examine where urgency is requested during the 911 call. Some guilty callers failed to express urgency throughout most of the call and only added weak requests for urgency after being prompted by the dispatcher. For example, after several minutes of conversation, dispatchers might inform the callers that the ambulance is approaching. If callers then respond weakly with "Tell them to hurry," after expressing no previous urgency, this response has been prompted and is not an indicator of urgency.

MR. AND MRS. HUNT CASE

Jake expressed No Urgency throughout his 911 call.

Innocent Indicators		Guilty Indicators
___ Urgency	n/a	_✓_ No Urgency

Reference

Olsson, J. (2004), *Forensic Linguistics: An Introduction to Language, Crime and Law*, Continuum International Publishing Group Ltd., London.

Is the Caller Fearful? 13

"Self-preservation is the first law of nature."
Samuel Butler

When street officers are dispatched to the scene of a violent assault or homicide, they routinely draw their service weapons on arrival at the location. Most homicide scenes are horrific in nature and therefore stressful for the responders; even seasoned officers reported being "scared to death" at gruesome murder scenes. The responding officers knew the offender might still be inside or near the premises, and their personal safety was at risk. Additionally, backup was not always available, and officers were often placed in situations where they had no alternative but to enter the premises on their own, locate the victims, and provide assistance. Upon entry, pairs of officers cleared each room in tandem until any direct threat was resolved. Only then would the officers holster their sidearms, cautiously attend to the victims, and search for evidence.

Innocent 911 callers exhibited the same Fear for their Own Safety that responding police officers display. The callers did not typically carry weapons, and they were naturally concerned about the victims and their own personal safety at the murder scenes. Innocent callers in these circumstances were scared and frequently expressed that fear through urgent demands to the dispatcher. Conversely, the guilty callers had no fear of assailants in the vicinity. They knew that no one but themselves and possible accomplices murdered the victims. No danger was lurking nearby.

When innocent 911 callers arrived on the scenes after violent attacks, the normal reaction was fear that an offender might be nearby and thus still pose a threat. Offenders might return to further injure the victim or attack the caller. A teenager discovered his friend stabbed to death and lying on the kitchen floor. The 911 dialogue revealed the caller's Fear for his Own Safety:

Dispatcher: *"We have help on the way, what color is the trailer?"*
Innocent Caller: *"IT'S WHITE, HURRY UP, HURRY UP PLEASE.* HE COULD STILL BE IN THE TRAILER COURT!"

73

The teenager in the previous case was clearly fearful that the assailant might still be present and could cause further harm to the victim or the caller.

In another example of Fear for Own Safety, a youth called 911 and stated that intruders had entered his home:

Dispatcher: "911. State your emergency."
Innocent Caller: "There's some—some guys. They're gonna kill my mom and dad. Can you come please? Can you come really fast? Please, please."
Dispatcher: "Can you tell me what happened?"
Innocent Caller: "They rang the door and they have guns to shoot my mom and dad."
Dispatcher: "Right now?"
Innocent Caller: "Yeah. Can you come really fast? Bring some cops."
Dispatcher: "I have them coming, hon. Listen okay?"
Innocent Caller: "Okay."
Dispatcher: "Listen to me. Take a deep breath. Where are you at in the house?"
Innocent Caller: "Um, inside the bathroom."
Dispatcher: "You're in the bathroom?"
Innocent Caller: "Yeah."
Dispatcher: "Who's with you?"
Innocent Caller: "My sister."
Dispatcher: "How old is she?"
Innocent Caller: "Six years old. Can you come really fast? Hurry up."
Dispatcher: "Yes, stay on the line with me. Don't hang up."
Innocent Caller: "Okay."

The caller was innocent and had locked himself and his younger sister in the bathroom in case the assailants returned. His call revealed Fear for Own Safety, as well as fear for his sister's safety. The call was also filled with Urgency. Both of the parents died of gunshot wounds. Two suspects unknown to the caller were apprehended and convicted of the double homicide.

A mother of a teenager called 911 to get help for her injured son. She was in fear for her son's life as well as her own.

Dispatcher: "911, what is the address of your emergency?"
Innocent Caller: "(Screaming) Oh, oh, oh! Yes, my son's been shot… 305 State Street. Please hurry."
Dispatcher: "I'm gonna ask you a few questions, OK? Stay on the line with me."
Innocent Caller: "Please hurry. I don't want him to die, please hurry!"
Dispatcher: "What's the problem, tell me exactly what happened."
Innocent Caller: "My husband came in and shot my son!"

Dispatcher:	*"Your husband did?"*
Innocent Caller:	*"Please, my husband yes, please hurry."*
Dispatcher:	*"Ma'am? Are you with your son now?"*
Innocent Caller:	*"Yes."*
Dispatcher:	*"How old is he?"*
Innocent Caller:	*"Thirteen."*
Dispatcher:	*"Thirteen?"*
Innocent Caller:	*"Yes."*
Dispatcher:	*"Is he conscious?"*
Innocent Caller:	*"No."*
Dispatcher:	*"Is he breathing?"*
Innocent Caller:	*"Yes, barely."*
Dispatcher:	*"Stay with me, OK? You're doing a great job. Just stay with me, OK? Where is your husband?"*
Innocent Caller:	*"He's in our bedroom."*
Dispatcher:	*"You're in the bedroom?"*
Innocent Caller:	*"I'm in my son's bedroom."*
Dispatcher:	*"Do you know where the gun is?"*
Innocent Caller:	*"My husband has it!"* (screaming)
Dispatcher:	*"He has the gun?"*
Innocent Caller:	*"Yes."*
Dispatcher:	*"Where did he shoot your son at?"*
Innocent Caller:	*"In the head! (crying) He's not breathing!"*
Dispatcher:	*"He's not breathing at all?"*
Innocent Caller:	*"No. Not that, I can't see any movement."* (crying hysterically.)
Dispatcher:	*"You don't see any movement. OK. I need you to stay inside that room where you're safe, OK? And we are gonna stay on the line with you until the police get there, OK?"*
Innocent Caller:	*"(screaming hysterically)* **OH OH OH OH NO!"** (gunshots heard in background)
Dispatcher:	*"OK. Ma'am, ma'am, is there a place in your son's room that you can hide? In the room that you're in, I want you to hide. Can you hide?"*
Innocent Caller:	*"I'm in the closet."*
Dispatcher:	*"Hide in the closet. Can he get into the room? Is the door locked?"*
Innocent Caller:	*"I've got the door locked."*
Dispatcher:	*"OK. You stay in the closet. Do not come out of the closet, OK?"*
Innocent Caller:	*"OK."*
Dispatcher:	*"I want you to stay in the closet. Do not answer him and be as quiet as you can, OK?"*
Innocent Caller:	*"OK."*

Dispatcher: *"I don't want him to know that you're in the closet, OK?"*
Innocent Caller: *"OK."*
Dispatcher: *"Is he still yelling?"*
Innocent Caller: *"Yes."*
Dispatcher: *"OK. You let him continue to yell, OK? You stay in the closet."*

When officers arrived, the father was still inside the house, holding his gun. The officers subdued the father and the mother was safe, but the medics could not save the 13-year-old son who died from the gunshot wound to his head. The father, who had earlier threatened to destroy the son, confessed to the murder.

In contrast to fearful innocent callers, guilty 911 callers usually displayed No Fear for their own safety at violent murder scenes. They remained on the line with the dispatchers for long periods of time without ever commenting on their safety or the suspects' possible proximity. Unlike innocent callers who were afraid because they did not know where the threat was, guilty callers knew there was no threat.

The No Fear indicator was present in 13% of the calls in the 911 study. As Figure 13.1 indicates, almost all of the callers who expressed No Fear were guilty (92%). Only 8% of the innocent callers expressed No Fear.

As an example of a caller with No Fear, a young man called 911 because his wife was shot in bed at 4 a.m. The wife was killed with a single shotgun blast as she slept. The husband told the dispatcher that he was in the shower when he heard a noise and came out of the bathroom to discover that his wife was dead. The husband never expressed fear for his own safety during the entire 911 call. In contrast, when the first deputy arrived on scene, he immediately grabbed his service rifle and later explained, *"I was scared. I thought the suspect could still be in the area."* Unlike the cautious deputy, the relaxed husband was sitting on the front porch in his shorts, smoking a cigarette. Although the husband had several guns in his trailer, he never felt the need to arm himself for defense. He was eventually convicted of his wife's murder.

No Fear

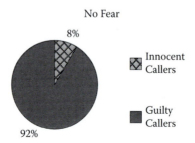

Figure 13.1 Percentages of Innocent vs. Guilty Callers in "No Fear."

In another case, a wife located her old boyfriend on Facebook and invited him to visit. She asked her husband if the "old friend" could stay with them for a week and the husband agreed. On the sixth day of the visit, the wife and boyfriend reported that they "discovered" the husband dead in the garage at 7 a.m. There had been a vicious, violent assault, and the scene was gruesome. The husband's head had been repeatedly bashed with a pipe causing the head to jellify. The wife called 911 but expressed No Fear for her safety. The wife and boyfriend were found guilty of the husband's murder.

A husband returned home from work and called 911 to report that he found his wife dead, lying nude on the kitchen floor. She had been stabbed multiple times, and the scene was horrifying. The husband stayed on the phone with the 911 dispatcher for seven minutes and expressed No Fear for his own safety. Instead, he calmly answered the dispatcher's questions and voiced concern about his children who were in school at the time. He was later convicted of homicide.

Many guilty 911 callers expressed No Fear for their own safety or the suspects' possible proximity because they knew there was no threat to their safety—because they were the killers.

MR. AND MRS. HUNT CASE

Jake was faced with a violent murder scene and displayed No Fear for his own safety. Innocent 911 callers facing Jake's situation would be expected to be fearful that the killer could still be nearby and might still be a threat.

Innocent Indicators		Guilty Indicators
___ Fear for Caller's Safety	n/a	✓ No Fear for Caller's Safety

Is the Caller in Close Proximity to the Victim?

14

"Why are you so far away?"

Unknown

The physical distance between the callers and the victims during the 911 calls can provide insight to their relationship. Most callers use cellphones or portable phones and are not restricted in their movement. Therefore, they can remain in close Proximity to victims while talking with dispatchers. Many offenders in the 911 study, however, moved away from the victims and called 911 when they were out of sight of the bodies.

Innocent 911 callers wanted to help the victims. Helping the victims involved seeking aid from 911, assessing the victims' condition, communicating changes to the dispatchers, and giving CPR and other medical aid as the dispatchers directed. Therefore, many Innocent Callers remained near the victims to offer help. When the victims were loved ones, innocent 911 callers stayed close, to cradle or hold the victims while on the phone with the dispatchers. This was especially true when the case involved an infant or small child, and the callers were parents or grandparents. In some emergencies, medics had to physically pry parents away from their children so they could attend to the victims. Evan after pronouncements of death, mothers and fathers clung to bloodied corpses and had to be forcefully pulled off their children to allow the coroner's team to remove the bodies.

Thirty-seven percent of callers in the 911 study remained in close Proximity to the victims. As shown in Figure 14.1, 72% of these callers were innocent and 28% were guilty.

The following case illustrates Proximity between the caller and the victim:

Dispatcher: *"911, what is your emergency?"*
Innocent Caller: *"GET AN AMBULANCE HERE NOW! MY BABY'S CHOKING! 18 FIRST STREET!"*
Dispatcher: *"Where is your child at Ma'am?"*
Innocent Caller: *"RIGHT HERE, IN MY ARMS, SHE'S NOT BREATHING!"*

79

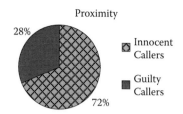

Proximity

28%

72%

Innocent
Callers

Guilty
Callers

Figure 14.1 Percentages of Innocent vs. Guilty Callers in "Proximity."

The Innocent Caller remained physically close to her baby who had choked on a small toy and later died at the hospital. The case was ruled an accident.

In another case, a mother and her five-month-old daughter were travelling in a car when a drive-by shooter accidentally shot into the mother's car. The bullet struck the child, and an innocent bystander called 911. After advising that help was on the way, the dispatcher tried to direct the caller to give CPR to the child:

Dispatcher: "OK...listen to me..."
Innocent Caller: "Oh, poor baby."
Dispatcher: "...you have to get her on the ground, listen to me."
                            (WAILING IN BACKGROUND)
Innocent Caller: "That's her mother holding her."
Dispatcher: "What part of her body was shot?"
Innocent Caller: "We don't know but she's—her mother won't turn her loose."
Dispatcher: "Okay, listen to me..."
Innocent Caller: "But she bleeding from her side."
Dispatcher: "Tell-tell the mother... the side of her stomach, okay... get a clean dry cloth or towel, you need to put it on the wound, apply firm and steady pressure and don't lift it up to look."
Caller to mother: "Yeah, you gotta stop the bl- - she just told me."
Dispatcher: "We have to give the baby mouth to mouth okay, you need to get her flat on her back."
Caller to mother: "Yeah, give her here, come here, give me the..."
Dispatcher: "You need to get her flat on her back."
Caller to mother: "Come here let me see. I'll give her mouth to mouth, give her here."

The mother did not want to release her baby who had died instantly from the gunshot wound. She cradled her close without concern for getting blood on herself. The mother's Proximity revealed that her focus was on her baby, and she could not bear to be parted from her.

In contrast to Innocent Callers, some guilty 911 callers revealed that they were physically distant from the victims. Such distancing is unexpected, especially when the victims were in medical distress, and the callers' proximity and immediate actions might have assisted them. Proximity to the victims could also aid in providing the dispatcher with ongoing, critical information for the first responders.

The following case is an example of a caller who had No Proximity to the victim:

Dispatcher:	*"911, what is your emergency?"*
Guilty Caller:	*"My, my son's not breathin'"*
Dispatcher:	*"What's your address sir?"*
Guilty Caller:	*"1271 Park Street."*
Dispatcher:	*"Do you know what's wrong with him sir?"*
Guilty Caller:	*"No, I don't know what happened."*
Dispatcher:	*"Does he have a pulse?"*
Guilty Caller:	*"I don't know, he's in the nursery."*

It is difficult to understand why parents would not be as close to the victim as possible, cradling their critically ill baby. In this case, the father of the baby was calling 911 from the living room as his son lay dying in the nursery. The autopsy revealed that the victim had a skull fracture, and the father was eventually convicted of his death.

In a similar case from Tennessee, a man called 911 to report that his girlfriend's baby was in distress:

Dispatcher:	*"911, what is your emergency?"*
Guilty Caller:	*"My step-daughter ain't breathing, get someone over here."*
Dispatcher:	*"I have you at 12 Hazel Street, is that correct?*
Guilty Caller:	*"Yeah."*
Dispatcher:	*"Are you holding her right now? Can you tell if she is breathing?"*
Guilty Caller:	*"She's lying on the floor in the den."*

The fact that the caller had No Proximity to the Victim revealed a physical distancing and the possibility of a distancing in the relationship. The mother's boyfriend later confessed that he shook the baby because she would not stop crying. The coroner stated that the victim's brain had bounced around the skull so violently that the shaking had killed the child within minutes.

In some instances, guilty 911 callers increased the distances between themselves and the victims by leaving the house. In the following case, a father called 911 to report his son's injuries:

Dispatcher:	*"911, what is your emergency?"*
Guilty Caller:	*"My son fell, fell outta bed"*
Dispatcher:	*"Gimmie your address."*
Guilty Caller:	*"I'm on Vine, 2322 Vine."*
Dispatcher:	*"All right and your house is marked? Is there anybody with your little boy right now?"*
Guilty Caller:	*"No, Ma'am. He's in there, in the house."*

The father in this case revealed that he was not in the house with the victim. Thus, it would be impossible to assess the victim's developing condition, communicate those developments back to the dispatcher, and give aid to the child. Instead of cradling and comforting his critically injured boy until help arrived, the father waited outside in the driveway for the medics. The father was found guilty of the murder of his son.

Considerations

Innocent and guilty indicators are not absolute; they must be considered in context. For example, when examining proximity, it is important to know if offenders might still be present. Innocent 911 callers may run to neighbors' homes or sit in locked cars because they fear for their own safety. In domestic violence cases in which offenders have injured or killed victims, it is common for callers to hide in locked bathrooms for protection while calling 911, thus necessitating distancing from the victims until help arrives.

Another proximity consideration applies when crime scenes are so horrific that it would be natural to leave the scene. For example, if a family member had been decapitated, burned beyond recognition, or in a stage of decomposition, it would be reasonable for callers to move away from the disturbing sights and smells at the scene.

MR. AND MRS. HUNT CASE
The Hunt case is an example of a scene with so much blood that many callers might want to step away from the sight. The Proximity indicator therefore does not apply.

Innocent Indicators		**Guilty Indicators**
____Proximity to Victim	(n/a)	____No Proximity to Victim

Does the Caller Begin with Initial Sounds or with Initial Delays?

15

"Defer no time, delays have dangerous ends."

William Shakespeare

Some innocent callers were so intent on getting immediate help that they uttered Initial Sounds or comments before the dispatchers completed their opening question. They cried, wailed, or shouted, *"No, no, no, no!"* The innocent callers' attention remained on the victims, and they repeated the victims' names in an effort to revive them. When dispatchers cued up the calls and began to ask their first question, the innocent callers frequently talked over them, demanding help while the dispatchers were still speaking. Most guilty callers in the 911 study, however, remained silent while waiting for the dispatchers. Other guilty callers responded to the dispatchers' first question with an Initial Delay.

In the following exchange, a desperate mother shouted at the dispatcher before the dispatcher had a chance to talk. The mother then talked at the same time as the dispatcher to expedite aid for her baby:

Innocent Caller: *"Pick up!!"*
Dispatcher: *"91-"*
Innocent Caller: *"Get the-"*
Dispatcher: *"-1 what is-"*
Innocent Caller: *"Get the ambulance to 873 Pine, my baby's not breathing!"*

The innocent mother knew her baby was in critical condition and did not waste valuable seconds waiting for the dispatcher to complete the first question. Her frantic efforts to get help were not enough to save the life of her child.

A caller seeking aid for a young suicide victim yelled to a friend before the dispatcher spoke:

Innocent Caller: *"I got 911!"*
Dispatcher: *"911, what is your emergency?"*

The caller, in crisis mode, could not remain quiet. She wanted her friend to know that she had already called 911. The victim had hung himself and did not live despite his innocent friend's continued efforts to revive him.

Before individuals ever pick up the phone to call 911, numerous events have already occurred at the scene. In many cases, the 911 callers were present when the incidents occurred and possessed eyewitness details such as the victims' conditions and the offenders' descriptions. Even if 911 callers arrived after the event, they may also have obtained crucial details that could save the victim's life if they were immediately shared with the dispatchers.

All 911 callers, whether innocent or guilty, will have conducted an assessment of the situation before deciding that the victims need medical attention. Although the thought process may vary depending on the event, these callers are under extreme stress while they perform a series of time-consuming actions. First, the caller must locate a telephone, then dial 911, and wait while the phone rings into the dispatch center. For innocent callers, each ring of the phone can seem like an eternity. When callers are focused on getting help in a crisis, time stands still. When the dispatcher finally asks, "911, what is your emergency?" the innocent callers' emotions have been pent up for so long that they are immediately expelled as a plea for help with details about the victim. Innocent callers often scream, cry, or yell on the 911 line before the dispatcher's opening question and rarely hesitate when answering. They may "talk over" the dispatchers' opening comments because they are focused on the victim and desperate to get aid. From their perspective, too much time has already passed.

Twenty-eight percent of callers in the 911 study made Initial Sounds before the dispatchers completed their first question. As illustrated in Figure 15.1, four times as many of the Initial Sounds were from innocent callers (80%) than from guilty callers (20%).

In the following case a father called 911 after discovering his child in medical distress:

Dispatcher:	"911, what is your emer—?"
Innocent Caller:	"GET AN AMBULANCE TO 897 FRAZIER STREET! MY TWO-MONTH-OLD ISN'T BREATHING! MY WIFE IS DOING CPR, GET THEM MOVING! NOW!"

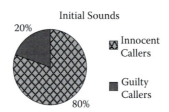

Initial Sounds

20%

⊠ Innocent Callers

■ Guilty Callers

80%

Figure 15.1 Percentages of Innocent vs. Guilty Callers in "Initial Sounds."

The caller did not delay when connected by the dispatcher. He focused on the victim by immediately demanding help and providing details. The investigation revealed that the mother was sleeping while the father watched a sporting event on television. As the father prepared for bed, he looked into the nursery to check on the baby. He noticed the baby was wedged between the mattress and the crib corner and he immediately turned on the bedroom light and approached the child. These actions took a few seconds. He assessed the child and realized that the baby was limp and lifeless. This took a few more seconds. He laid the baby on the changing table and observed that the child was not breathing. These mental and physical actions took several more seconds. The husband yelled out to his wife to wake up and he initiated CPR on his son. The wife entered the room and took over CPR as the husband located his phone and called 911. These actions took additional seconds. The frantic father waited for the dispatcher to finally answer the phone and when the dispatcher asked, *"911, what is your emergency?"* the caller interrupted. He screamed out a demand for help, adding details about the victim and the event. The investigation revealed that the child rolled into the corner of the crib causing his head to become wedged between the mattress and the wooden frame. The child died at the scene, and the death was ruled an accident.

In the following case, a teacher called 911 after a student was shot at an elementary school:

Dispatcher:	*"911, what is your emer-"*
Innocent Caller:	*"Start a medic to Lincoln Elementary School, a student's been shot! He's bleeding really bad, he's shot in the back. We're in the playground, hurry up, hurry up please!"*

The teacher was inside the school when the shooting occurred. She heard the shot, looked out of the window toward the playground, and saw several students standing around the victim. She ran outside, asked the students what had happened, got the information, began assessing the victim's condition by lifting his shirt and examining his wound, and determined that he needed immediate medical attention. The process so far had taken over a minute. More time passed as the anxious teacher comforted and aided the panicked victim and pulled out her cell phone to call 911. The phone rang into the dispatch center four times while the desperate teacher waited. The 911 dispatcher began to ask, *"911, what is your emer-."* The caller immediately blurted out a demand for help and the details about the victim and the location, making Initial Sounds by interrupting before the dispatcher completed her question.

In contrast to innocent callers, some guilty callers remained silent as they waited for the dispatchers to complete their introductions. There appeared to

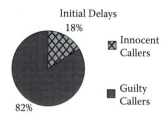

Figure 15.2 Percentages of Innocent vs. Guilty Callers in "Initial Delay Indicator."

be no emergency, as guilty callers patiently lingered on the line, allowing the dispatchers to take the lead. Unlike innocent callers who were on their toes, ready for battle by urgently pleading for aid, many guilty callers were back on their heels, stalling. The Initial Delay Indicator occurs when callers hesitate before providing vital information that would hasten the response for assistance. The most important comments the caller will make occur in the opening seconds when urgency can save a life. Therefore, callers who delayed were not focused on the victim's survival.

The Initial Delay Indicator was present in 31% of the calls in the 911 study. Of these calls, 82% were made by guilty callers and 18% were by innocent callers as illustrated in Figure 15.2.

In the following four cases, guilty callers used Initial Delays in their 911 calls regarding their family members:

Dispatcher:	"911, what is your emergency?"
Guilty Caller:	"*Well, uh, you see*, my girlfriend drowned in the tub."

…

Dispatcher:	"911, Dispatcher Kendra, what is the emergency?"
Guilty Caller:	"*Ah, yes, Officer. Um*, I just came home from the store and it looks like my husband is deceased."

…

Dispatcher:	"911, what's your emergency?"
Guilty Caller:	"*What's your name Ma'am?*"

…

Dispatcher: *"This is Dispatcher Crown, what's your emergency?"*
Guilty Caller: *"<u>The thing is that</u> my cousin shot himself."*

Each of the four callers used Initial Delays by beginning with unnecessary words and delivering them in a leisurely fashion. In subsequent trials, all four of the callers were found guilty of the murders.

MR. AND MRS. HUNT CASE
Jake exhibited neither Initial Sounds nor Initial Delays in his 911 call.

Innocent Indicators		**Guilty Indicators**
___ Initial Sounds	n/a	___ Initial Delays

Does the Caller Use Aggressive Demands or Passive Defenses?

16

"Defensive behavior is a primary barrier to effective communication."

Kathryn Yarborough

Like frantic, adrenaline-filled mothers who lifted cars to save their toddlers' lives, most innocent callers were Aggressive and Demanding when seeking lifesaving aid for family or friends. If callers sensed that dispatchers did not comprehend the magnitude of the situation or if the emergency response was delayed, they used Aggressive Demands to get results. Conversely, some guilty 911 callers were Passive and Defensive despite the traumatic nature of the situation.

Sixteen percent of callers in the 911 study used Aggressive Demands. Innocent callers were over six times more likely to be Aggressive and Demanding than were guilty callers (87% vs. 13%), as shown in Figure 16.1.

In the following case, a caller's friend was shot in the hallway of an apartment building. The caller was frustrated at the delay in emergency response and he became increasingly demanding.

Dispatcher:	*"911, what is your emergency?"*
Innocent Caller:	*"Guy been shot—dude been shot!"*
Dispatcher:	*"Sir, listen, did you say somebody's been shot?"*
Innocent Caller:	*"Yes! Yes!"*
Dispatcher:	*"OK, who's been shot?"*
Innocent Caller	*"My friend's been shot! Come on, please hurry!"*
Dispatcher:	*"Do you know who did it?"*
Innocent Caller:	*"No! Come on, hurry!"*
Dispatcher:	*"OK, sir, listen to me. I'm gonna get the police out there, just try and help me out."*
Innocent Caller:	*"Come on, NOW!"*
Dispatcher:	*"I got the police, the run has been sent up there and as soon as they dispatch it they'll be out, but I'm trying to help you. Where was he shot?"*
Innocent Caller:	*"IN THE CHEST! COME ON! HE'S BLEEDING OUT!"*

Figure 16.1 Percentages of Innocent vs. Guilty Callers in "Aggressive Demands."

Despite the caller's frantic efforts to get immediate aid, the victim died en route to the hospital. The caller, who used clear indicators of innocence in his call, was not involved in his friend's death.

Consider the following call from an innocent woman calling about an unresponsive man in a hotel:

Dispatcher: *"911, what is your emergency?"*
Innocent Caller: *"We need an ambulance at the Ranch Inn, there's a guy in the room and he's on the bed and he ain't movin'. He's in room number 41.* HURRY PLEASE!"
Dispatcher: *"What's wrong with him?"*
Innocent Caller: *"I'm the house keeper and I hadn't seen him for two days, I got worried and I keyed into the room and he's purple and he ain't moving. He uses a lot of drugs. There's usually people coming and going from that room all night long.* IS THE AMBULANCE COMING?"
Dispatcher: *"They're on the way. What kind of drugs does he use?"*
Innocent Caller: *"I don't know but the guy that brings it here is named Dion and he drives a black Mazda.* I'VE CALLED YOU GUYS ABOUT HIM BEFORE BUT YOU NEVER DO ANYTHING ABOUT IT!! WHERE'S THE AMBULANCE?"

The caller became more Aggressive and Demanding as the call continued, as the caller realized that the victim might die due to repeated lack of emergency response. Although the ambulance arrived shortly after this call, the victim died of a self-inflicted drug overdose and *"Dion"* was convicted of trafficking in heroin.

The next caller began to talk before the 911 operator had a chance to answer the phone, an example of an Initial Sounds indicator. He then made Aggressive Demands as he desperately pleaded with the dispatcher for immediate medical help for his wife:

Innocent Caller: *"Hey!"*

Dispatcher: *"911 what's your emergency"*

Innocent Caller: *"My wife just shot herself.* She's still breathing, please send somebody now!*"*

Dispatcher: *"Okay. What's your address?"*

Innocent Caller: *"550 Templeton Road!"*

Dispatcher: *"Okay, what's going on there?"*

Innocent Caller: *"She just shot herself!"*

Dispatcher: *"What's going on?"*

Innocent Caller: *"She just shot her fucking self!"*

Dispatcher: *"Okay, what's her name?"*

Innocent Caller: *"She's still fucking breathing. Please send a God damn ambulance now!"*

Dispatcher: *"Okay what's going on?"*

Innocent Caller: *"God damn it, she shot herself!"*

Dispatcher: *"She shot herself—okay."*

Innocent Caller: *"She's still breathing!"*

Dispatcher: *"Hold on—stay on the line."*

Innocent Caller: *"NOW!"*

Dispatcher: *"All units stand by for a medical page."*

Innocent Caller: *"HELP—HELP!"*

Dispatcher: *"Stay on the line okay—just stay on the line with me."*

Innocent Caller: *"She's still breathing. I can see her moving and everything.* Please send somebody NOW!*"*

Dispatcher: *"Attention to Medics, please respond to 550 Templeton Road."*

Innocent Caller: *"Send an ambulance now! HELP!"*

Dispatcher: *"We got 'em going okay? Hold on."*

Innocent Caller: *"Please hurry—please!"*

Dispatcher: *"Stay on the line."*

Innocent Caller: *"She's choking! Hey!"*

Dispatcher: *"Hold on."*

Innocent Caller: *"Ma'am, help us!"*

Dispatcher: *"Okay."*

Innocent Caller: *"SHE'S STILL BREATHING—SHE'S STILL MOVING! PLEASE SEND SOMEBODY TO HELP!"*

Dispatcher: *"Sir?"*

Innocent Caller: *"SHE'S CHOKING!"*

Dispatcher: *"Okay, she's choking? Is she lying flat on the ground?"*

Innocent Caller: *"YES!"*

Dispatcher: *"And where exactly can you tell me where she shot herself—in the head?"*

Innocent Caller: *"I DON'T KNOW. I SEE THE BLOOD—I SEE THE GUN—EVERYTHING!"*
Dispatcher: *"Okay."*
Innocent Caller: *"SHE'S CHOKING!"*
Dispatcher: *"Okay, just stay on the line with me."*
Innocent Caller: *"SHE'S REALLY CHOKING! SHE'S MAKING ALL SORTS OF WEIRD NOISES! SEND SOMEBODY NOW!!"*

The husband was frantically trying to speed up emergency aid and although the medics responded immediately, his wife died before they reached the location. The death was ruled a suicide, and the caller was found to be innocent.

One might predict that course language would be used by more guilty 911 callers than by innocent callers. Although this could be true in other criminal suspect statements, it was not true in the 911 study, for in homicide cases, expediency saved lives. The Aggressive Demands of innocent callers included swearing at dispatchers to prompt faster emergency responses, as the next call by an innocent wife demonstrates.

Dispatcher: *"911, what is your emergency?"*
Innocent Caller: *"Get to 672 Allen Park now! My husband was hanging here in the garage! Get an ambulance here now!"*
Dispatcher: *"Slow down Ma'am, you said somebody hung themselves?"*
Innocent Caller: *"DAMN IT! MY HUSBAND TRIED TO HANG HIMSELF GET THE FUCKIN' MEDICS HERE NOW!"*
Dispatcher: *"OK Ma'am, what did he use to do it?"*
Innocent Caller: *"AN EXTENSION CORD! HURRY! I CUT HIM DOWN BUT I CAN'T GET A PULSE! DO YOU HAVE THEM COMING? HURRY!"*

The wife immediately went on the offense with her Aggressive Demands. She was an innocent caller trying desperately, but unsuccessfully, to save her husband.

To return to the football analogy, consider again the similarities between 911 callers and offensive or defensive players. Just as the offensive football players' strategy is to aggressively move the ball forward, innocent 911 callers aggressively act to save the lives of victims. Unlike offensive players, however, defensive backs can only react by back-pedaling and warding off threats. Guilty callers overwhelmed by dispatchers' questions may respond with verbal back-pedaling in hopes of deflecting suspicion. For guilty callers in the 911 study, Passive Defenses included the following five indicators: Defendant Mentality, Ingratiating Remarks, Insults or Blames Victim, Mental Miscues, and Minimizes. Each defensive approach will be discussed individually, although they are often used in conjunction as cohorts in deception.

Defendant Mentality

"The sin that is most destructive in your life right now is the one you are most defensive about."

Tim Keller

In the 911 study, callers with the singular mission of saving a life did not worry about their own image. In contrast, some guilty callers were so concerned with crafting an innocent image of themselves that they accomplished the opposite objective—revealing their guilt. Through their inadvertent comments and questions, guilty callers revealed their Defendant Mentality.

Fourteen percent of the calls in the 911 study contained Defendant Mentality. Guilty callers were responsible for almost all instances of Defendant Mentality (96% vs. 4%), as illustrated in Figure 16.2.

A woman expressed Defendant Mentality in her 911 call concerning her husband. She told the dispatcher that her husband had attacked her and that she had no choice but to shoot him. The dispatcher asked the following question to verify the caller's actions:

Dispatcher: *"You said your husband tried to kill you so you shot him?"*
Guilty Caller: *"He's going to die isn't he? Ma'am is he going to die? <u>Am I going to jail for the rest of my life</u>?"*

The wife's Defendant Mentality revealed that she realized the severity of her actions, the probability that she would be found guilty, and her possible sentence.

In a similar domestic violence homicide case, a boyfriend called 911 and claimed that he shot his girlfriend after she assaulted him:

Dispatcher: *"Sir, where is she injured at?"*
Guilty Caller: *"<u>I'll end up in hell</u>."*

Figure 16.2 Percentages of Innocent vs. Guilty Callers in "Defendant Mentality."

The caller focused on himself, and instead of answering the dispatcher's question, he revealed his guilt with an incriminating statement. Both the wife who shot her husband and the boyfriend who shot his girlfriend argued at trial that they were the victims; however, evidence confirmed their guilt and both were convicted of the homicides.

In the following case, a husband and wife were involved in a dispute with a friend, resulting in the friend's death. The wife called 911 and advised that a shooting had occurred at her residence, without identifying the offender:

Dispatcher: *"Is the shotgun still in the living room?"*
Guilty Caller: *"We're not murderers—I never hurt anybody."*

An innocent caller would be expected to relay the facts of the event without caution or self-preservation. However, the wife revealed that she had the word "murder" on her mind, and she did not want to be identified as a murderer. She added, *"I never hurt anybody,"* which was technically true, as she did not pull the trigger. Because only the wife, the husband, and the victim were at the scene, the wife inadvertently implicated her husband. The investigation showed that the husband was the shooter; however, the wife was also involved and attempted to obstruct the investigation. The husband was convicted of murder, and the wife was convicted of conspiracy to commit murder.

In addition to Defendant Mentality regarding themselves, some guilty 911 callers showed Defendant Mentality regarding their involvement in the crime scene itself. The following statements regarding the crimes were made by guilty callers:

1. "Don't worry, I'm not touching anything!"
2. "I have a little blood on me."
3. "I can't do CPR, I don't want to touch anything."
4. "I touched the gun, my prints are gonna be on it."
5. "I touched the door knob, just so you know."
6. "I came in through the window, cause the door was locked so the window's been moved open."

Innocent 911 callers did not feel obligated to volunteer why they were on scene, why their fingerprints or DNA was present, or why they had blood on themselves. However, to avoid culpability, many guilty callers felt compelled to make such Defendant Mentality statements to the dispatcher.

Ingratiating Remarks

"If a person is too nice to you, is he trying to sell you something?"

Unknown

When drivers are pulled over for traffic violations, they are often irritated, short-tempered, and discourteous with the police. Street officers understand that rude behavior is common with these citizen interactions, and they have learned to expect it. Occasionally, however, officers interact with traffic violators who greet them with ingratiating language. Experienced officers know instinctively that these overly polite drivers are probably "rolling dirty," with license suspensions, warrants, or illegal drugs in the vehicle. Traffic violators who are too polite to street officers are often hiding something.

Many organizations require employees to take random drug tests. As part of the process, the employees must drive to the clinic, complete forms, sit in the waiting room for long periods of time, and be searched before submitting to a urinalysis. Employees rarely enjoy the process and often become annoyed by the time they are called into the testing area. Just as with experienced police officers, experienced nurses understand that employees' agitated behavior is the norm. Thus, when employees enter the testing area and greet the nurse with ingratiating compliments, the clinic staff becomes suspicious and closely monitors these employees.

As an example of ingratiating language, a truck driver, mandated by law to undergo periodic drug screening, recently visited a clinic in Dayton, Ohio. After a lengthy stay in the waiting room, he entered the testing area and greeted the nurse with atypical comments:

> *"Hello darling! How you doing on this beautiful day? Have you lost weight since I was here last? Your hair is different too, I love it."*

Immediately, the nurse suspected that the employee was "dirty" and directed him to open his pants before entering the bathroom. The employee complied, and as he unzipped his pants, a plastic bag containing "clean" urine fell to the floor. Like traffic offenders and guilty employees taking drug tests, ingratiating 911 callers are often hiding something.

Individuals who begin their 911 calls with, *"Hi,"* or end them with, *"Bye, bye,"* are overly polite and ingratiating. Also, callers who apologize with, *"I'm sorry,"* and *"Pardon me,"* are too apologetic for the circumstances. In a true emergency, etiquette becomes secondary to urgency.

the dispatcher in this manner. The Lieutenant had staged the scene and was convicted of the homicide.

Guilty callers' attempts to "win the dispatcher over" through ingratiating politeness can obscure the callers' deception. This strategy is often employed by individuals who try to manipulate others, as illustrated by a pedophile during a counseling session. The pedophile, who was convicted of abusing numerous children, described his strategy of using politeness toward his targets' parents: *"I used niceness as a camouflage for my deviance"* (Salter, 2012).

...

Considerations

A simple *"Thank you"* at the end of the 911 call is not considered to be inappropriately polite, particularly if the caller has received valuable assistance from the dispatcher. This expression of gratitude in closing does not delay medical help, unlike excessive politeness during the call. Callers who receive the emergency service they sought are grateful and relieved when the medics pull up to the residence. Many innocent callers end their calls with a heartfelt *"Thank you."*

Insults or Blames Victim

"You don't have to disrespect and insult others simply to hold your own ground. If you do, that shows how shaky your own position is."

Red Haircrow

People suffering from violent assaults, accidents, serious medical events, and suicide attempts are at the most vulnerable and weakest moments in their lives. Innocent 911 callers focus on the victims' survival, seek immediate help for them, and often attempt to give aid and comfort to them. Sometimes innocent callers even compliment the victim for fighting to stay alive while clinging to life. The following case of a husband speaking to his dying wife illustrates an encouraging compliment:

| Dispatcher: | *"OK sir, keep the pressure on the wound, use more towels if you need to."* |
| Innocent Caller: | *"You're doing good Kathy, they're almost here, hang with me...you're going to be OK, you're doing good..."* |

In contrast to the previous case, some callers Insulted or Blamed the victims, thus revealing friction or even hostility. Insulting or Blaming individuals

Insults or Blames Victim

Figure 16.4 Percentages of Innocent vs. Guilty Callers in "Insults or Blame."

who were critically injured was unexpected, particularly when these actions replaced providing aid to victims.

The Insult or Blame indicator was found in 12% of the calls in the 911 study. Guilty callers made all of these calls, as seen in Figure 16.4.

A wife made the following comment to the 911 dispatcher when asked where her husband's injury was located:

Guilty Caller: *"It must be on his head cause I looked at the back of his head, and it's all bloody and gross, and, you know, so…"*

To refer to her husband's head as *"gross"* while he lay dying on the floor was not helpful and was insulting to the victim. The wife was involved in her husband's death.

In another case, a boyfriend called 911 after his girlfriend allegedly shot herself in the head and lay dying on the kitchen floor:

Dispatcher: *"911, what's your emergency?"*
Guilty Caller: *"My girlfriend shot herself. The crazy bitch shot herself in the head."*

Instead of asking for help for the victim and focusing on her survival, the boyfriend insulted his girlfriend by referring to her as a *"crazy bitch."* There was no evidence that the victim suffered from emotional or mental issues; however, even if she did have such a disability, the comment was not beneficial to the victim or the dispatcher. Instead, it was designed to convince the dispatcher that the victim committed suicide. The case facts proved otherwise, and the boyfriend was convicted of homicide.

Even if victims were responsible for putting themselves in unsafe situations, no innocent 911 callers in the 911 study blamed the victims for the situations that eventually caused their deaths. However, guilty 911 callers did occasionally blame victims for their circumstances. In the following case, a mother who escaped a house fire called 911 to report that her child was still inside the burning home. She continued with the following comment:

Guilty Caller: *"I told him not to light the candles in his room!"*

The mother needlessly blamed her child for his fatal situation. In this case, the child was not responsible for the fire, and the mother was convicted of arson and murder.

In the following case, a stepfather called 911 because his four-year-old stepdaughter was in severe distress. She was having seizures and foaming at the mouth with her eyes rolled back as the father made the following comments to the 911 dispatcher:

Dispatcher: *"Do you know what's wrong with your daughter?"*
Guilty Caller: *"Not even a clue."*
Dispatcher: *"Has she taken any medications?"*
Guilty Caller: *"She might have. She's very, very sneaky. She threw a HUGE temper tantrum earlier. She might have taken something."*

Later in the call the dispatcher asked the caller:

Dispatcher: *"OK, and has she ever done this before?"*
Guilty Caller: *"She's had some ep...she...she's seeing a psychiatrist, she's got a really bad case of RAD, she has temper tantrums, she zones out. But this...this is the worst I've ever seen it."*
Dispatcher: *"OK. Just do what you can."*
Guilty Caller: *"She can't keep her eyes open. Like I said, she had a really, really bad episode tonight. Ummmm, she's foaming at the mouth now."*
Dispatcher: *"OK, have you given her any medication that would do this?"*
Guilty Caller: *"No, no medication whatsoever. She takes stuff all the time. She might have taken something."*

Instead of demanding help and focusing on his stepdaughter's survival, the father repeatedly Insulted and Blamed the four-year-old for her condition. The father felt the need to share that the victim had been *"seeing a psychiatrist, she's got a really bad case of RAD, she has temper tantrums, she zones out."* None of these negative comments were beneficial to aiding the victim in her current critical condition. As the little girl was dying in front of him, the father referred to her as *"very, very sneaky"* and emphasized that she *"threw a HUGE temper tantrum."* The father's insults and his use of the intensifying adjectives *"very, very"* were meant to convince the dispatcher that the victim was a bad child who misbehaved and probably brought the event upon herself. The father was found guilty of homicide.

Insulting and Blaming the victim during the 911 call provides insight into the relationship between the caller and the victim, as demonstrated by a call concerning a four-month-old baby:

Dispatcher:	*"911, state your emergency."*
Guilty Caller:	*"Um, I have a daycare and I have a daycare boy here, he's... ahh, he had <u>kind of been ridiculous</u> the last couple of days, but anyways when I change his diaper he gets <u>kinda crazy</u>... he was <u>screamin', pissed off</u>...like he was just <u>SCREAMING</u>, I mean like <u>throwing a RIDICULOUS fit which is kinda how he acts</u>."*

As the baby was dying, the caller described his behavior as *"kind of been ridiculous"* and *"kinda crazy."* It is difficult to think of a dying four-month-old in these terms, and the insults are not helpful in describing details relevant to the victim's medical event. The emphasis the caller placed on the words *"SCREAMING"* and *"RIDICULOUS"* later in the 911 call revealed that it was likely the caller who was "pissed off" instead of the infant. Had the officers and detectives analyzed the 911 call at the initial stages of the investigation, they would have quickly focused on the caller's insults and formed an interview strategy incorporating the challenges of dealing with a screaming baby. Eventually, the caller was arrested and convicted of murder.

Minimizes

"If anybody asks, I wasn't here."

Unknown

Innocent 911 callers concentrated on getting medical aid for victims, but some guilty callers Minimized their involvement in the incident by starting the call with, *"I just..."* or *"I've only..."* The words *"<u>just</u>"* and *"<u>only</u>"* are adverbs designed to mitigate the described action. *"Just"* can mean *"only"* or *"recently,"* but both meanings are inappropriate because they focus on the callers' actions in emergency situations. Unless specifically asked about themselves, callers should focus on the victims. It does not benefit the victims for 911 callers to inform the dispatcher that they *"just got home."*

The following comments by guilty callers served to Minimize the callers' involvement in the offense:

1. *"<u>I just got home</u> and my wife is dead."*
2. *"<u>I've only been here a few minutes</u>, I don't know what's wrong with the baby."*
3. *"<u>I just came downstairs</u> and found my girlfriend on the floor."*
4. *"<u>I just came in</u> from the deck and the baby ain't breathing."*

By providing details of their previous location and their recent arrival on scene, guilty callers Minimized their involvement to create distance and provide alibis. In contrast, innocent 911 callers rarely found it necessary to volunteer such irrelevant information. Dispatchers were typically uninterested in the prior location of the callers; this extra information could confuse them and slow down the emergency response.

The Minimizes indicator was present in 20% of the calls in the 911 study. Guilty callers made 82% of these calls and innocent callers made 18%, as depicted in Figure 16.5.

The following dialogue occurred when a subject called 911 to report his wife's condition:

Dispatcher: *"911, what is your emergency?"*
Guilty Caller: *"I just came home and my wife is on the floor and there's blood all over, I don't know what to do."*

The first comment uttered by the husband was *"I just came home."* The caller Minimized his involvement in the situation even before advising that his wife was on the floor with *"blood all over."* It was imperative for the caller to create distance between himself and the offense by immediately inserting Minimizing into the call. The subsequent investigation revealed that the husband had hired two men to kill his wife. The husband knew his wife was dead even before he arrived home and he was truthful when he said, *"I just came home."* He was eventually convicted of first-degree murder.

In the following case, a police officer called 911 to report that his wife had committed suicide:

Dispatcher: *"Where is she shot at, sir?"*
Guilty Caller: *"I've only been home for five minutes, I've been at work all day, I'm not sure."*

It was important for the husband to establish the fact that he had *"only been home for five minutes,"* a true statement. The investigation later revealed

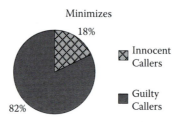

Figure 16.5 Percentages of Innocent vs. Guilty Callers in "Minimizes."

that the husband, who was having an affair, killed his wife earlier in the day and staged the scene to resemble a suicide.

...

Consideration

The Minimizes Indicator is most significant when callers present it in the opening lines of a 911 call, when the primary focus should be on the victims, not the callers. Additionally, minimizing is not an indicator of guilt unless it is spontaneous. If dispatchers asked specific time-related questions, the callers' answers would not be considered minimizing, as in the following example:

Dispatcher: *"OK, help is on the way. How long have you been there?"*
Innocent Caller: *"I just got here a minute ago."*

Mental Miscues

Under stress from committing a murder, some guilty callers voiced thoughts they did not intend to reveal. This indicator is called Mental Miscues and it includes Freudian Slips and Non Sequiturs. Alert investigators can gain insight to what is in the callers' minds by closely examining these unintended utterances.

Mental Miscues occurred in 7% of the calls in the 911 study. All 15 occurrences of this indicator were by guilty callers. See Figure 16.6.

Freudian Slips

"A slip of the foot you may soon recover, but a slip of the tongue you may never get over."

Benjamin Franklin

Freudian Slips occurred when callers accidentally used words that revealed their unconscious thoughts. By studying the use of Freudian Slips, investigators

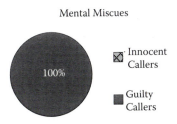

Figure 16.6 Percentages of Innocent vs. Guilty Callers in "Mental Miscues."

gain insight to what is in the callers' minds, as evidenced in the following examples:

Dispatcher:	*"911, what is your emergency?"*
Guilty Caller:	*"The baby woke up in a cough and starting, <u>like, uh choking out</u>."*

(The caller choked the victim.)

...

Dispatcher:	*"OK, will you try CPR?"*
Guilty Caller:	*"I'll <u>take a stab</u> at it."*

(The caller stabbed the victim.)

...

Dispatcher:	*"...have you guys been having problems?"*
Guilty Caller:	*"We had our <u>head above water</u>."*

(The caller drowned the victim in a river.)

...

Dispatcher:	*"911, what is your emergency?"*
Guilty Caller:	*"Yeah, <u>We have a death on our hands</u>."*

(The female caller and her husband choked and beat the female's grandmother.)

...

Dispatcher:	*"Is he an infant?"*
Guilty Caller:	*"Infant, no, he's not breathing, his stomach isn't moving but every once in a while he will <u>jerk</u>, and he will kinda move or <u>jerk real quick</u>...then he won't move but he'll <u>kinda jerk</u>."*

(The caller shook the baby with repeated jerking motions.)

...

Dispatcher:	*"911, what is your emergency?"*
Guilty Caller:	*"A guy came in the house, he shot me and he shot my father."*
Dispatcher:	*"I know your dad real well."*
Guilty Caller:	*"Oh, then, I'm sorry for you."*
Dispatcher:	*"Do you know if your dad knew the guy?"*
Guilty Caller:	*"I don't know. He's a cop. <u>Who knows how many people hated him?</u>"*

(The caller shot and killed his father, slightly grazed himself, and then called in to the department where his father worked as a police officer. The dispatcher who took the call was a personal friend of the officer and knew the father–son relationship had been contentious.)

In each of the previous examples, the callers revealed more information than they intended. Their Freudian Slips disclosed the manner of the deaths, and all of the quoted callers were found guilty of homicide. Despite the ironic nature of these subconscious *"confessions,"* investigators should never ignore them.

Compare the following two cases of parents who called 911 regarding their children with cerebral palsy:

Case #1 Call Made by a Mother

Dispatcher:	*"911, what is your emergency?"*
Innocent Caller:	*"Send an ambulance to apartment 7 at Larkspur my son is breathing very shallowly— start them now!"*
Dispatcher:	*"OK, what's going on with him?"*
Innocent Caller:	*"My son is four years old, he has cerebral palsy. Do you have them coming? He is struggling. It's OK Tommy, you're OK. HURRY UP! HURRY UP!"*

Case #2 Call Made by a Father in a Separate Case

Dispatcher:	*"911, what is your emergency?"*
Guilty Caller:	*"My son is unresponsive."*
Dispatcher:	*"What's your address, sir?"*
Guilty Caller:	*"Apartment 11, Dayton Towers."*
Dispatcher:	*"What's going on there, sir?"*
Guilty Caller:	*"My girlfriend watches my son, he's barely breathing.....please."*
Dispatcher:	*"And she was supposed to take care of your children?"*
Guilty Caller:	*"Well I've only got son and he's a handicap."*
Dispatcher:	*"What's wrong with your son?"*
Guilty Caller:	*"He has cerebral palsy."*

Both parents from the previous examples were faced with emergency situations involving children with cerebral palsy who experienced breathing problems. The innocent mother demanded help immediately, expressed urgency, volunteered important details, and attempted to comfort her son by using his name and telling him. *"It's OK Tommy, you're OK."*

Unlike the innocent mother, the guilty father did not request help, express urgency, volunteer important details, or comfort his child. Further, the father referred to his physically challenged son by stating, *"Well I've only got son and he's a handicap,"* instead of stating, *"I've only got one son and he is handicapped"* or simply, *"I've only got one son."* The father's Freudian Slip provided insight regarding his resentment of caring for the sick child.

The first child died of complications from cerebral palsy and the mother was innocent. The second child died of suffocation and the father was convicted of his murder.

Non Sequiturs

"I find that highly illogical"

Mr. Spock

Some of the guilty callers in the 911 study provided misleading comments in an effort to convince dispatchers of their innocence. Then, instead of focusing on the victims as most innocent callers did, a few guilty callers focused on supporting their false assertions with illogical statements, known as Non Sequiturs. This was a flawed strategy, however, for under scrutiny the Non Sequiturs crumbled.

A husband used a Non Sequitur in the following 911 call regarding his wife:

Dispatcher:	*"911, what is your emergency?"*
Guilty Caller:	*"Oh my God, Oh my God!"*
Dispatcher:	*"Slow down, what's the problem, sir?"*
Guilty Caller:	*"My wife is dead!"*
Dispatcher:	*"What's your address?"*
Guilty Caller:	*"985 Garden Drive."*
Dispatcher:	*"Tell me what's going on sir."*
Guilty Caller:	*"My wife broke her neck!"*
Dispatcher:	*"Is she breathing?"*
Guilty Caller:	*"I don't think so."*
Dispatcher:	*"OK."*
Guilty Caller:	*"And her neck, I think it's broken <u>because she's in the tub</u>."*

The husband changed his response from *"My wife broke her neck!"* to *"And her neck, I think it's broken."* These are very different statements. In the first statement, the husband provided specific information about his wife's injury that he had not meant to disclose. In the second statement, he attempted to retract the conviction of his first statement. In order to support the revised contention that he only thought the neck was broken, he needed to explain how he came to this possible conclusion, so he added, *"because she's in the tub."* This Non Sequitur failed to support the assertion. Much more information would be needed to make the connection between a broken neck and a woman in the tub. An autopsy showed that the wife's injuries were not consistent with a fall, but she did have a broken neck. Investigation revealed that the husband committed the murder and he was found guilty.

In the following case, a husband called 911 regarding his wife's condition:

Dispatcher:	*"911, what is your emergency?"*
Guilty Caller:	*"My wife has been shot."*
Dispatcher:	*"Is she conscious right now?"*
Guilty Caller:	*"No, she's not."*
Dispatcher:	*"Is she breathing?"*
Guilty Caller:	*"Umm, no."*
Dispatcher:	*"OK, are you able to get near her so that we can do CPR, sir?"*
Guilty Caller:	*"No, there's way too much blood all over the place."*
Dispatcher:	*"Could you check if she has a pulse?"*
Guilty Caller:	*"No, there's way too much blood."*

The husband asserted that he was unable to get near his wife to attempt life-saving measures. He supported this contention by stating that he was prevented from helping her because *"there's way too much blood"* at the scene. This response sounded illogical to the dispatcher, who expected the husband to take every possible step to save his wife's life. The dispatcher then asked if the husband could check for a pulse, and he repeated his Non Sequitur.

Investigators learned that the 911 caller, an attorney and a pastor who had been consorting with prostitutes in his law office, bought a rifle and convinced a relative to kill his wife. He left the back door unlocked and told the relative where the victim would be sleeping. The relative entered the home and shot the victim in the eye but failed to kill her. The relative then got a butcher knife from the kitchen and stabbed the wife to death. Both the husband and the relative were convicted of the murder.

In the following case, a wife called 911 to report that she had arrived home to find her husband dead:

Dispatcher:	*"911, what is your emergency?"*
Guilty caller:	*"I just came home and my husband is dead!"*
Dispatcher:	*"What's wrong with him?"*
Guilty caller:	*"I don't know."*
Dispatcher:	*"Does he have health problems?"*
Guilty caller:	*"Noooooooooooo."*
Dispatcher:	*"Did somebody break in?"*
Guilty caller:	*"I don't know."*
Dispatcher:	*"When's the last time you saw him?"*
Guilty caller:	*"This morning before I left."*
Dispatcher:	*"Have you talked to him on the phone?"*
Guilty caller:	*"No, cause I was at work."*

Unless one of the spouses had an unusual job, the fact that the wife was at work should not preclude her from calling her husband. Therefore, her explanatory comment, *"No, cause I was at work,"* is a Non Sequitur. When law enforcement arrived at the scene, the deceased husband was still in bed, shot in the back of the head. The investigation revealed that the wife had participated in her husband's murder by convincing her boyfriend to kill him.

Another 911 caller used a Non Sequitur in a call about his wife:

Dispatcher:	*"911, what is your emergency?"*
Guilty Caller:	*"I just got back from California, I was on a business trip and I came home and found my wife dead."*
Dispatcher:	*"Your wife is dead?"*
Guilty Caller:	*"Yes."*
Dispatcher:	*"Is there anything we can- do you want to try CPR?"*
Guilty caller:	*"No, no, it's too late."*
Dispatcher:	*"What happened?"*
Guilty Caller:	*"(crying) It looks like she committed suicide."*
Dispatcher:	*"How long ago do you think it happened?"*
Guilty Caller:	*"I don't know. I've been gone for a week."*
Dispatcher:	*"Did you talk to your wife?"*
Guilty Caller:	<u>*"No, I was on a business trip out of state."*</u>

When asked if he had talked with his wife during his trip, the husband realized that his phone records could be checked, so he truthfully responded *"No."* Because the caller was the offender, he knew his wife was dead, and any calls to her would have been futile. However, he needed to explain his decision not to call, so he added, *"I was on a business trip out of state."* This Non Sequitur is illogical; many spouses speak to each other on the phone when one of them is out of town. The investigation confirmed that the husband killed his wife before he left for California.

Deception is complicated. Guilty callers have little time to plan their responses to dispatcher's direct questions and inadvertently utter Non Sequitur comments. These comments, missing from innocent calls in the 911 study, are insightful clues for investigators.

MR. AND MRS. HUNT CASE

Jake began his call with the Minimizes indicator: *"I just got to my in-laws house."*
His priority was to inform the dispatcher that he had been elsewhere instead of focusing on the needs of his in-laws.

Innocent Indicators:

___ AGGRESSIVE DEMANDS

Guilty Indicators:

PASSIVE DEFENSES:

___ Defendant Mentality
___ Ingratiating Remarks
___ Insults or Blames Victim
___ Mental Miscues
✔ Minimizes

Reference

Salter, A. (2012), "Truth, Lies and Sex Offenders," September 24.

Does the Caller Show Cooperation with Dispatcher or Resistance to Dispatcher?

17

Cooperation with Dispatcher

> *"Alone we can do so little; together we can do so much."*
>
> Helen Keller

Innocent callers in the 911 study were more likely than guilty callers to show Cooperation with Dispatchers by opening the faucet to let the information flow. Their cooperation was in sharp contrast with guilty callers who displayed Resistance to Dispatchers, closing the information faucet entirely or allowing only a trickle of facts to seep out.

Innocent callers displayed Cooperation with Dispatchers by following dispatchers' instructions to provide information or take actions that expedited aid to the victims. These instructions included obtaining full addresses, opening front doors, and turning on outside lights to assist the first responders in locating the emergency.

Almost all (94%) of the callers in the 911 study who showed Cooperation with Dispatchers were innocent and only 6% were guilty, as shown in Figure 17.1. This indicator was present in 16% of the calls.

A young woman arrived at her aunt's home to visit her and the aunt's new baby. The aunt was not home and a babysitter was caring for the aunt's child. When the young woman saw the baby and realized the child was unresponsive, she immediately called 911 but was unable to provide the address of the aunt's home:

Dispatcher: *"You don't know the address?"*
Innocent Caller: *"No, this is my aunt's house!"*
Dispatcher: *"OK, we need you to find the address, look outside."*
Innocent Caller: *"It's 97 Sunnyview—97 Sunnyview! I found some mail with the address on it!"*

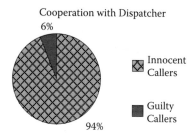

Cooperation with Dispatcher

Innocent Callers

Guilty Callers

Figure 17.1 Percentages of Innocent vs. Guilty Callers in "Cooperation with Dispatcher."

By the time the first responders arrived, the babysitter had fled the scene and the child had died. The babysitter was located, arrested, and eventually confessed to killing the child. The caller was innocent.

In another example of Cooperation with Dispatcher, a farmer called 911 to get help for his father. He lived in a rural area, and his cooperation helped the responders find his farm:

Dispatcher: *"Sir, are you off of Heritage Road?"*
Innocent Caller: *"Yes, tell them to come down Heritage all the way to the end, we're right across from the school. Hurry up!"*
Dispatcher: *"They're on the way, Sir. What color is your house?"*
Innocent Caller: *"It's white, there's a black truck in the driveway, hurry!"*
Dispatcher: *"Is the front door unlocked? Go unlock it if it isn't."*
Innocent Caller: *"OK, the door's unlocked now—just please hurry!"*

The caller's Cooperation with the Dispatcher enabled the first responders to reach the victim without delay, although efforts to save the victim were unsuccessful. The previous two callers, both innocent, were instrumental in expediting the emergency response through their Cooperation with the Dispatchers.

In the following case, a woman called 911 when her neighbor's child was accidentally shot:

Dispatcher: *"911, what is your emergency?"*
Innocent Caller: *"Get an ambulance to 2211 Stratford Lane, a boy was shot in the back. He's unconscious and bleeding bad!"*
Dispatcher: *"OK, I'm sending them. What was he shot with?"*
Innocent Caller: *"A rifle. He is bleeding bad! Hurry up!"*
Dispatcher: *"Can you put a clean towel on the wound?"*
Innocent Caller: *"OK, I have a towel on it. Now he's turning gray!"*

The innocent caller Cooperated with the Dispatcher by pressing a folded towel on the victim's wound. Although the caller treated the victim until medics arrived and the bleeding was controlled, the victim did not survive. The caller was innocent.

Resistance to Dispatcher

"If I have resistance to something it means something's wrong. The resistance, to me, is a sign of fear."

Billy Corgan

While innocent callers gushed forth details, guilty callers used the following 11 resistance techniques to withhold the truth: Dispatcher Confusion, Diversion, Equivocation, Evasion, Hangs Up, Only Answers What's Asked, Pauses, Repetition, Self-interruption, Short Answers, and Unintelligible Comments. Each indicator will be discussed individually, although, like Passive Defenses indicators, they are frequently used in tandem throughout guilty calls.

Dispatcher Confusion

"If you can't convince them, confuse them."

Harry S Truman

Dispatcher Confusion occurred when callers persisted in their use of resistance techniques so that dispatchers, adept at obtaining information, were confused. Some guilty callers reported burglaries within the first few seconds of the call, but withhold information about homicides. Dispatchers thought they were sending responders to home intrusions and learned much later about the loss of lives. Other guilty callers initially described their own minor wounds and only after probing questions did dispatchers learn of additional victims with life-threatening injuries.

Dispatcher Confusion was evident in 9% of the calls in the 911 study. As Figure 17.2 illustrates, most of this confusion was caused by guilty callers (94%) rather than innocent callers (6%).

In the following call, a young woman intentionally omitted information while the confused dispatcher tried repeatedly to help her.

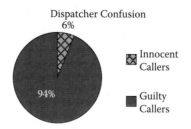

Figure 17.2 Percentages of Innocent vs. Guilty Callers in "Dispatcher Confusion."

Dispatcher:	*"911."*
Guilty Caller:	*"He's trying to kill me."*
Dispatcher:	*"Who's trying to kill you?"*
Guilty Caller:	*(Inaudible)*
Dispatcher:	*"What?"*
Guilty Caller:	*"He's going to kill me."*
Dispatcher:	*"I can't help you if I don't understand what's going on."*
Guilty Caller:	*"He's trying to kill me." (inaudible)*
Dispatcher:	*"Ma'am, I can't understand what you're saying."*
Guilty Caller:	*"(Inaudible) is breathing, I don't know."*
Dispatcher:	*"Who's breathing?"*
Guilty Caller:	*"I don't think he's breathing."*
Dispatcher:	*"Who ma'am?"*
Guilty Caller:	*"My dad, I don't think my dad's breathing."*
Dispatcher:	*"Ma'am?"*
Guilty Caller:	<u>*"He tried to kill me. He's trying to kill me."*</u>
Dispatcher:	*"Ma'am?"*
Guilty Caller:	*"He's not moving."*
Dispatcher:	*"I can't understand what you're saying. Is there anyone else there I can speak to?"*
Guilty Caller:	*"Yeah."*

The dispatcher was confused because the caller intentionally withheld information about the nature of the emergency and tried to portray herself as the victim. The dispatcher could not tell if the actions had already occurred or were occurring during the call because the caller did not clarify this. (*"He tried to kill me. He's trying to kill me."*) After the dispatcher asked to speak with someone else, the caller's mother came on the line and clearly explained that the father had been shot and needed an ambulance. The daughter was unharmed and was subsequently convicted of premeditated murder.

Diversion

"The eye is diverted from the real business, it is caught by the spectacular action that means nothing—nothing at all."

Agatha Christie

Innocent callers had nothing to fear from the dispatchers' questions, so they cooperated to the best of their ability, knowing this strategy helps the victim. In contrast, guilty callers were very concerned about the 911 dispatchers' questions, and they employed Diversion techniques to avoid making comments that could implicate them. These techniques allowed callers to block dispatchers' questions and divert attention away from themselves and toward other suspects. Guilty 911 callers employed this "sleight of hand" by asking unanswerable "Who" and "Why" questions to redirect attention from uncomfortable lines of questioning.

Diversion was present in 6% of the calls in the 911 study. Guilty callers made all of these calls, as seen in Figure 17.3.

As an example of Diversion, in the following 911 call, a husband said he returned home and found his wife dead on the bathroom floor:

Dispatcher: *"How long has she been laying there?"*
Guilty Caller: *"I don't know, I was on a business trip."*
Dispatcher: *"When did you talk to her last?"*
Guilty Caller: *"Oh my God! Who would do such a thing to her?"*
Dispatcher: *"OK, Sir...calm down, help is coming."*

By using Diversion, the husband effectively blocked the line of questioning about his timeline and countered with an unanswerable "Who?" question. He was later found guilty of killing his wife.

In the following case, a woman called 911 to report that her elderly boyfriend had been shot in his yard. The caller gave conflicting stories about her location at the scene, and the dispatcher repeatedly questioned the woman to learn her exact position:

Figure 17.3 Percentages of Innocent vs. Guilty Callers in "Diversion."

Dispatcher:	*"Is your boyfriend inside or outside right now?"*
Guilty Caller:	*"I don't know, I can't see nothing. It's dark but I think I see him laying over here on the ground but I don't know."*
Dispatcher:	*"Are you outside too?"*
Guilty Caller:	*"Marvin has a heart condition, he's 81 years old."*
Dispatcher:	*"Are you outside with him?"*
Guilty Caller:	*"Why did this happen to us?"*
Dispatcher:	*"I don't know Ma'am...the ambulance is almost there."*

The 911 caller effectively diverted the line of questioning by replying with a "Why?" question that the dispatcher could not possibly answer. Diversion techniques redirect attention from what should be the primary issues, the critical needs of the victims.

Equivocation

> *"A sudden lie may be sometimes only manslaughter upon truth; but by a carefully constructed equivocation, truth always is with malice aforethought deliberately murdered."*
>
> Christopher Morley

Unlike truthful callers who provided spontaneous details, some guilty callers offered equivocal terms to resist commitment. These callers were not fully committed to their narratives. Equivocation conveys vagueness by using ambiguous terms with varying interpretations. Cautious guilty callers qualified their responses with words like "apparently," "appeared," "assumed," "kind of," "maybe," "seemed," "something," and "whatever."

The use of equivocal words violates the basic rules of communication—that speakers should be explicit without ambiguity. Communication should be clearly understood by listeners; a lack of clarity in a 911 call may indicate that the caller does not desire to be understood. Guilty callers in the 911 study used equivocation to obscure their culpable actions.

Lying is difficult for most people. Because telling a lie is a more complicated cognitive process than telling the truth, deception can cause stress. As a result, guilty individuals may attempt to avoid outright falsification, knowing that this can be disproven by skilled investigators. It is less stressful to simply omit part of the truth, such as the callers' involvement in the homicide, than to fabricate a story and remember that fabrication. However, when questioned by experienced dispatchers, guilty callers may be forced to provide a false version of events, often accompanied by equivocation.

This technique avoids the negative alternatives: a direct lie or a truthful confession.

In a comprehensive study of deception, the most statistically significant finding was that deceptive individuals were not totally committed to their discourse (DePaulo et al., 2003). Instead, their communication contained vague references, evasive answers, irrelevant material, and distant involvement; conversely, discourse judged to be truthful contained clear commitment and specific details (DePaulo et al., 2003). The art of equivocation can be an effective technique to avoid offending another person. However, when used during an emergency call for a critically injured person, the use of equivocation can have dire consequences. It not only causes confusion but also can delay the medics' lifesaving measures.

Thirty-six percent of the calls in the 911 study contained Equivocation. Almost six times as many guilty callers used Equivocation (85%) as did innocent callers (15%), as depicted in Figure 17.4.

A mother called 911 concerning her teenage daughter who was not breathing:

Dispatcher: "911, what is your emergency?"
Guilty Caller: "I need an ambulance at 4127 Walker Lane. Please."
Dispatcher: "And what's the problem?"
Guilty Caller: "Um, my daughter _I believe_ has, uh, taken some pills."

Instead of describing her daughter's breathing difficulty, the mother tried to inform the dispatcher that her daughter had overdosed. However, the mother weakened her assertion with the equivocal phrase, "I believe" as well as with the hesitations "um" and "uh." A thorough investigation uncovered not only the fact that the mother poisoned her daughter but also that she had poisoned two previous husbands. She was convicted of all three offenses.

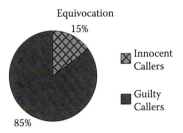

Equivocation

15%

Innocent Callers

Guilty Callers

85%

Figure 17.4 Percentages of Innocent vs. Guilty Callers in "Equivocation."

In the following case, a man called 911 concerning events at his parents' home.

Dispatcher:	*"911, what's your emergency?"*
Guilty Caller:	*"Yes, uh, I have a break-in <u>I guess</u>."*
Dispatcher:	*"What's your address?"*
Guilty Caller:	*"1717 Lee Highway."*
Dispatcher:	*"In Bakersfield?"*
Guilty Caller:	*"Yes."*
Guilty Caller:	*"I'm their son I got my daughter here we just got here and their... both their heads have been cracked open."*

The son advised that he had a break-in, then immediately stepped back from full commitment with the equivocal phrase, *"I guess."* He wanted the dispatcher to believe there was a break-in, but he knew otherwise. Only later in the call did he mention that his mother and father both had life-threatening head injuries. The caller was not initially focused on his parents, who both died. Instead, his priority was to establish the fact that someone had broken into the house, thereby introducing a probable suspect. However, because lying is difficult, the son could not bring himself to state this fact with certainty. Examine the photographs of the door in Figures 17.5 and 17.6, where the intruder would have entered. Notice the lack of forced entry evidence.

Figure 17.5 Door with no sign of forced entry.

Figure 17.6 Lock with no sign of forced entry.

The call was made by the victims' older son, and the investigation focused on a younger son who was recently forced out of the family home by the parents. The younger son had stolen a family heirloom and pawned it. Two detectives spent five hours in the interview room with the younger son, who refused to admit guilt. A new detective who had received training in 911 call analysis two months before the double homicide noticed guilty indicators in the older son's call. Using the insight from the analysis, the detective quickly obtained a full confession from the older son who had killed both parents.

Equivocation can also be used to avoid identifying an assailant. Consider the next case of a wife who called 911 regarding her husband.

Dispatcher: *"911, what is your emergency?"*
Guilty Caller: *"<u>Someone</u> came in and hurt my husband."*

The choice of the noun "someone" is equivocal. Was the person male or female, old or young, tall or short? What was the person's race and description? Deceptive callers who alleged that they witnessed an attack were more likely to describe fictitious assailants with vague terms such as "someone," rather than with specifics, such as "a tall man with a black beard." The subsequent investigation revealed that the wife was involved in the death of her husband.

In addition to using the equivocal word "someone" to describe an assailant, the same word might be used to describe a victim. In the following case, a man called 911 regarding an injured person he identified initially only as "someone."

Dispatcher:	*"911, what is your emergency?"*
Guilty Caller:	*"Yes, I have an emergency. <u>Someone</u> is...ah, injured here."*
Dispatcher:	*"How did they get injured?"*
Guilty Caller:	*"I don't know, there is blood all over the floor, I just came upstairs."*
Dispatcher:	*"Who...You say there is blood all over the floor?"*
Guilty Caller:	*"Yes."*
Dispatcher:	*"Is it your roommate that is hurt or what?"*
Guilty Caller:	*"I'm sorry, it is my wife."*

The dispatcher surmised that the caller may be referring to a roommate, since the equivocal word "someone" was used. The revelation that the victim was the caller's wife confused the dispatcher, who would have expected the husband to immediately identify the victim as his wife. The dispatcher had to specifically ask the husband who was hurt to gain this important information. During the call, the husband stated that only he and his wife were present in their home at the time his wife was "injured." The wife had been shot in the head, but the husband never said that his wife shot herself. The investigation revealed that the husband shot his wife, and he was eventually convicted of the murder.

Considerations
Equivocal words often precede numbers in everyday speech. It is normal for individuals to approximate times and ages; for example, 911 callers might provide the time as "around 11 pm," or estimate an age as "about 35 years old." Because these are examples of normal conversation, such vague words preceding numbers in 911 calls are not considered to be equivocal indicators of guilt.

Evasion

"What you resist, persists"
C.J. Jung

Guilty 911 callers placed themselves in precarious situations by posing as innocent callers. It was complicated for them to paint false pictures of events because deceivers had not experienced their fabrication and therefore could not rely on their memories.

Instead of focusing on the victims, the guilty callers' goal was to survive the 911 call without implicating themselves. Some guilty 911 callers rehearsed their "story" before making the 911 call, but they could not duplicate the pressure they felt under direct questioning by dispatchers. The guilty callers' dilemma was that they could not be totally honest because this would constitute a confession. They therefore remained guarded; one wrong answer could be catastrophic, leading to life in prison or the death penalty. Some guilty callers used Evasion to avoid the dire consequences by resisting divulging the whole truth.

Guilty callers in the 911 study employed the following Evasion strategies:

1. Repeating the dispatcher's question:

Dispatcher:	*"911, what is your emergency?"*
Guilty Caller:	*"My babysitter just left and my baby's not responding."*
Dispatcher:	*"OK, what's the baby sitter's name?"*
Guilty Caller:	*"<u>The, the baby sitters name?</u>"*

2. Answering a different question:

Dispatcher:	*"911, what is your emergency?"*
Guilty Caller:	*"My girlfriend's been shot...."*
Dispatcher:	*"Who shot her?"*
Guilty Caller:	*"I did, it was an accident."*
Dispatcher:	*"Have y'all been fighting?"*
Guilty Caller:	*"<u>It was an accident</u>."*

3. Providing a partial or confusing answer:

Dispatcher:	*"911, what is your emergency?"*
Guilty Caller:	*"Two guys just jumped the fence in my backyard and one of 'em hit my wife with a baseball bat!"*
Dispatcher:	*"Which way did they go?"*
Guilty Caller:	*"They ran out my back yard."*
Dispatcher:	*"I know, but which way did they run?"*
Guilty Caller:	*"<u>Ahh, ahh...Across. Parallel. Away</u>."*

4. Screaming or crying instead of answering:

Dispatcher:	*"911, what is your emergency?"*
Guilty Caller:	*"<u>AAAHHHHHHHHH!</u>"*
Dispatcher:	*"HELLO! What is your emergency?"*
Guilty Caller:	*"<u>OHHH, AAAHHHHH! My girlfriiiiieeend.</u>"*
Dispatcher:	*"What's going on there?"*
Guilty Caller:	*"<u>OOOHHhhhhhh!</u>"*

5. Substituting distracting noises for answers:

Dispatcher:	*"911, what is your emergency?"*
Guilty Caller:	*"We crashed our car..."*

Dispatcher:	*"Is anybody hurt?"*
Guilty Caller:	*"(Coughing noises for three seconds)"*
Dispatcher:	*"Is anybody hurt?"*
Guilty Caller:	*"She's still in there (coughing noises for four seconds)."*
Dispatcher:	*"Who's in there?"*
Guilty Caller:	*"My (coughing noises for three seconds) my (coughing)."*
Dispatcher:	*"Is somebody hurt?"*
Guilty Caller:	*"My (coughing noises for three seconds) wife is in there."*

The previous five examples were from callers who were later convicted of the homicides. Their Evasion tactics provided only temporary protection.

Evasion often occurred when callers resisted providing the address of the emergency. This delaying tactic ensured that medics' lifesaving attempts would be futile, and the victim would not be a witness against the 911 caller.

Evasion was present in 21% of the calls in the 911 study, and it was almost exclusively used by guilty callers (98% vs. 2%). See Figure 17.7.

Evasion techniques are evident in the following case in which a son called 911 to report that his father had committed suicide:

Dispatcher:	*"911, what's your emergency?"*
Guilty Caller:	*"My Dad!"*
Dispatcher:	*"What's wrong with your Dad?"*
Guilty Caller:	*"My Dad, my Dad, send someone."*
Dispatcher:	*"What's your address?"*
Guilty Caller:	*"OH MY GOD!"*
Dispatcher:	*"Sir, what is your address?"*

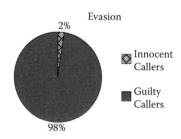

Figure 17.7 Percentages of Innocent vs. Guilty Callers in "Evasion."

Guilty Caller: "(_Wailing into the phone_)"
Dispatcher: "_Sir, I need to know your address to get help started._"
Guilty Caller: "_I can't, I can't......._"
Dispatcher: "_Give me your address!_"
Guilty Caller: "_Gratiot._"
Dispatcher: "_Sir, where on Gratiot?_"
Guilty Caller: "_Oh my God, Oh my God!_"

The caller used Evasion twice when asked about the victim's condition and four times when asked for the location of the event. Either of these topics would have been of paramount importance if the son actually wanted to get help for his father. Without knowing what happened to the victim or the exact location of the event, the dispatcher was powerless to aid the victim.

When the first responders arrived at the scene, they discovered the caller's father had been shot in the head. A pistol was lying on the victim's lap and the son stated that his father had committed suicide. At first glance the scene appeared appropriate, but the coroner found that the trajectory of the bullet did not match the scene. Subsequent investigation revealed that the son would become the sole beneficiary of a multimillion-dollar estate, including an expensive home and other real estate properties. After a year-long investigation, the son was arrested, prosecuted, and convicted of his father's murder.

Considerations

The Evasion indicator does not apply if the caller and the dispatcher were talking simultaneously, and it might have been difficult for the caller to hear the question. Further, if loud background noises are present (i.e., screaming, machinery, music, and vehicular traffic), Evasion is not relevant.

Another consideration applies when the dispatcher asks an irrelevant question. Even though the caller ignores the question, this is not Evasion if the caller focuses on more important information, as in the following case:

Dispatcher: "_911, what is your emergency?_"
Innocent Caller: "_Get an ambulance to 32 McCall, a guy's been shot, send them now!_"
Dispatcher: "_OK, what's your phone number sir?_"
Innocent Caller: "_The dude that shot him just drove off in a white van. He's a fat, white dude._"
Dispatcher: "_WHAT'S YOUR PHONE NUMBER SIR!_"
Innocent Caller: "_937-535-1000, send the cops too!_"
Dispatcher: "_Do you know how many shots were fired?_"
Innocent Caller: "_OH! HE JUST STOPPED BREATHIN'!_
                    WHERE THE AMBULANCE AT, MAN?"

Dispatcher: *"It's on the way, does he have a pulse?"*
Innocent Caller: *"Yes! I feel one, but he ain't breathin' and he's turnin' gray."*

The caller did not answer two questions posed by the dispatcher because he was focused on the victim's breathing and the suspect. The caller was an innocent witness to the drive-by shooting.

Hangs Up

"Sometimes I just stop talking, and that solves everything."
Unknown

Some 911 calls were terminated before dispatchers had received all necessary information. This often occurred with guilty callers when the line of questioning became focused on specifics about the offender and the crime. Hanging up on dispatchers was the ultimate form of resistance, for the callers no longer had to provide potentially incriminating information.

In the 911 study, callers hung up on the dispatchers in 13% of the calls. Guilty callers hung up more than twice as often as innocent callers (69% vs. 31%), as illustrated in Figure 17.8.

The timing of the disconnections was instructive. Innocent callers who hung up had typically provided all the needed information before the disconnection, while guilty callers had not.

The following conversation ended abruptly when the caller hung up on the dispatcher:

Dispatcher: *"How many times was your wife shot?"*
Guilty Caller: *"Two times, in the chest!"*
Dispatcher: *"OK, what did the shooter look like sir?"*
Guilty Caller: *"... ah... ah... (dial tone)."*
Dispatcher: *"Hello? ... Hello?"*

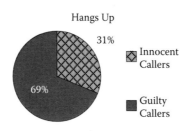

Figure 17.8 Percentages of Innocent vs. Guilty Callers in "Hangs Up."

The dispatcher had posed a difficult question for the caller, since the caller was the shooter. The caller was convicted of homicide.

Only Answers What's Asked

"There comes a time when silence is betrayal."
Martin Luther King Jr.

Most innocent callers in the 911 study freely volunteered details; some guilty callers, however, Only Answered What's Asked. They resisted providing full information, and their answers lacked relevant facts, necessitating follow-up questions from dispatchers.

The Only Answers What's Asked indicator was a strong indicator of guilt in the 911 study. Over a quarter of all the calls (26%) contained this method of resistance, which was almost exclusively used by guilty callers (94% vs. 6%), as depicted in Figure 17.9.

On the surface, it may appear that guilty callers are cooperating by answering the dispatchers' questions. However, when examined closely, it becomes obvious that these callers are focused on withholding information rather than on providing information to aid the victims. The communications between the dispatchers and guilty callers often resemble hostile witnesses being questioned in the courtroom, after receiving legal advice to answer only what is specifically asked.

In the following case, a resident of an apartment complex called 911 to report that his neighbor was unresponsive:

Dispatcher: *"911, what's your emergency?"*
Guilty Caller: *"My, my name is Dave. My neighbor is lying on his floor."*
Dispatcher: *"OK, what happened to him?"*

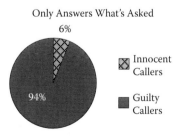

Figure 17.9 Percentages of Innocent vs. Guilty Callers in "Only Answers What's Asked."

Guilty Caller:	"He and I got into an argument, and then I left, OK, and then I came back and everything was fine and then somebody came in and his head is all bloody."
Dispatcher:	"Is he breathing?"
Guilty Caller:	"No, he's not breathing right now."
Dispatcher:	"Are there any weapons around him?"
Guilty Caller:	"Yes, there's a knife lying by his arm."
Dispatcher:	"Has he been stabbed?"
Guilty Caller:	"Yes, he's got cuts all over his neck."

The caller had to be specifically asked about what happened to his neighbor, whether he was breathing, and if there were weapons around him. These relevant details should have been volunteered. Additionally, his use of the word *"somebody"* revealed Equivocation. The caller was eventually arrested for the murder, and he confessed that he had killed the victim after an argument about drug money.

Pauses

"When truth is replaced by silence, the silence is a lie."
Yevgeny Yevtushenko

Innocent 911 callers were often frantic when a friend or family member was in severe medical distress. They rarely permitted silence during their calls because they filled any voids with demands, details, updates, and shouts to the victim.

The following call is from a man whose child was sledding down a hill. He was alerted to a car accident involving the sledders and immediately called 911. As he walked toward the scene, he suddenly realized the victim was his son:

Dispatcher:	"911, what is your emergency?"
Innocent Caller:	"I'm calling because a little boy got hit here on Spring Valley Road. Someone said he was hit by a car, I'm almost there now. You might want to send someone."
Dispatcher:	"Is he hurt?"
Innocent Caller:	"Anybody know if the kid is hurt? (yelled to other subjects at the scene). Yes, you better send an ambulance, they said he is hurt."
Dispatcher:	"OK, tell me exactly where he is at."

Innocent Caller: *"I'm walking up to the corner of Holden—THAT'S MY SON! WHAT HAPPENED? GET THE AMBULANCE HERE NOW! DID A CAR HIT YOU? AMBULANCE NOW! THIS IS MY SON, GET THEM HERE NOW! WE'RE AT THE CORNER OF SPRING VALLEY AND HOLDEN! HE'S BLEEDING, I THINK HIS LEG IS BROKEN!"*

The father's stress and urgency dramatically increased after he learned the victim's identity. There were no pauses or periods of silence, either before or after he learned the victim was his son. Despite the father's frantic efforts, the child died of his injuries.

In contrast, some guilty 911 callers used Pauses during calls, leaving periods of unexpected silence. Pauses are a form of resistance in which callers remained silent for three seconds or more while waiting for the dispatcher's next question. Instead of providing a continuing flow of information to benefit the victim, these callers allowed voids that hampered the dispatchers' effectiveness. The Pauses allowed callers to carefully edit their information to avoid incrimination. In the 911 study, a few callers paused as often as 20 times during their calls.

The pattern of Pauses during 911 calls was one of the strongest indicators of guilt in the 911 study. Over a third of the calls (34%) contained Pauses, and almost all of the pauses were by guilty callers (97% vs. 3%). See Figure 17.10.

In the following case, a woman called 911 to report that her boyfriend's three-year-old daughter was missing:

Dispatcher: *"911, what's your emergency?"*
Guilty Caller: *"Yes, Ma'am. Hi. Um. (three-second pause) I just woke up and our backdoor was wide open and I think (three-second pause) and I can't find our daughter."*
Dispatcher: *"What's your address?"*
Guilty Caller: *"Lot 33, Greenly Mobile Home Courts."*

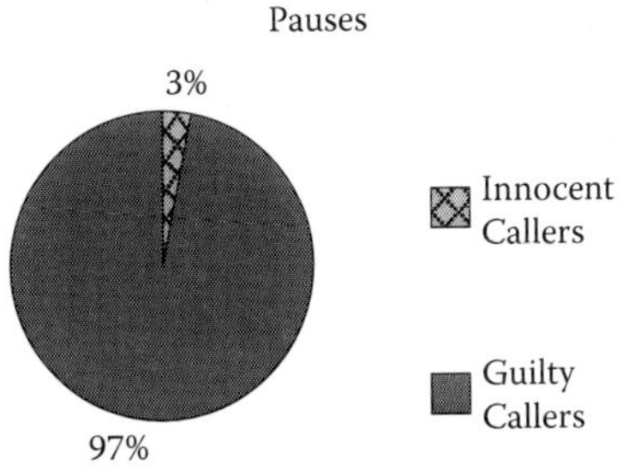

Pauses

3%

Innocent Callers

Guilty Callers

97%

Figure 17.10 Percentages of Innocent vs. Guilty Callers in "Pauses."

Dispatcher:	*"OK when did you last see her?"*
Guilty Caller:	*"Um, we like just, you know (two second pause) it was about nine o'clock (three-second pause). She was sleeping (four-second pause). I was cleaning."*

The caller used four long pauses, each at least three seconds in length, during the first portion of the 911 call. The caller also used Initial Delays (*"Hi. Um,"*). These guilty indicators were used in tandem to resist answering the dispatcher's relevant questions about the victim but disappeared when answering the question regarding the address. The caller was found guilty of homicide.

In the following case, a husband called 911 to report that his wife was missing:

Dispatcher:	*"911, what is your emergency?"*
Guilty Caller:	*"Hey, how are ya? Can you send the cops over here?"*
Dispatcher:	*"What happened?"*
Guilty Caller:	*"My wife went to the store (three-second pause) and she never came home."*
Dispatcher:	*"What was she wearing?"*
Guilty Caller:	*"She had a running suit on (four-second pause). I think it was blue."*

The husband used two Pauses during the opening segment of the 911 call, and each was when the dispatcher asked about the victim. These questions should have resulted in free-flowing information delivered with Urgency. Instead of fully answering questions or volunteering details regarding his wife's height, weight, hair color, race, and clothing, the caller was content to pause and provide minimal information. Like the previous caller, he also used an Initial Delay (*"Hey, how are ya?"*). The wife's body was located in a ravine three months later, and the husband admitted to strangling her.

While a few guilty callers used Pauses in the middle of their sentences, the most common use of the Pause indicator occurred at the end of replies. Instead of exhibiting Urgency, volunteering Sensory Details, and updating victim information throughout the call, some guilty callers in the 911 study inserted long pauses after their replies. These pauses often continued until the dispatcher asked the next question.

In some cases, guilty 911 callers were asked to hold while dispatchers alerted the street officers of the situation or transferred the call to other dispatchers. These holds lasted up to a minute, and guilty callers were often content to remain on the line silently waiting for the dispatchers.

In the following case, a mother called 911 when her son was in medical distress:

Dispatcher:	*"911, what's your emergency?"*
Guilty Caller:	*"(Spoken very slowly) Yes, umm, we need an ambulance (three-second pause)."*
Dispatcher:	*"Okay. What's the address?"*
Guilty Caller:	*"It's 686 West Circle Avenue (four-second pause)."*
Dispatcher:	*"Okay."*
Guilty Caller:	*(four-second pause)*
Dispatcher:	*"Okay, what's going on there?"*
Guilty Caller:	*"Um, our son is on an apnea monitor and the alarm is going off (three-second pause). He's not breathing (three-second pause)."*
Dispatcher:	*"Okay, how old is he?"*
Guilty Caller:	*"He's three months (three-second pause)."*
Dispatcher:	*"Have you started CPR?"*
Guilty Caller:	*"Ah, no, not yet. Oh, my husband's doing it."*
Dispatcher:	*"County Medic, need you to respond to 686 West Circle Avenue. Reference infant that's not breathing, Medics 303 and 622 respond from Station 1. Mother advises that the child suffers from apnea and the alarm is going off. Clear Medic 303, clear Medic 622. And you said he's three months old, ma'am?"*

(The caller waited silently for 24 seconds while the dispatcher alerted the medics.)

Guilty Caller:	*"Yes (five-second pause)."*
Dispatcher:	*"(Speaking to medics) Go ahead 303.........Unit 2 will you respond with medic 303 to 686 West Circle Avenue, three month old not breathing.*
	And when did you notice he wasn't breathing?"

(The caller waited silently for 14 seconds while the dispatcher spoke to the medics.)

Guilty Caller:	*"He's on an apnea monitor, it goes off when he stops breathing."*
Dispatcher:	*"Okay, is your husband doing CPR now?"*
Guilty Caller:	*"Yes (three-second pause)."*
Dispatcher:	*"Does he know how to do CPR?"*
Guilty Caller:	*"Yes, he does (three-second pause)."*
Innocent husband:	*"(Yelling at the caller) Tell 'em to get here, COME ON! Tell 'em it just keeps going off! TELL THEM TO COME ON!"*

Guilty Caller:	*"He's—he's not breathing, it's just—just going off."*
Dispatcher:	*"Okay, how's his color? Is he bluish?"*
Guilty Caller:	*"I imagine he's probably bluish by now (<u>four-second pause</u>)."*
Dispatcher:	*"And how does he feel to your husband—is he cool?"*
Guilty Caller:	*"Is he cool? They're asking questions, is he cool or not?"*
Innocent husband:	*"YES, PLEASE HELP US, WHERE ARE THEY?"*
Dispatcher:	*"What's your son's name, ma'am?"*
Guilty Caller:	*"Noah (<u>three-second pause</u>)."*
Innocent husband:	*"COME ON NOAH, COME ON! WHERE ARE THEY?"*
Dispatcher:	*"What's your name?"*
Guilty Caller:	*"Tiffany (<u>four-second pause</u>)."*
Dispatcher:	*"Okay. Can your husband hear any kind of breathing coming from him or see a rise and fall in his chest, anything like that?"*
Husband:	*"TELL THEM TO GET THEIR ASSES HERE! HE'S NOT BREATHING!"*
Dispatcher:	*"Did the baby choke on anything?"*
Guilty Caller:	*"No (<u>three-second pause</u>)."*
Dispatcher:	*"Did the machine just start going off?"*
Guilty Caller:	*"No (<u>four-second pause</u>)."*
Dispatcher:	*"Does the baby have a medical condition?"*
Guilty Caller:	*"No (<u>three-second pause</u>)."*
Dispatcher:	*"Okay, I have two squads en route and my sergeant, okay?"*
Guilty Caller:	*"Okay (<u>five-second pause</u>)."*
Dispatcher:	*"Is that the officer?"*
Guilty Caller:	*"Okay, they're here."*

The 911 caller used 16 Pauses during her communication with the dispatcher. Remarkably, she also waited quietly for 24 and 14 seconds while the dispatcher attended to other tasks. The mother could have used the time to demand medical assistance, express Urgency, provide Sensory Details, or describe the event. Instead, she used the numerous and lengthy Pauses to resist supplying information that could have saved her child's life. She also included an Initial Delay at the beginning of her opening comment. In contrast to the mother, the child's father screamed Aggressive Demands for medical aid and provided victim updates while he was attempting CPR.

The investigation revealed that the mother suffocated her child in a Munchausen by proxy case. The investigation also disclosed that the mother had previously killed two of her other children. She confessed that she thought the deaths of her three children would provide sympathy and attention from her husband. She was convicted of homicide.

Repetition

"Repetition does not transform a lie into a truth."
Franklin D. Roosevelt

Guilty 911 callers could not fully prepare for the onslaught of dispatcher questions, particularly questions that might cause callers to incriminate themselves. They needed time to think of safe answers so they often repeated words as a stalling technique. Guilty callers in the 911 study used Repetition by repeating words or phrases three or more times in sequence, in response to a dispatcher's question.

Repetition was used by 8% of the callers in the 911 study. Guilty callers used Repetition in 88% of these calls, and innocent callers used this indicator in 12% of the calls, as illustrated in Figure 17.11.

In the following case, a husband used Repetition when reporting his wife's suicide:

Dispatcher: *"911, what's your emergency?"*
Guilty Caller: *"Oh my God, my wife committed suicide! I just got in from work."*
Dispatcher: *"Where is your wife at right now?"*
Guilty Caller: *"She's in the bathroom."*
Dispatcher: *"Why would she do this?"*
Guilty Caller: *"<u>Oh my God, Oh my God, Oh my God</u>, I just got in from work and there's blood everywhere, <u>Oh my God</u>. She's been depressed."*

The husband answered questions without delay until the dispatcher asked him why his wife would commit suicide. The caller immediately responded with Repetition in order to gain time to think of an appropriate response. An innocent caller could have spontaneously answered the dispatcher's question by explaining the victim's mental state and previous actions. The husband

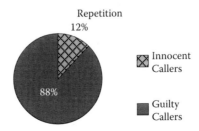

Figure 17.11 Percentages of Innocent vs. Guilty Callers in "Repetition."

eventually confessed to the murder after investigators learned that he had taken out a large insurance policy on his wife three months before her death.

In the following case, a wife called 911 after her husband was shot and killed in their home while he was watching television:

Dispatcher:	*"911, what is your emergency?"*
Guilty Caller:	*"SOMEBODY JUST SHOT MY HUSBAND!"*
Dispatcher:	*"Where is he shot at Ma'am?"*
Guilty Caller:	*"He's shot in the head, OH MY GOD!"*
Dispatcher:	*"Is he breathing Ma'am?"*
Guilty Caller:	*"I don't know, I think he's dead!"*
Dispatcher:	*"What is your address?"*
Guilty Caller:	*"48 Crestview Street!"*
Dispatcher:	*"Ma'am, what did the guy look like?"*
Guilty Caller:	*"Keep breathing, Doug. I'm in the back bedroom. Keep breathing, Doug. Keep breathing, Doug. Keep breathing, Doug. Keep breathing, Doug."*
Dispatcher:	*"What did the guy look like?"*
Guilty Caller:	*"It was dark, I don't know, It was dark."*

The wife quickly answered all of the dispatcher's questions until she was asked about the offender's description. She was unable to describe the fictitious offender's race, height, weight, hair style, facial hair, or clothing. The question about the offender required creativity and thus was too difficult for the caller to answer on the spur of the moment, so she used Repetition to stall and then to avoid answering at all. The investigation revealed that the wife had planned her husband's homicide and convinced her lover to help her. Both were convicted of the murder.

In the following case, a wife called 911 after her husband was shot in their front yard:

Dispatcher:	*"911, what is your emergency?"*
Guilty Caller:	*"Help! My husband has been shot, he's a cop!"*
Dispatcher:	*"What's your address?"*
Guilty Caller:	*"21 Ivy Lane. My husband's been shot!"*
Dispatcher:	*"Where is he shot at?"*
Guilty Caller:	*" I don't know."*
Dispatcher:	*"What's his name?"*
Guilty Caller:	*"Kevin."*
Dispatcher:	*"Did you see what happened?"*
Guilty Caller:	*"He's a cop, he's a cop! He's a cop!"*
Dispatcher:	*"Where is he bleeding from?"*
Guilty Caller:	*"He is bleeding from his back."*

Dispatcher:	*"Where were you when he got shot?"*
Guilty Caller:	*"Oh please! I love you so much, I love you so much, oh Kevin, I love you, I love you!"*

The wife answered questions without difficulty until the dispatcher asked if she saw what happened. She then responded with Repetition: *"He's a cop, he's a cop! He's a cop!"* As the 911 call progressed, the wife again answered the dispatcher's questions without delay until she was asked where she was when her husband was shot. For the second time, the wife responded with Repetition. The investigation revealed that the wife had paid her niece's boyfriend to kill the husband. The wife, the niece, and the boyfriend were all convicted of the murder.

Self-Interruption

"Evil is the interruption of a truth by the pressure of particular or individual interests."

Alain Badiou

Innocent 911 callers, because they had nothing to hide, offered comments without considering their choice of words. Guilty callers, however, had a different priority. Self-preservation demanded that they communicate with caution. Sometimes they began comments and stopped themselves midword or midsentence to change the direction of their statements, thus using the Self-interruption indicator.

The Self-interruption indicator was present in 47% of the calls in the 911 study. Guilty callers used Self-interruption more than twice as often as did innocent callers (68% vs. 32%), as shown in Figure 17.12.

In the following case, a husband called 911 to report that his wife committed suicide:

Dispatcher:	*"911, what is your emergency?"*
Guilty Caller:	*"Oh my God, Oh my God, my wife—I just drove home from a trip and my wife killed herself. Oh my God, Oh my God."*

The husband began to talk about his wife but then interrupted himself midsentence and changed direction to focus on himself. It was important to him to Minimize his involvement by inserting, *"I just drove home from a trip."* Once the husband accomplished his priority of Self-preservation, he addressed what should have been the true priority—his wife's condition. When the first officers arrived on scene, the husband quickly provided

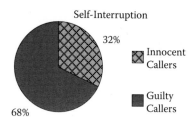

Figure 17.12 Percentages of Innocent vs. Guilty Callers in "Self-interruption."

several travel receipts in an attempt to establish an alibi. The investigation revealed that the husband had killed his wife before leaving town for his trip.

In the next case, a wife called 911 after she returned home from work and discovered her husband dead on the floor:

Dispatcher: *"911, what is your emergency?"*
Guilty Caller: *"My <u>husb—I</u> just came home and my husband is dead."*

Instead of beginning her 911 call with an immediate plea for help for her husband, the wife used Self-interruption on the second word of her opening sentence. She started to comment about her husband, interrupted herself midword, and then changed direction to Minimize her own involvement by stating that she just came home. The case investigator, who knew the principles of 911 Homicide Call Analysis, recognized indicators of guilt and decided to examine the wife's personal life. Further investigation disclosed that the wife had a boyfriend, and she had convinced him to shoot her husband while she was at work. She planned to call 911 when she got home, while posing as an innocent spouse. As directed, the boyfriend shot the victim and then fled the scene. When the wife entered her house after work, she expected to find her husband dead from a small gunshot wound, but instead she encountered an appalling scene. The boyfriend had used a shotgun. The first blast severed the husband's leg from his body and the second struck him squarely in the stomach. The wife found her deceased husband lying with his intestines in his hands. Although horrified at the condition of her husband, the wife was still careful to use Self-interruption to edit her comment and Minimize her involvement. Both the wife and boyfriend were convicted of the husband's murder.

When analyzing Self-interruption, it is helpful to examine where this indicator is located within the phone call. Some callers interrupted themselves almost immediately, as in the previous two examples (*"My wife—I just drove home,"* and *"My husb—I just came home."*) The callers could not wait until completing their first sentence to establish the fact that they had just arrived at the scene. The need to protect themselves was greater than the need to expedite help. Other guilty callers interrupted themselves later in the calls; their Self-interruptions were triggered by specific questions from dispatchers.

In the following case, a man returned home from work and discovered that his wife had been killed. He used Self-Interruption immediately as well as repeatedly throughout the call:

Dispatcher:	*"911, what is your emergency?"*
Guilty Caller:	*"There's a <u>murd—my</u> wife has just been killed I think."*
Dispatcher:	*"Where's she at?"*
Guilty Caller:	*"This is Lieutenant Brady!"*
Dispatcher:	*"Is this 212-5660?"*
Guilty Caller:	*"Yeah, just got home, all I know is my wife's on the bed, the pillow is over her face and there's blood and she's cold. I think she's been shot, I don't know."*
Dispatcher:	*"OK."*
Guilty Caller:	*"Somebody get here quick but I think <u>she's—I don't</u> know if somebody's committed <u>burg—all</u> my guns are laying out in here, in my house and everything."*
Dispatcher:	*"Do you know if somebody shot her?"*
Guilty Caller:	*"It looks like somebody's been through my house!"*
Dispatcher:	*"Is there a gun by her?"*
Guilty Caller:	*"I <u>can't</u>—I don't know!"*
Dispatcher:	*"Units have been dispatched right now, go see if she's breathing or not and see where she's been shot."*
Guilty Caller:	*"(Sigh) God Damn I don't know if this <u>guy—somebody's</u> still in the house."*

The caller began the 911 call with a Self-interruption. He likely started to say the word murder, but he interrupted himself midword and changed the crime to a less severe action and then ended with Equivocation: *"There's a murd—my wife has just been killed I think."* He also shifted the attention from a burglary to unattended guns: *"I don't know if somebody's committed burg—all my guns are laying out."*

The caller interrupted himself after the following two questions that he found difficult to answer: *"Do you know if somebody shot her?"* and *"Is there a gun by her?"* He avoided answering either question. Instead, he continued to edit his comments, using Self-Interruption a total of five times during this portion of the call.

The caller's last Self-interruption is the most revealing: *"I don't know if this guy—somebody's still in the house."* The caller made a catastrophic error at this point in the call. He began to make a comment about a specific suspect, a single male but then stopped, changed direction, and described the offender with the Equivocal word, "somebody." He knew more than he wanted to share.

The investigation confirmed that the caller had arrived home and discovered his wife's body. She had been sexually assaulted and murdered. He reported the offense to 911 and seemingly cooperated with investigators. The case was unsolved for the next nine years until a Cold Case Task Force discovered new information. Evidence confirmed that the caller, who was at work when the death occurred, had organized the burglary of his own home to frighten his wife into moving to a new location. Instead, the "burglar" assaulted and killed the wife. Had the original investigators analyzed the 911 call, the case might not have gone cold. The caller's Self-interruption regarding the suspect was damning. It was introduced at trial and contributed to a guilty verdict.

Investigators who recognize Self-interruptions in calls and examine where they occur can gain insight to the caller's focus. This insight can be used to plan effective interview strategies to uncover the whole truth.

Short Answers

"Silence becomes cowardice when occasion demands speaking out the whole truth and acting accordingly."

Mahatma Ghandi

Innocent callers had much to say to the 911 dispatchers, and they were determined to say it all. While focusing on the victims, they freely communicated relevant facts. They were often verbose and fervent when conveying details of injuries, updates on victims' conditions, crime scene information, and offender descriptions. The extreme stress of the events caused them to be vociferous as they broadcasted any and all information that might assist the dispatchers to help the victims.

In the following case, a man called 911 to get help for a shooting victim:

Dispatcher: *"911, what is your emergency?"*
Innocent Caller: *"Get the cops up here on Third Street and bring the ambulance! They just rolled up on this boy and shot him two times! He's down, he's bleeding, he needs help!"*
Dispatcher: *"What's the cross street, sir?"*
Innocent Caller: *"(Yelling at another witness) WHAT'S THE CROSS STREET RIGHT THERE?*
                   (Speaking to dispatcher)

It's on Third Street just east of Kent. Oh, he's shot in the back! This guy is hurt bad! Do you have them coming?"

Dispatcher: *"They are on the way sir."*

Innocent Caller: *"The dude that done it is in a gray van and he pulled up next to the boy and started shooting. He was a black dude and he had a white shirt on. I didn't get the tag but it was an Ohio plate!"*

Dispatcher: *"Is the victim conscious?"*

Innocent Caller: *"NO! He aint' breathin' and there's a lady here checkin' on him and she say he ain't got no pulse either! I don't hear no sirens, where are they?"*

The caller witnessed a drive-by gang shooting as he walked out of a grocery store. He immediately called 911 and volunteered crucial information regarding the victim, the event, and the suspect. He had never met the victim, but he freely conveyed vital information to the dispatcher and urgently demanded help. The victim died at the scene. The caller was innocent, and the drive-by suspect was later arrested and convicted of the murder.

In contrast, guilty 911 callers were often reluctant to share victim information, crime scene details, and offender specifics. They provided the dispatchers with limited information by using Short Answers to avoid incriminating themselves with facts. The Short Answer indicator is defined as a pattern of short answers by callers who used replies of three words or less in at least 25% of their call. While technically answering the questions, a pattern of Short Answers lacked essential details. The verbal exchange during these calls resembled an interrogation, as dispatchers attempted to pry needed information from resistant callers.

Thirteen percent of the calls in the 911 study contained a pattern of Short Answers. Guilty callers made most of these calls (92%), and innocent callers made 8% of the calls, as illustrated in Figure 17.13.

The following case illustrates the short answer pattern by a husband who resisted the dispatcher's questions:

Figure 17.13 Percentages of Innocent vs. Guilty Callers in "Short Answers."

Dispatcher:	"911, what is your emergency?"
Guilty Caller:	"Yes, Ma'am, can, I need some help here."
Dispatcher:	"What's the problem sir?"
Guilty Caller:	"_It's my wife_." (three-second pause)
Dispatcher:	"What's wrong with your wife, sir?"
Guilty Caller:	"I don't know, she said she wasn't feeling well."
Dispatcher:	"OK, does she have any medical conditions?"
Guilty Caller:	"_No_." (two-second pause)
Dispatcher:	"Let me talk to her, sir."
Guilty Caller:	"She's out of it, she can't talk."
Dispatcher:	"Is she—is she conscious?"
Guilty Caller:	"_No, she isn't_." (three-second pause)
Dispatcher:	"OK, I'm sending the medics, hold on."
Guilty Caller:	"_OK_." (five-second pause)
Dispatcher:	"Where is she now?"
Guilty Caller:	"_She's in bed_." (three-second pause)
Dispatcher:	"Do you have any idea what's wrong with her? Tell me what's going on."
Guilty Caller:	"She's been real sick lately and takes lots of medicines. She mighta taken too much, she's been so sick."
Dispatcher:	"Sick how? What's wrong with her? Does she see a doctor for something?"
Guilty Caller:	"_She threw up_." (two-second pause)
Dispatcher:	"What kind of medicine is she on?"
Guilty Caller:	"_Methadone_." (three-second pause)
Dispatcher:	"Who's her doctor?"
Guilty Caller:	"She's been seeing Dr. Craft down at University Hospital for two years now. She was there last week to see him."
Dispatcher:	"Is your wife breathing?"
Guilty Caller:	"_I can't tell_." (three-second pause)
Dispatcher:	"OK, get her on her side and tell me if she's breathing or not."
Guilty Caller:	"_OK_." (two-second pause)
Dispatcher:	"Is she breathing sir?"
Guilty Caller:	"No she's not. Do you have someone coming?"
Dispatcher:	"Yes, they're pulling in now, you should see them."
Guilty Caller:	"_They're here_."

The husband had 16 opportunities to speak, and on 10 of these he replied to the dispatcher with three or fewer words.

In conjunction with Pauses, the Short Answers allowed the husband to resist providing vital information about his wife. The dispatcher had to extract additional information by asking follow-up questions throughout the call. By wasting precious time, the husband's guarded strategy protected him but delayed aid to his wife.

The investigator assigned to this case, trained in 911 Homicide Call Analysis, recognized the guilty indicators in the call. After interviewing the husband, the investigator sent the following note to the authors:

> After a long interview, I told the husband about 911 Call Analysis. He just looked at me like I had no clue what I was talking about. Then I dropped your articles on 911 Analysis on the table and he confessed. He admitted that he gave his wife the methadone that caused her death. Thanks for making me think outside of the box.

Considerations

The Short Answer indicator does not apply if 911 callers were providing CPR to the victims while on the phone with the dispatchers. For example, in the following case, a 911 caller gave CPR to a coworker while talking to the dispatcher:

Dispatcher: "911, what is your emergency?"
Innocent Caller: "Start the ambulance to Point West Office Center, I think one of our employees is having a heart attack, he's passed out, he's had heart surgery before."
Dispatcher: "OK, does he have a pulse?"
Innocent Caller: "No pulse and he ain't breathing! Start the ambulance!"
Dispatcher: "OK, the medics are already coming, tilt his head back a little so it's easier for him to breathe. Put your palms in the center of his chest and pump 15 times and then give two quick breaths while pinching his nose shut."
Innocent Caller: "OK."

> Caller can be heard placing the phone down, pumping the victim's chest and making two breaths.

Dispatcher: "OK, does he have a pulse now?"
Innocent Caller: "No!"
Dispatcher: "OK, do it again."
Innocent Caller: "I am."
Dispatcher: "Do you feel a pulse?"
Innocent Caller: "No pulse yet!"
Dispatcher: "The ambulance is almost there, do it again, don't stop."
Innocent Caller: "OK."
Dispatcher: "Have somebody go outside and flag down the medic when they pull up."

Innocent Caller: *"OK."*

> *Caller is heard yelling to someone to go outside and flag down the medics, and then continuing with CPR.*

Dispatcher: *"You still with me?"*
Innocent Caller: *"He's turning blue!"*
Dispatcher: *"They're pulling up now sir. You're doing a great job."*
Innocent Caller: *"Hurry!"*

In this case, the caller gave short answers on 8 of his 10 turns to speak but all related to CPR. Brevity benefited the victim.

Unintelligible Comments

> *"Whatever you say, say it with conviction."*
> Mark Twain

Innocent callers' voices were typically loud and demanding; guilty callers' voices were weaker and more fragile, trailing off at the end of sentences. Instead of speaking with clarity and strength, some guilty callers mumbled with such little confidence that keywords became Unintelligible. Figure 17.14 illustrates the Continuum of Demands to Unintelligible Comments. When callers who had been communicating clearly up to this point changed their pattern and responded to the dispatchers' questions with Unintelligible Comments, they revealed a lack of conviction in their responses. In fact, they may not have wanted to be understood. This strategy allowed guilty callers to resist the dispatchers' critical questions, and it benefited themselves instead of the victims.

A quarter of all calls in the 911 study contained Unintelligible Comments. Guilty callers uttered almost all of the Unintelligible Comments, at a rate of over 11 times that of innocent callers (92% vs. 8%). See Figure 17.15.

In the following case, a male called 911 when his girlfriend's baby was in distress:

Dispatcher: *"911, what is your emergency?"*

Figure 17.14 Continuum of demands to unintelligible comments.

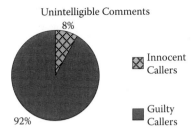

Figure 17.15 Percentages of Innocent vs. Guilty Callers in "Unintelligible Comments."

Guilty Caller:	*"My son I mean my girlfriend's son he been (<u>unintelligible</u>) and I really don't know what to do"*
Dispatcher:	*"What's going on?"*
Guilty Caller:	*"The baby was eatin' and threw up and somebody needs to come out here."*
Dispatcher:	*"When did you feed the baby last?"*
Guilty Caller:	*"(Two second pause) probably about (<u>unintelligible</u>)."*
Dispatcher:	*"What?"*

In the beginning of the 911 call, the guilty caller avoided giving a clear explanation of the child's condition by answering with Unintelligible Comments. He then spoke with clarity when stating that the victim *"was eatin' and threw up."* When the dispatcher asked about the last time the caller fed the baby, the reply was again Unintelligible. The caller was unwilling to commit to an answer that might implicate him. The caller later confessed to shaking the baby after the child threw up on the floor, and he was convicted of murder.

Unintelligible Comments often appeared at the end of replies to dispatchers. Some guilty 911 callers began to answer questions appropriately, then became quieter and trailed off with hushed murmurs. Their answers often lacked confidence and avoided commitment. In the following case, a woman called 911 to report that her stepdaughter was unresponsive:

Dispatcher:	*"911, what is your emergency?"*
Guilty Caller:	*"Yes, Sir, I – send an ambulance to 90 Catalpa Drive!"*
Dispatcher:	*"OK, what's the problem, Ma'am?"*
Guilty Caller:	*"My stepdaughter fell in the kitchen (three-second pause)."*
Dispatcher:	*"OK, where is she hurt?"*
Guilty Caller:	*"The back of her (<u>unintelligible</u>)."*
Dispatcher:	*"The back of what?"*
Guilty Caller:	*"The back of her head is all (<u>unintelligible</u>)."*

Dispatcher:	*"Speak up Ma'am, I can't understand what you're saying."*
Guilty Caller:	*"The back of her head is all mushy."*
Dispatcher:	*"Did you say 'mushy'?"*
Guilty Caller:	*"Yes (three-second pause)."*
Dispatcher:	*"What did she hit her head on?"*
Guilty Caller:	*"I was in the other room, I think it (<u>unintelligible</u>)."*
Dispatcher:	*"What did she hit her head on?"*
Guilty Caller:	*"I think she hit in on the floor because (<u>unintelligible</u>)."*

Each time the stepmother was asked a question about the victim's injury, she started the reply in a clear fashion, but then her garbled endings made the answers indiscernible to the dispatcher. She used four Unintelligible Comments to complete her answers. Instead of helping the victim by clearly demanding aid and providing details of the injury, the caller protected her own interests by resisting questions with Unintelligible Comments, a Delay, and Pauses. The investigation revealed that the stepmother assaulted the child, causing the victim's head to strike the corner of the kitchen table. She later pled guilty to a murder charge.

Considerations
Occasionally, the callers' crying and screaming at the beginning of the 911 call made their words difficult to understand. Once dispatchers took control by getting frantic callers to calm down, the callers usually became coherent. This situation was most common when innocent mothers called 911 to demand help for their unresponsive babies. Incoherent opening sounds are not examples of the Unintelligible Comments indicator.

A consideration in child death investigations is that these deaths were generally not premeditated, and the actions that caused the deaths were often immediately regretted. The 911 callers in such cases were often temporary caregivers at the time of the incidents, primarily boyfriends, stepfathers, or daycare providers. These 911 calls thus contained both urgent pleas and signs of resistance. The callers needed the victims to live, but they could not tell the whole truth.

MR. AND MRS. HUNT CASE

Jake showed Resistance to the Dispatcher in four areas:

He used Equivocation when referring to the burglary: *"there's been a break-in, I think."* This Equivocation did not make sense because Jake later confirmed the break-in.

Jake employed Evasion by answering a different question than he was asked.

Dispatcher: *"Who did you say is dead?"*
Jake: *"Someone broke in."*

He included Repetition in the following exchanges:

Dispatcher: *"What happened to them, sir?"*
Jake: *"Oh my God, oh my God, oh my God"*

. . . .

Dispatcher: *"Are you sure they're both gone, are they breathing…do they have pulses?"*
Caller: "I don't know. *Oh my God, oh my God, oh my God."*

Jake also used Self-interruption so he would not have to finish the description of where he found his in-laws: "*I found them in the—there's been a* break-in, I think!"

Innocent Indicators

____COOPERATION WITH DISPATCHER

Guilty Indicators

RESISTANCE TO DISPATCHER

____Dispatcher Confusion

____Diversion	✓ Equivocation
✓ Evasion	____Hangs Up
____Only Answers What's Asked	____Pauses
✓ Repetition	✓ Self-interruption
____Short Answers	____Unintelligible Comments

Reference

DePaulo, B. M., Lindsay, J. J., Malone, B. E., Muhlenbruck, L., Charlton, K., and Cooper, H. (2003), "Cues to deception," *Psychological Bulletin*, 129 (1), 74–118.

Independent Guilty Indicators V

Attempts to Convince

18

"I figured that if I said it enough, I would convince the world that I really was the greatest."

Muhammad Ali

There is a difference between conveying information directly and making exaggerated attempts to convince (Rabon, 1996). Individuals who are telling the truth have no need to try to convince others that the information is accurate; truthful speakers assume that the information will be accepted as factual. Guilty 911 callers providing false narratives, however, realized they were on shaky ground and needed to bolster their "stories." Some made Attempts to Convince the dispatchers by repeating key phrases such as *"I was at the store"* in an effort to support their fictitious messages. Often these phrases by themselves are true, but they are meant to obscure the whole truth. The Attempts to Convince indicator is defined as statements repeated three or more times in an effort to persuade the dispatchers.

Even under inordinate stress, innocent 911 callers realized that the best way to aid the victims was to convey only relevant information. Few Attempts to Convince were made in innocent calls.

In the following case, an innocent woman called 911 to seek aid for her neighbor. She conveyed information by sharing pertinent facts regarding the victim and the victim's condition:

Dispatcher: *"911, what is your emergency?"*
Innocent Caller: *"Get an ambulance to 19 Johnson Place! My neighbor's down in his yard!"*
Dispatcher: *"What's going on?"*
Innocent Caller: *"He was cutting his grass and I looked outside and he was down. He has heart problems; he had heart surgery last year. Do you have an ambulance coming? Hurry!"*
Dispatcher: *"Yes, they are on the way. Is he breathing?"*
Innocent Caller: *"He wasn't breathing but my husband is giving him CPR. His bracelet says he takes Nitro. He's had two heart attacks before, please hurry, he's gray."*
Dispatcher: *"They're coming honey, as fast as they can."*

147

Innocent Caller: *(yells to victim)* *"Ernie! Ernie! Can you hear me? Squeeze my hand Ernie!"* *"PLEASE HURRY, he's feeling really clammy and he's sweating really bad."*

The innocent caller focused on getting help for the victim and providing critical information to the 911 dispatcher. The caller volunteered facts about the victim's past medical issues, his Nitro medication, and his current condition. The call contained no Attempts to Convince. Despite the caller's efforts to get immediate aid, the victim died at the scene and an autopsy revealed that he suffered a massive heart attack.

In contrast to innocent callers who simply conveyed critical information regarding the victim, some guilty 911 callers Attempted to Convince the dispatchers of a theme about themselves. The theme often centered on the callers' alibis and consisted of phrases repeated throughout the 911 call to try to persuade the dispatcher that the callers were innocent. They offered such statements as, *"I just got back from shopping,"* or *"I just got back from McDonalds,"* repeating this theme throughout the call to convince the dispatchers that they were not present during the murder. Their goal was to distance themselves from suspicion.

In the 911 study, the Attempts to Convince indicator was present in 15% of the calls. Guilty callers used this indicator nine times more often than did innocent callers (90% vs. 10%), as depicted in Figure 18.1.

In the following case, a husband said he returned home and found his wife lying in the back yard in the snow:

Dispatcher:	*"911, what is your emergency?"*
Guilty Caller:	*"936 St. Cloud Drive, my wife's out on the ground. I just got home from a baseball game in, in town."*
Dispatcher:	*"Yes."*
Guilty Caller:	*"The wife's out on the back yard out on the ground and she's ice cold."*

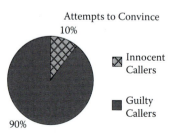

Attempts to Convince

Figure 18.1 Percentages of Innocent vs. Guilty Callers in "Attempts to Convince."

Dispatcher:	*"Okay just stay on the line I just want to get an ambulance started first please."*
Guilty Caller:	*"What's that?"*
Dispatcher:	*"I want you to stay on the phone line; do you know if she's ah, she's unconscious, is she breathing?"*
Guilty Caller:	*"No."*
Dispatcher:	*"Okay, um, I can give you CPR instructions if you believe that she's ah, not breathing."*
Guilty Caller:	*"I, I know CPR."*
Dispatcher:	*"Do you?"*
Guilty Caller:	*"But she's ice cold, she's ice cold man. <u>I just got back from the game</u>. I don't know how long she's been out here."*
Dispatcher:	*"Okay, when did you last see her?"*
Guilty Caller:	*"<u>I left like six, seven o'clock to go to…down to go to the baseball game</u>, the Barons game."*

Three times during the 911 call, the husband advised the dispatcher that he was at a baseball game. It was very important to him to Attempt to Convince the dispatcher that he was not at the scene of the offense when it occurred. He focused on providing an alibi instead of sharing critical information and details regarding his wife and her condition. The dispatcher had no idea whether the victim suffered a medical event, was involved in an accident, or was assaulted. However, the fact that the caller was at a game was made very clear. This may have been truthful information, but the overexaggerated attention on the alibi was unusual. When the first responders arrived on scene, the husband quickly provided them with a ticket stub from the baseball game. He was also wearing a brand new team jersey and had the receipt for the jersey in his pocket. The investigation revealed that the caller's wife had been struck with an object and suffered a fractured skull. The husband was eventually convicted of the murder, which he committed before going to the baseball game.

In the following case, a wife called 911 to report that her husband had been assaulted. As a practice exercise, look for repeated phrases that reveal the caller's Attempts to Convince the dispatcher:

Dispatcher:	*"911, what's your emergency?"*
Guilty Caller:	*"My, my husband has been, it looks like shot or stabbed or something. My house has been ransacked."*
Dispatcher:	*"Okay, Ma'am. Ma'am, where are you at right now? 991—"*
Guilty Caller:	*"I'm at—I said 991 Varchi, V-A-R-CH-I. Our last name is Campbell, C-A-M-P-B-E-L-L."*
Dispatcher:	*"Okay. Now when you came home did you find anything in the house?"*

Guilty Caller:	*"I was..."*
Dispatcher:	*"Was the door open?"*
Guilty Caller:	*"... in the gym. I was in—we have a gym out back and I was working out in the gym. I heard some noise, and I came in. My husband's lying in the middle of the floor and (unintelligible)—he's not moving. I don't know if he's even alive and the house has been ransacked. Please, please hurry and get here."*
Dispatcher:	*"All right, all right, ma'am."*
Guilty Caller:	*"I'm sorry. Please."*
Dispatcher:	*"All right, ma'am. We have officers—"*
Guilty Caller:	*"Please."*
Dispatcher:	*"—coming, okay?"*
Guilty Caller:	*"I'm pleading for my life. This man's my life."*
Dispatcher:	*"Okay. And you said he's unconscious, right? Right, ma'am? You said he's unconscious?"*
Guilty Caller:	*"(Unintelligible) I think he's dead. I think my husband might be dead but if you hurry, maybe he's alive and you can help him."*
Dispatcher:	*"Okay, ma'am. We have the—uh, Rescue is responding right now."*
Guilty Caller:	*"I was in the gym out back when it happened."*
Dispatcher:	*"Okay."*
Guilty Caller:	*"I heard a noise. I came in. I called his name. He's been watching golf. He's been trying to stay awake to watch the Super Bowl. Oh, my God. Oh, my God, oh, my God."*
Dispatcher:	*"Okay. Now did you see anybody leave the house or anything?"*
Guilty Caller:	*"No, I didn't see anything. I came out of the gym (unintelligible), no, no. Please, please (unintelligible)."*
Dispatcher:	*"Okay, ma'am. Where are you right now in the house?"*
Guilty Caller:	*"I am outside in my car 'cause I didn't know whether to go back in or not."*
Dispatcher:	*"Okay. Go back in and see if your husband is conscious, okay, ma'am?"*
Guilty Caller:	*"I did. I've already checked for a pulse. I couldn't feel—I didn't feel for one."*
Dispatcher:	*"Okay."*
Guilty Caller:	*"But then he doesn't look like he is. He's—his eyes—"*
Dispatcher:	*"Okay. But where—does he look like he was shot, stabbed?—"*
Guilty Caller:	*"I can't tell. It looked like he was either shot or he was stabbed. Please help me, please. Please help me."*
Dispatcher:	*"Okay, ma'am. We're coming right now. We have officers on the way right now."*

Guilty Caller:	*"Thank you."*
Dispatcher:	*"—but I'm gonna need you to take a deep breath and tell me exactly what happened. Okay? So you didn't see anyone leave the house, you didn't see anyone running, you didn't see any vehicles, right?"*
Guilty Caller:	*"Nothing, nothing. I was working out at the gym. I heard a noise."*
Dispatcher:	*"What kind of noise did you hear?"*
Guilty Caller:	*"It was like a pop. And I was like, 'What is that?' So I came in from the gym."*
Dispatcher:	*"Okay."*
Guilty Caller:	*"I—I—I (unintelligible) saw him laying there in a pool of blood. I was like, 'What the fuck?' and I ended up going to him. I was, like, (unintelligible) to see if he was alive and I (unintelligible)."*
Dispatcher:	*"Okay, ma'am. Let me get your name. What's your name, ma'am?"*
Guilty Caller:	*"My name is Sherri Becker. I am his wife."*
Dispatcher:	*"Okay. And what…"*
Guilty Caller:	*"We love each other. This man is my life."*
Dispatcher:	*"Okay. I understand, ma'am, but, you know, you need to help me as best as possible and I'm gonna need you to, you know, take a deep breath and give me everything that you've got, okay? What's your last name?"*
Guilty Caller:	*"It's Campbell, C-A-M-P-B-E-L-L."*
Dispatcher:	*"Okay, ma'am."*
Guilty Caller:	*"I'm sorry."*
Dispatcher:	*"We have an ambulance on the way as well. Um, what's your husband's name?"*
Guilty Caller:	*"I can't live without this man."*
Dispatcher:	*"Okay. I understand, ma'am. What is your husband's name?"*
Guilty Caller:	*"It's Garry. It's Garry C. Becker and he loves me and I love him. And this cannot be happening."*
Dispatcher:	*"Okay."*
Guilty Caller:	*"This cannot be happening."*
Dispatcher:	*"Now do you see any, um, ambulance coming outside or anything?"*
Guilty Caller:	*"I can hear them. I can hear…"*
Dispatcher:	*"Okay. 'Cause I can hear it in the background as well. Do you see them coming down the street?"*
Guilty Caller:	*"No. No."*
Dispatcher:	*"Okay, ma'am. Let me get a phone number for you if we lose connection or anything."*

Guilty Caller: *"Call me on my cell. It's 709-0672. Everything else I didn't*
                     wanna touch in the house. They tore it to (unintelligible)."
Dispatcher: *"That's—that's a good idea, ma'am. Do not touch anything in*
                     the house because if someone came in and tried to burglarize
                     your house, we need to get the fingerprints."
Guilty Caller: *"(Unintelligible). You've gotta help me."*
Dispatcher: *"Now are you still outside by your vehicle?"*
Guilty Caller: *"I'm standing by my vehicle."*
Dispatcher: *"Did you see any weapons on the floor? Did anyone drop*
                     anything?"
Guilty Caller: *"I don't see—there's cops (unintelligible) by. There goes a cop*
                     car."
Dispatcher: *"Okay, are they there?"*
Guilty Caller: *"Yes, thank you."*

Many indicators of guilt are contained in the above call, including No Immediate Plea for Help, Focus on Caller, Acceptance of Death, No Urgency, No Fear, Self-interruptions, Extraneous Information, Blood and Brains, and Unintelligible Comments. Perhaps the most obvious indicator was the caller's continued Attempts to Convince the dispatcher that she was in the gym when her husband was attacked. The caller included two additional Attempts to Convince: her house was ransacked and the couple loved one another. The wife stated six times that she was in the gym, in an effort to convince the dispatcher that she was nowhere near the scene of the crime. She repeated the burglary theme three times and variations of the love theme four times. These themes were meant to convince the dispatcher and law enforcement that she could not possibly be a suspect because she was nowhere near the crime, that someone burglarized her home, and that she and her husband were deeply in love. The subsequent investigation revealed that the crime scene was illogical and the burglary was staged. Investigators learned that the couple was recently married, and the wealthy elderly husband was much older than his young wife, a former prostitute. The wife, who would have received a large estate as her husband's beneficiary, was later convicted of murdering her husband.

Considerations

Attempts to Convince were only considered as indicators of guilt if they were unprompted. For example, when dispatchers expressed skepticism about the victims' conditions, innocent callers repeated their descriptions of injuries to persuade the dispatchers of the need for immediate emergency response. Because these were not spontaneous utterances, they were not Attempts to Convince indicators.

MR. AND MRS. HUNT CASE

Jake Attempted to Convince the dispatcher that intruders had been in his in-laws home by repeating a burglary theme.

"*there's been a break-in, I think!*"

"*Somebody broke in and tore up their house.*"

"*There is stuff everywhere.*"

Guilty Indicators

✓ Attempts to Convince

Reference

Rabon, D. (1996), *Investigative Discourse Analysis*, Carolina Academic Press, Durham, North Carolina.

Awkward Phrases

19

"Truth is ever to be found in simplicity, and not in the multiplicity and confusion of things."

Isaac Newton

Innocent and guilty 911 callers were both under stress when speaking to dispatchers. However, even during the crisis, most innocent callers were able to quickly convey information without having to carefully choose their words. In contrast, some guilty callers tried to edit their comments while under stress, resulting in Awkward Phrases. In response to dispatchers' questions regarding the victims and the scenes, these guilty callers' words were clumsy and confusing.

As an example of the typical innocent callers' spontaneous and concise clarity, examine the following case of a wife calling 911 regarding her husband's medical event:

Dispatcher: *"Tell me what happened."*
Innocent Caller: *"He grabbed his chest and fell and he's lying on the floor near the couch."*

The dispatcher could immediately visualize what happened and ask the proper follow-up questions. The victim died of a heart attack and the caller was innocent of the death.

After reporting that his wife was suffering from a medical event, the following caller was given the same instruction as the previous caller.

Dispatcher: *"Tell me what happened."*
Guilty Caller: *"I woke up...I slept in, and I, I, she had gotten up earlier this morning and I went out...<u>finally now to the living room and she was fallen,</u>...between the, um, like the ottoman and the wall."*

Instead of using a quick, concise phrase in his reply, the caller edited his comments as he was speaking to the 911 dispatcher. He began by focusing on himself, using *"I"* four times in the first sentence before mentioning his wife. The caller described the location of the victim as *"finally now to the living room and she was fallen.*" This awkward, lengthy comment contrasts with the previous call. However, the callers are both saying the same thing: the victim was lying on the floor. In this case, the husband had killed his wife and he was convicted of his crime.

In the 911 study, Awkward Phrases were present in 14% of the calls. Almost all of the Awkward Phrases were uttered by guilty callers (93% vs. 7%). See Figure 19.1.

In many homicides, suicides, drug overdoses, and accidents, the victims' blood was visible at the scene. Contrast the next two calls, made by callers at scenes with large amounts of blood.

Dispatcher: *"What's wrong with him?"*
Innocent Caller: *"He's bleeding from his mouth and nose."*

....

Dispatcher: *"What happened to him?"*
Guilty Caller: *"It's all bloody on his head."*

The first caller clearly described the injury and its location. The second caller, however, used an Awkward Phrase that did not clearly describe the injury.

A husband also answered the dispatcher's question with an Awkward Phrase when he was asked about his wife:

Dispatcher: *"Was she there by herself?"*
Guilty Caller: *"Her head is open."*

Not only did the caller fail to answer the question, but he also used an Awkward Phrase that did not adequately describe his wife's wound.

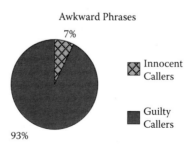

Figure 19.1 Percentages of Innocent vs. Guilty Callers in "Awkward Phrases."

Similarly, a caller reporting that his wife committed suicide was asked a direct, logical question by the 911 dispatcher. He replied as follows:

Dispatcher: *"Did you see her do it? Just explain the situation."*
Guilty Caller: *"I see (two-second pause) everything in the face."*

The caller, editing his comments while speaking, responded with an Awkward Phrase. This confusing phrase was neither direct nor concise, and it did not benefit the victim or the dispatcher. Awkward Phrases provide clues to callers' inner turmoil.

MR. AND MRS. HUNT CASE
Jake used no Awkward Phrases.
<u>Guilty Indicators</u> ___ Awkward Phrases

Conflicting Facts

20

Mark Twain

Some guilty callers provided Conflicting Facts during their 911 calls by stating information that conflicted with information they previously provided. These Conflicting Facts, or lies, ranged from the obvious to the subtle.

All of the calls with Conflicting Facts in the 911 study were made by guilty callers, as shown in Figure 20.1. Twenty-one percent of all calls contained Conflicting Facts, another strong indicator of guilt.

To illustrate an obvious conflict, the following case involves a wife who called 911 to report that intruders entered her home and shot her husband:

Dispatcher:	*"How many broke in?"*
Guilty Caller:	*"<u>Three men broke in</u>...Oh my God...there were <u>three of them</u>. Oh my God, they shot my husband, he's dead!"*
Dispatcher:	*"What did they look like? What were they wearing?"*
Guilty Caller:	*"I don't know, it was dark...Oh my God!"*
Dispatcher:	*"Is your husband breathing?"*
Guilty Caller:	*"Noooooo, Oh my God."*
Dispatcher:	*"Ma'am, calm down, which way did they go?"*
Guilty Caller:	*"<u>Both of them</u> took off through the back yard."*

Not only did the wife provide Conflicting Facts about the number of intruders, she also failed to give specific descriptions of the offenders (race, height, weight, etc.) and their clothing. An innocent caller should, at a minimum, be able to provide a general description of the relative sizes of the intruders.

Some Conflicting Facts are subtle and can be easily missed, as in the following case. A mother called 911 because her baby was not breathing:

Dispatcher:	*"911, what are you reporting?"*
Guilty Caller:	*"My daughter <u>just stopped breathing</u>."*
Dispatcher:	*"When did this happen?"*
Guilty Caller:	*"<u>I don't know, my boyfriend just called and woke me up</u>."*

Conflicting Facts

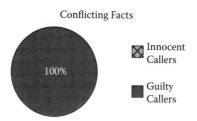

Figure 20.1 Percentages of Innocent vs. Guilty Callers in "Conflicting Facts."

An investigator rushing through an analysis of the previous 911 call could easily miss the conflict revealed by the mother. Her first comment was that her daughter *"just stopped breathing."* However, in her next statement, she negated the first comment by stating that she was asleep and did not know when the baby stopped breathing. No matter how obvious or subtle the conflicts, both are indicators of guilt. The subtle Conflicting Facts reveal why it is imperative to have written, line-numbered transcripts available with the audios of the 911 calls, to effectively analyze the callers' words. If detectives do not have staff who can complete accurate transcriptions, it is important that detectives do it themselves. Although typing exact transcripts takes time, the accuracy of the transcriptions will be assured.

Considerations

Some callers provided facts that they later learned were inaccurate. Correcting inaccurate information as new details were gained was a spontaneous correction rather than a Conflicting Fact. The following call illustrates a spontaneous correction by a caller when additional details revealed a discrepancy. The caller heard a noise in his apartment building and walked down the hall to investigate. Through an open apartment door, he saw a person lying face down. He ran back to his own apartment and called 911 to get help.

Dispatcher: *"911, what is your emergency?"*
Innocent Caller: *"There's a man been shot down the hall of my apartment."*
Dispatcher: *"Can you check and see if he has a pulse?"*
Innocent Caller: *"OK." (Caller checks victim.)*
Innocent Caller: *"I thought it was a man, but it's a lady,* and I didn't feel a pulse."

The innocent caller did not know the victim and had assumed that the person was male. After a closer look and learning additional information, he corrected his previous inaccuracy about the victim's gender. A murderer is not likely to think through the complicated events of killing a woman, calling 911 to report that a neighbor was shot, falsely describing the victim as a male, and finally changing the gender of the victim to reclassify her as a female. In fact, the offender could not have known that the dispatcher was going to direct him to go back to the body, so there would be no reason for the complicated ruse. Note that this innocent caller showed Cooperation with the Dispatcher by following directions and checking for the victim's pulse.

A second call also illustrates the use of spontaneous correction:

Dispatcher: *"Where's he shot at?"*
Innocent Caller: *"This guy's been shot in his stomach. He's down."*
Dispatcher: *"Did you see anyone leaving the area?"*
Innocent Caller: | *"No, no—he's shot in the head.* | *The bloods leakin' down."*

The caller had walked into a business and noticed the victim in a sitting position on the floor, leaning against a couch. The victim was heavyset, and blood had pooled on the top of his large stomach. When the caller first saw the victim, he noted the pooling blood and assumed that was where the victim was shot. However, as the caller was speaking to the dispatcher, he noticed that the victim had a gunshot wound behind his left ear, and he quickly corrected himself. The autopsy revealed that the victim had been shot with a .22 caliber bullet; blood from the wound trailed down the victim's neck and chest, pooling above his stomach. The subsequent investigation revealed that the caller was innocent of the crime. As in the previous case, a murderer is not likely to provide inaccurate information and then spontaneously correct it.

MR. AND MRS. HUNT CASE
Jake used no Conflicting Facts.
Guilty Indicators __ Conflicting Facts

"Huh?" Factor 21

"Open your eyes, ears, mind, and consciousness for the truth is right in your face. You can see it but only if you would pay attention!"

Kenneth G. Ortiz

Innocent 911 callers did not need to deceive the dispatchers when seeking help to save victims' lives. Because they did not care what questions were posed as long as they expedited aid to the victims, they answered the questions immediately, without fear of incrimination. In contrast to spontaneous truthful callers, deceptive callers needed time for crafting their responses. After narrating fabricated events to dispatchers, guilty callers struggled to recall the details of their stories during dispatchers' rapid fire questions. They may have anticipated some of the questions to be asked by dispatchers, but guilty callers could not predict every question. They worked hard to remain in character, continually editing their words as they tried to respond like innocent persons during their 911 calls. Because their fabricated stories were not experienced and stored in their memories, some guilty callers replied to dispatchers' key questions with words like "Huh?" or "What?" These words are examples of the "Huh?" Factor, a confused response that reveals the callers' difficulty in tracking their own false narratives.

The "Huh?" Factor was present in 15% of the calls in the 911 study, and almost all of these calls (97%) were made by guilty callers. Only 3% of the calls with "Huh?" Factors were made by innocent callers, as depicted in Figure 21.1.

The following call by a husband illustrates the "Huh?" Factor.

Dispatcher:	*"911, what's your emergency?"*
Guilty Caller:	*"My wife fell down the stairs, she's hurt bad, she's not breathing."*
Dispatcher:	*"How many stairs did she fall down?"*
Guilty Caller:	*"Huh?"*

The husband had bludgeoned his wife to death with a metal rod and then staged her body at the bottom of the stairs. He fabricated the stairs story to the dispatcher, not anticipating her logical follow-up question. When asked how many stairs his wife fell down, the caller did not track his previous comment. Momentarily confused, he responded with *"Huh?"* Although providing an exact number of stairs would be difficult, an innocent caller would

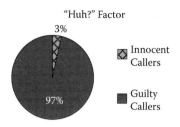

Figure 21.1 Percentages of Innocent vs. Guilty Callers in "Huh?" Factor.

have known if the victim fell down an entire flight of stairs or only a few stairs at an entranceway.

The following startled responses that reveal callers' inability to track their false narratives are included as "Huh?" Factors: Huh? What? What's that? Say what now? Eh? Pardon?

In the next case, a husband called 911 concerning his wife:

Dispatcher:	*"911, what is your emergency?"*
Guilty Caller:	*"Hi, I need some help, my wife went running this morning and never came back."*
Dispatcher:	*"Like jogging?"*
Guilty Caller:	<u>*"What's that?"*</u>

The caller told the dispatcher that his wife went *"running"* in the morning and failed to return home. When the dispatcher followed up with the logical clarifying question, *"Like jogging?"* it confused the husband. He was not tracking his fabricated story, and he replied with a "Huh?" Factor. Readers will also recognize the husband's first word, *"Hi,"* as an example of an Initial Delay. Guilty calls usually contained more than one guilty indicator.

In this case, the investigation revealed that the husband had killed his wife and placed her in a dumpster. His wife never went *"running,"* and he therefore could not track his lie when communicating with the dispatcher. The husband was convicted of his wife's murder.

In the following case, a 911 caller contacted the dispatch center to report that his five-year-old stepdaughter was having a seizure:

Dispatcher:	*"911, what is your emergency?"*
Guilty Caller:	*"I'm at 4200 Kendall Street, my daughter is having some type of seizure, she won't respond to me at all."*
Dispatcher:	*"What's going on with her?"*
Guilty Caller:	*"She is shaking like crazy, really shaking bad. She is breathing real shallow, I'm scared."*

After sending the medics to 4200 Kendall Street, the dispatcher turned her attention back to the caller and asked about the victim:

Dispatcher: *"OK, is she still shaking?"*
Guilty Caller: *"Is she <u>what</u>?"*

The caller was not tracking his previous story and was confused by the dispatcher's logical question regarding his stepdaughter's condition. In fact, the caller had assaulted the child and concocted the story about a medical event involving "seizures." He was eventually convicted of his stepdaughter's murder.

In the next call, a mother contacted 911 to report that her baby was in distress:

Dispatcher: *"911, what is your emergency?"*
Guilty Caller: *"Um, our son's not breathing."*
Dispatcher: *"Okay, how old is he?"*
Guilty Caller: *"He's three months old."*
Dispatcher: *"Has CPR been started?"*
Guilty Caller: *"<u>Huh</u>?"*
Dispatcher: *"Have you started CPR?"*
Guilty Caller: *"Ah, no, not yet."*
Dispatcher: *"And you said he's three months old, ma'am?"*
Guilty Caller: *"Yes."*
Dispatcher: *"Okay, how is his color?"*
Guilty Caller: *"His <u>what</u>?"*

The mother told the dispatcher that her baby was not breathing, and the dispatcher followed up with a logical question concerning the victim's survival, *"Has CPR been started?"* The caller, not tracking her story, replied with a *"Huh?"* An innocent mother, however, would have been totally focused on her baby and the event transpiring before her. The dispatcher asked another pertinent question regarding the victim's color. However, the mother was still not tracking her fabricated narrative. Confused by the question, she responded with a second "Huh?" Factor *"His what?"* The mother eventually confessed to killing her baby and she was convicted of the offense.

Considerations
When 911 calls have loud background noise (music, traffic, screaming, etc.), it is possible that the callers cannot hear the dispatchers' questions. No "Huh?" Factors would apply in these cases.

MR. AND MRS. HUNT CASE

During Jake's 911 call, the dispatcher was worried for his safety and asked a relevant question, *"Are you hurt?"* Jake failed to track the dispatcher's question and responded with *"Huh?"*

Guilty Indicators

✓ "Huh?" Factor

"I Don't Know"

22

"I say 'I don't know' to everything when I'm not in the mood to talk."

Unknown

The optimal dialogue between 911 dispatchers and callers is an information-gathering exercise focused on sharing details for the victims' benefit. Innocent callers answered questions and volunteered relevant information even when not specifically asked. They provided updates about the victims' conditions, such as changes in breathing, pulse, bleeding, and body temperature.

In contrast to innocent callers, guilty callers often resisted providing information that would benefit the victims, even when the victims were close family members. In some calls, guilty callers initially claimed ignorance by using the phrase *"I Don't Know"* when asked a relevant question. This response was problematic when the callers immediately followed up with information indicating that they "did know." The guilty callers' automatic *"I Don't Know"* default may be an effort to distance them from culpability for the crime.

The *"I Don't Know"* indicator was present in 22% of the calls in the 911 study. Guilty callers used this indicator over five times as often as did innocent callers (84% to 16%) as illustrated in Figure 22.1.

In the following case, a mother called 911 to report an incident regarding her one-year-old stepson:

Dispatcher: *"911, what is your emergency?"*
Guilty Caller: *"My son ain't breathin.'"*
Dispatcher: *"What's wrong with him?"*
Guilty Caller: *"I don't know. He hit his head earlier."*

When asked, *"What's wrong with him?"* the mother immediately defaulted to *"I don't know."* However, she then indicated that she did know by providing information regarding a significant event that might have caused the child's injuries. The investigation revealed that the father violently shook the child in the mother's presence, causing the child's head to hit a wooden chair, a fatal injury. The father eventually confessed to the offense.

167

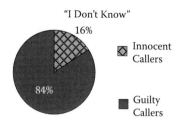

Figure 22.1 Percentages of Innocent vs. Guilty Callers in "I Don't Know."

In the following case, a husband who had just returned from military duty called 911 to report that his wife committed suicide.

Dispatcher: *"Now what's going on there?"*
Guilty Caller: *"I don't know. We just had an argument and I confronted her about sleeping with another guy while I was in the Navy and she shot herself in the head!"*

When the dispatcher asked about the nature of the event, the husband immediately defaulted to *"I don't know."* He then added relevant information, indicating that he actually did know *"what's going on there."* The husband confessed that he killed his wife because he suspected her of adultery while he was deployed; he was convicted of the murder.

In another alleged suicide case, a son called 911:

Dispatcher: *"911, what is your emergency?"*
Guilty Caller: (sobbing) *"My Dad, my Dad."*
Dispatch: *"What's going on there?*
Guilty Caller: *"My dad, I don't know."*
Dispatcher: *"OK tell me where you're at."*
Guilty Caller: (sobbing) *"I'm on Ridge Road."*
Dispatcher: *"OK, what is wrong with your dad?"*
Guilty Caller: (sobbing)
Dispatcher: *"What is wrong with him?"*
Guilty Caller: *"He, he shot himself."*

When the dispatcher asked, *"What's going on there?"* the son immediately responded, *"My Dad, I don't know."* Seconds later the son was asked, *"OK, what is wrong with your dad?"* and he answered, *"He, he shot himself."* The son's response indicated that he actually did possess significant information regarding the event. The investigation revealed that the son, the sole heir to the family fortune, killed his father and staged the scene to resemble a suicide.

The "I Don't Know" indicator can precede or follow the information about which the callers deny knowledge. In the following example, a young man called 911 concerning his girlfriend. He provided information and then claimed that he did not know the information he just provided.

Dispatcher: *"Did you see her get hit?"*
Guilty Caller: *"Yes and I saw her go down."*
Dispatcher: *"You saw her get hit?"*
Guilty Caller: *"I don't know. I'm not for sure after all."*

MR. AND MRS. HUNT CASE

Although Jake stated *"I don't know what's going on here!"* he did not follow this claim of ignorance with an indication that he did know. Therefore, this is not an example of the "I Don't Know" indicator.

Guilty Indicators

___ "I Don't Know"

Isolated "Please"

23

"Words empty as the wind are better left unsaid."

Homer

The word *"please"* was frequently heard during 911 calls, but innocent and guilty callers tended to use it differently. Innocent callers often used *"please"* with a demand, as in *"Please send an ambulance!"* Guilty callers were more likely to use *"please"* in isolation, to avoid providing information.

As an example of an innocent caller's use of *"please,"* a mother called 911 for help for her baby:

Dispatcher: *"911, what is your emergency?"*
Innocent Caller: *"Get me an ambulance now! My baby's sick. Hurry, please!"*

The *"please"* used by this mother was accompanied with a clear demand for urgency, and *"please"* served to accentuate the demand.

In the next call, a woman used the word *"PLEASE"* with an appeal for assistance in aiding a victim.

Dispatcher: *"OK, we have help coming, I want you-"*
Innocent Caller: *"HIS LIPS ARE TURNING BLUE, PLEASE TELL ME WHAT TO DO!"*

In this case, a desperate innocent caller was trying unsuccessfully to save a life and was pleading with the dispatcher for help. Because the caller used *"please"* in conjunction with a demand for assistance in aiding the victim, this was not an Isolated "Please."

Unlike the previous two innocent callers, some guilty callers repeatedly uttered or screamed *"please"* during 911 calls without making demands to the dispatchers. At first glance, these screams may mistakenly be interpreted as urgent pleading. Instead, these Isolated "Pleases" are empty words that act as "fillers" by allowing callers to say something without saying anything at all.

Isolated "Please"

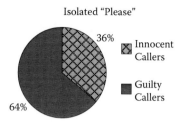

Figure 23.1 Percentages of Innocent vs. Guilty Callers in Isolated "Please."

Eleven percent of the calls in the 911 study contained Isolated Pleases. Sixty-four percent of these calls were made by guilty callers and 36% were made by innocent callers, as depicted in Figure 23.1.

In the following case, a man called 911 to report that his girlfriend was injured:

Dispatcher:	*"911, where is your emergency?"*
Guilty Caller:	*"1510 Pine Street. Please!"*
Dispatcher:	*"What happened?"*
Guilty Caller:	*"My girlfriend had an accident."*
Dispatcher:	*"What kind of accident?"*
Guilty Caller:	*"She fell down the basement stairs. Please!"*
Dispatcher:	*"OK, somebody's dispatching the medics while I ask you questions."*
Guilty Caller:	*"Please, Please!"*
Dispatcher:	*"Is she awake now?"*
Guilty Caller:	*"Ahh....ahh.."*

(Caller disconnects.)

The previous 911 caller uttered four Isolated "Pleases!" Each "Please!" was empty, adding no additional details or demands. The caller was found guilty in the death of his girlfriend.

Earlier chapters discussed guilty callers' resistance to answering dispatchers' questions. Isolated "Pleases" are similar to resistance, for the *"pleases"* can allow callers to avoid providing critical information. As an example, a woman called 911 to report that an unknown suspect broke into her home and shot her husband:

Dispatcher:	*"Listen to me, listen to me...Was he white or black?"*
Guilty Caller:	*"Please!"*
Dispatcher:	*"What was he wearing?"*
Guilty Caller:	*"Please, please!"*

Under careful review, it becomes apparent that the caller did not use *"Please!"* for Urgency but rather to sound distressed while evading the questions about the alleged intruder. The wife was convicted of killing her husband.

In the following case, a wife called 911 after her husband was shot in the driveway at their residence:

Dispatcher:	*"911. Do you need police, fire, or ambulance?"*
Guilty Caller:	*"Somebody just shot my husband."*
Dispatcher:	*"I can't hear you. What's the address?"*
Guilty Caller:	*"165 St. Clair. <u>Please, please.</u>"*
Dispatcher:	*"What's going on?"*
Guilty Caller:	*"He got shot. <u>Please.</u>"*
Dispatcher:	*"Who? All right, I'm saying who got shot?"*
Guilty Caller:	*"My husband. <u>Please, please.</u>"*
Dispatcher:	*"The police are coming. Who shot your husband?"*
Guilty Caller:	*"<u>Please.</u> (inaudible)"*
Dispatcher:	*"Ma'am, they are coming."*
Dispatcher:	*"The police are coming. Who shot him?"*
Dispatcher:	*"Who shot him?" (long pause)*
Guilty Caller:	*"I don't know."*
Dispatcher:	*"Listen, ma'am. Stop saying please. The police are coming. Can you give us some more information?"*
Guilty Caller:	*"Oh my God. <u>Please.</u> Baby, Baby, Baby. I love you."*
Dispatcher:	*"Okay. The police are coming."*
Guilty Caller:	*"I love you. I love you. I love you."*
Dispatcher:	*"The police are coming, ma'am."*
Guilty Caller:	*"<u>Please.</u> He...He got dead."*
Dispatcher:	*"They're on their way. They are on their way."*
Guilty Caller:	*(inaudible)*
Guilty Caller:	*"<u>Please.</u>"*
Dispatcher:	*"They are on their way. Where's he shot at?"*
Guilty Caller:	*"He's a firefighter. He's...I don't know."*
Dispatcher:	*"Where's he shot at?"*
Guilty Caller:	*"He's in the driveway."*
Dispatcher:	*"No. I mean on his body."*
Guilty Caller:	*(crying) "Please help. Please help me. Please help me."*
Dispatcher:	*"Ma'am, they're on their way. They are on their way, okay?"*
Guilty Caller:	*"Baby, I love you. I love you."*
Dispatcher:	*"What's your husband's name?"*
Guilty Caller:	*"Tim Spencer. He's a firefighter. <u>Please.</u> I love you. I love you. I love you. I love you. Can you hear me? <u>Please, please, please.</u> Oh my God. <u>Please.</u>"*

Dispatcher:	*"Ma'am, police is coming and EMS is coming. Okay?"*
Guilty Caller:	*"Okay. He's a firefighter. <u>Please</u>."*
Dispatcher:	*"They are on their way. They are en route."*
Guilty Caller:	<u>*"Please. Please."*</u>

(Caller disconnects.)

The caller gave No Immediate Plea for the Victim, expressed No Urgency, used Self-interruptions, added an Awkward Phrase (*"He got dead."*), and Attempted to Convince the dispatcher that she loves the victim. The caller also uttered 17 Isolated "Pleases" during the 911 call. Each of the Isolated "Pleases" was used to fill a gap in the exchange between the caller and the dispatcher; however, they were vacuous and did not provide details regarding the victim or the event. At one point during the call, however, the caller did use *"please"* accompanied with requests: *"Please help me. Please help me. Please help me."* Note that this use of *"please"* was an indication of Focus on the Caller, not Focus on the Victim. The subsequent investigation revealed that the wife had shot her husband.

MR. AND MRS. HUNT CASE

Jake used Isolated Pleases to avoid answering questions about his in-laws. These "pleases" were not accompanied by demands for help or for urgency.

Dispatcher:	*"Did...Did you say somebody is dead? Who is dead?"*
Caller:	<u>*"Please*</u>*, oh my God...<u>please!</u>"*

Guilty Indicators

✓ Isolated Please

Lack of Contractions 24

"If time be of all things the most precious, wasting time must be the greatest prodigality."

Benjamin Franklin

To obtain medical aid as quickly as possible, most innocent 911 callers answered dispatchers' questions in abrupt, concise manners. Relaying vital details rapidly was the best strategy for saving the lives of victims and shortening two words into contractions reduced time.

The Lack of Contractions indicator appeared in 13% of the calls in the 911 study. More than twice as many guilty callers used Lack of Contractions (68%) than did innocent callers (32%). See Figure 24.1.

An innocent mother used contractions to describe her emergency to a 911 dispatcher:

Innocent Caller: *"My baby's choking, hurry, she's one year old and she's choking, there's nobody else here and I don't know what to do."*

The caller provided vital information in the fastest manner possible. Examine how the previous call would appear if the mother used no contractions:

"My baby is choking, hurry, she is one year old and she is choking, there is nobody else here and I do not know what to do."

The rewording of the mother's call by eliminating contractions would significantly slow the information transfer.

Note the lack of contractions when a husband called 911 to report that his wife had been shot. He also spoke in a slow, monotone fashion:

Dispatcher: *"911, what's your emergency?"*
Guilty Caller: *"My wife has been shot, I do not know who did it."*
Dispatcher: *"Your wife's been shot?"*
Guilty Caller: *"Yes (three-second delay)."*
Dispatcher: *"Where's she shot at?"*
Guilty Caller: *"Um, uh, I think she is shot in the back."*
Dispatcher: *"OK, do you live at 1091 Meadowlark apartments?"*

Figure 24.1 Percentages of Innocent vs. Guilty Callers in "Lack of Contractions."

Guilty Caller: *"Yes (two-second delay)."*
Dispatcher: *"OK, the ambulance is on the way, is she breathing?"*
Guilty Caller: *"I don't think that <u>she is</u> breathing."*
Dispatcher: *"She's not breathing?"*
Guilty Caller: *"Um, no....she <u>is not</u>."*

The husband gave No Immediate Plea for Help for Victim, displayed No Urgency, expressed No Fear, used Equivocation, and five times failed to use contractions. This caller's slow responses contrasted with the dispatcher's rapid questions that were filled with contractions. The investigation revealed that the husband had recently purchased a large insurance policy on the victim without her knowledge. The husband was also skimming funds from the family business and was near bankruptcy. Evidence at the scene confirmed the husband's guilt, and he was convicted of the murder.

In a different set of circumstances, a husband called 911 and reported that he and his wife were attacked while walking in a park at night:

Dispatcher: *"911, what is your emergency?"*
Guilty Caller: *"Yes, I—yes I need some help <u>we are</u> hurt..."*
Dispatcher: *"You're on a cell phone, where are you at?"*
Guilty Caller: *"<u>We are</u> at Colby Park, at the trails. <u>I am</u> by the front gate, the wooden ones."*
Dispatcher: *"OK, what's the problem, sir?"*
Guilty Caller: *"Me and my wife were attacked. I <u>am hurt</u> and <u>she is</u> hurt bad."*
Dispatcher: *"Are you with your wife?"*
Guilty Caller: *"No, I'm at the front gate, tell them to meet me here and <u>I will</u> show them were <u>she is</u> at."*
Dispatcher: *"You're not with your wife?"*
Guilty Caller: *"NO! <u>I will</u> take them back to her when they come."*
Dispatcher: *"Is your wife injured?"*
Guilty Caller: *"Yes, <u>she is</u> injured, they beat her very badly."*

The husband displayed the Focus on Caller indicator, gave No Immediate Assessment of Victim, expressed No Urgency, and used a Lack of Contractions nine times. English was his first language, so his Lack of Contractions was unusual.

The caller, a college professor, beat his wife to death on the hiking trail and fabricated a story accusing two unknown males of the offense. The street officers began a search for the suspects, and the investigators canvassed the area, conducting interviews regarding potential offenders. Eventually, the husband's story unraveled and he was arrested and convicted of the murder. Had the dispatcher, street officers, and investigators been trained in 911 homicide call analysis, they might have questioned the husband more thoroughly at the outset and saved time, effort, and resources.

Considerations
Context is critical when examining Lack of Contractions. Innocent 911 callers sometimes omitted contractions later in their calls, when doing so did not delay help. Other innocent callers in the 911 study used contractions to add emphasis to their declarations or to add clarity when identifying themselves. When the purposes of omitting the contractions were obvious, as in adding emphasis or clarity, these instances did not qualify as Lack of Contractions indicators.

As an example of a Lack of Contraction with a clear purpose, an innocent wife omitted a contraction in order to emphatically drive home an important point to the dispatcher. Her husband had been shot in the chest, and she called 911 to demand medical aid. She willingly cooperated with the dispatcher's CPR instructions:

Innocent Caller: *"Where's the ambulance? Tell them to come in!"*
Dispatcher: *"I want you to keep pumping on his chest and do not stop till the medics get inside, OK?"*
Innocent Caller: *"I will not give up on him!"*

The dispatcher instructed the wife to continue with chest compressions, and the wife immediately and adamantly declared that she would not give up on her husband. Her statement, *"I will not give up on him!"* was more emphatic than stating *"I won't give up on him!"*

The victim in the next case was a very large man who had a history of heart disease. His petite wife called 911 when she found him in medical distress, seated cross-legged in the bathtub leaning against the wall:

Innocent Caller: *"AHHHhhhhh!"*
Dispatcher: *"911, what's your emergency?"*
Innocent Caller: *"My husband's having a heart attack, he's sitting in the tub, he's had two heart surgeries, send the ambulance, hurry!"*

Dispatcher:	*"Can you get him out of the tub?"*
Innocent Caller:	*"I can't, he's stuck in the tub, hurry!"*
Dispatcher:	*"Can you pull him out?"*
Innocent Caller:	*"I CANNOT GET HIM UP, HE'S STUCK IN THE TUB!"*

The wife immediately demanded help for her husband. She expressed Urgency and used five contractions to speed up her communications with the 911 dispatcher. When the caller was asked if she could get her husband out of the tub, she quickly replied using contractions, *"I can't, he's stuck in the tub, hurry!"* The dispatcher directed the caller, for a second time, to pull the victim out of the tub. In her second reply to the same question, the anxious wife answered with an adamant, loud declaration, *"I CANNOT,"* to make the point that she was incapable of completing the task alone. The victim died at the scene, and the coroner ruled that the death was from natural causes.

The following case is an example of omitting a contraction to add clarity when identifying oneself. The caller had a long criminal history, including a prior homicide conviction. He spent 14 years in prison for the offense and might therefore have a valid reason to feel anxious when law enforcement requested his identity.

Dispatcher:	*"Do you know what's wrong with her?"*
Innocent Caller:	*"She ain't breathin', where's the medics?"*
Dispatcher:	*"What's your name, sir?"*
Innocent Caller:	*"My name is Mark Carson."*

This caller, with a previous homicide conviction, was not hesitant to identify himself at the scene of a dying victim. He gave his full name with confidence and strength. The omission of a contraction in this context added clarity to his response and was not a delaying tactic. The investigation revealed that the caller was not involved in the victim's death.

MR. AND MRS. HUNT CASE

Jake's Lack of Contractions slowed down the communication with the dispatcher.

"There is stuff everywhere."
"There is blood everywhere."

Guilty Indicators

✓ Lack of Contractions

No Modulation

25

"*The way in which we say something is often more important than what we say.*"

Sydney J. Harris

Voice volume, tone, pitch, and pace varied with the speakers' psychological and physiological states. These speech variations, known as Modulation, were amplified in times of great emotion, and Modulation was heard frequently in innocent 911 callers' voices. In contrast, some guilty callers had No Modulation as they spoke in flat, unemotional, or robotic tones.

Innocent 911 callers desperately seeking aid for critically injured persons had substantial changes in voice Modulation throughout their calls. Often, callers' voice modulation increased significantly as the calls progressed, particularly when callers felt that medics were not responding quickly enough or when the victims' condition deteriorated. In addition to analyzing written transcripts of the 911 calls, investigators can gain key insight listening to the voice modulation in the calls.

In the following call, a depressed woman used a handgun to shoot herself in the temple in her husband's presence. The husband immediately called 911 and screamed at the dispatcher to send an ambulance to his house. He yelled that his wife shot herself and he refused to accept her death, even though the gunshot separated her skull cap and brains from her body. The husband, using modulation throughout the call, interrupted the dispatcher by shrieking:

"*SHE'S STILL FUCKIN' BREATHING. GET A GODDAMN AMBULANCE HERE NOW!*"

Even though the victim, in fact, was dead, her body experienced a postmortem muscle contraction that looked like breathing. Thus, the innocent husband did not give up hope that his wife could live, and he viewed the contraction with optimism.

The next case is an example of increasing modulation when a mother believed assistance was not arriving fast enough. She frantically wailed into the phone after discovering her baby early in the morning, stiff and cold in his crib:

"*WHAT THE FUCK IS TAKING THEM SO LONG? WHAT THE FUCK IS TAKING THEM SO LONG? COME ON, COME ON!*"

The autopsy revealed that the baby had accidentally suffocated during the night. Even though the baby had been dead for hours by the time his mother found him, she never gave up hope and her voice was modulated throughout the call.

Surprisingly, many guilty callers exhibited no modulation during the 911 calls. They simply reported the events in robotic, emotionless manners, often without specifically seeking help for the victims. These calls did not appear to be about emergencies, and the callers' comments seemed detached from the critical nature of the events.

Twenty-nine percent of the callers in the 911 study expressed No Modulation in their voices. Six times as many guilty callers had No Modulation (86%) than innocent callers (14%), as illustrated in Figure 25.1.

In the following call, a father violently shook his infant and called 911 after the baby's brain began to swell, resulting in the infant's death. The father's words to the dispatcher were spoken in a slow, robotic tone:

Dispatcher: "911, what is your emergency?"
Guilty Caller: "Yes, my daughter, my daughter was crying, OK? And it's like she had to catch her breath."
Dispatcher: "Is she OK?"
Guilty Caller: "No, her heart not beating."
Dispatcher: "How old is she?"
Guilty Caller: "She's like two and a half months."
Dispatcher: "Two and a half months?"
Guilty Caller: "Yes Ma'am."
Dispatcher: "And what's your name?"
Guilty Caller: "My name, my name is Darius." (whimpering at the mention of his own name)

At a time that many would consider to be the most horrific moment of a father's life, this caller answered questions about his dying daughter without using modulation. As his own biological child died in his presence, the father continued to communicate with the dispatcher in a monotone manner. He astonishingly uttered the words, "No, her heart not beating," without varying his volume or pitch.

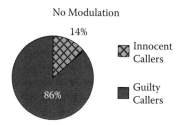

Figure 25.1 Percentages of Innocent vs. Guilty Callers in "No Modulation."

Although the father calmly commented about his dying baby without voice inflection, he did express slight modulation at one point in the 911 call. When the dispatcher changed the focus from the victim to the caller by asking for the caller's name, the father finally showed emotion as he whimpered, "My name, my name is Darius." He was very uncomfortable providing his name to the dispatcher. Guilty 911 callers often became reticent when dispatchers changed focus and asked for the callers' names. In many cases, guilty callers only provided their first name when asked, "What is your name?" Innocent callers rarely hesitated to provide their full names clearly because their focus was on the victims, not on themselves.

It is noteworthy that in addition to the father expressing No Modulation throughout the call, with the exception of one change from monotone to whimpering, the father never sought help for his daughter or displayed Urgency. His opening comments were in Inappropriate Order. He began by stating that his daughter *"was crying,"* then *"had to catch her breath,"* and finally *"no, her heart not beating."* The fact that his daughter had no heartbeat should have been his opening comment, to communicate the gravity of the emergency.

In another tragic case, an infant died in a house trailer fire. Six people called 911 as flames engulfed the residence. The first five callers demanded help, focused on the victim, and displayed intense modulation. They screamed at the dispatcher as follows:

Caller #1: *"THERE'S A BABY IN THE TRAILER! THERE'S A BABY IN THE TRAILER! HURRY! HURRY!"*

....

Caller #2: *"WHERE ARE THEY? THERE'S A BABY IN THERE!"*

....

Caller #3: *"GOD DAMN YOU, WHERE THE FUCK IS THE FIRE DEPARTMENT, THERE'S A KID IN THERE!"*

....

Caller #4: *"WHERE'S THE FIRE DEPARTMENT? THE STATION IS A FUCKING MILE FROM HERE, WHERE ARE THEY?"*

....

Caller #5: *"GET THE FIRE DEPARTMENT HERE NOW! NOW! THE WHOLE TRAILER IS ON FIRE, I THINK THERE'S A BABY IN THERE!"*

The sixth caller, however, sounded very different. This caller had No Modulation, No Urgency, No Immediate Plea for Help, and never even mentioned the victim:

Caller #6: *"There's a trailer fire at 19 Garrison. It's a green trailer with white trim. It's at the corner of Garrison and Delcour Roads."*

The sixth caller's voice was slow, robotic, and devoid of emotion. The sixth caller was the baby's mother. She had killed her child and set the fire to conceal the crime.

In the following case, a mother called 911 from her place of employment to report an incident. Her voice was calm with No Modulation as she communicated with the dispatcher:

Dispatcher: *"Springfield Police, you dialed 911?"*
Guilty Caller: *"Yes, I did."*
Dispatcher: *"How may I help you?"*
Guilty Caller: *"I'm at 2900 Rice Road, at Christian University (2 second pause) I just went out, I just went out to my car a few minutes ago (two second pause) realized (two second pause) that I left my baby in the car and she died."*

During the entire call, the mother never changed her inflection. She gave No Immediate Plea for Help for the Victim and expressed No Urgency. She even had to be asked, "How may I help you?" before she provided any information. The mother Minimized her involvement in the event and provided information in an Inappropriate Order. What was most shocking was that the mother could utter the words "she died" with No Modulation whatsoever.

Six months before this incident, in the same city, another mother left her baby in a car and the infant died. The event drew a large media response, and commentators from newspapers, television, and radio talk shows debated the appropriate punishment for the mother. A segment of the community believed that the mother should be charged with child neglect for leaving her infant in the car, causing the death. An equally large part of the community believed that she had suffered enough and should face no charges. The two sides argued publicly in the media, and after months of contention, the prosecutor held a press conference to announce his decision. With the mother at his side, the prosecutor stated that justice would not be served by moving forward with criminal charges, as the mother had been through enough.

As the media storm blazed, the second mother watched the news from her home. She was six months pregnant, alone, with financial problems. She was under great stress from the critical attitudes of her coworkers at the religious institution where she worked. Several months after learning that the prosecutor did not pursue charges on the other mother, this mother left her own baby in a car. After several hours in a hot car, this baby also died. Neither of the mothers' 911 calls were analyzed during the cases and neither mother was charged with a crime.

Some guilty 911 callers talked in rushed, out-of-breath patterns. These quick cadences could be attempts to falsely convince the dispatcher of a sense of urgency. However, the rushed and breathless speech patterns of guilty callers often lack modulated pitch, a phenomenon that was rare in the innocent calls studied.

Identifying the difference between genuine modulation and faked breathlessness can be difficult. True modulation was random, not uniform; therefore, callers with a consistently breathless pattern of speech should be carefully scrutinized.

As an example of a 911 call with a consistent and breathless speech pattern, examine a call from a man reporting that his wife had an accident:

Dispatcher:	*"911, what is your emergency?"*
Guilty Caller:	*"My wife fell down the stairs AHHHH!"*
Dispatcher:	*"OK, give me your address."*
Guilty Caller:	*"She fell down the stairs AHHHH!"*
Dispatcher:	*"Is she hurt?"*
Guilty Caller:	*"Yes! AHHHH!"*
Dispatcher:	*"Where is she hurt?"*
Guilty Caller:	*"I don't know AHHHH!"*
Dispatcher:	*"Is she breathing?"*
Guilty Caller:	*"I don't know, I can't tell AHHHH!"*
Dispatcher:	*"OK, OK, are you on 345 Blumen Lane?*
Guilty Caller:	*"Yes, yes, AHHHH!"*

Note that the caller displayed a consistent pattern throughout the 911 call. He used the same inflection and breathless tone at the same location each time he answered the dispatcher's question. The scripted response was not genuine, and the husband later confessed to assaulting his wife and staging her body at the bottom of the stairs.

Another indication of faked modulation occurred when callers exhibited extreme inflection variations throughout the calls and then unexpectedly slipped out of this pattern and uttered comments without modulation. As an illustration, a husband had a rushed, breathless, uniform cadence throughout the call. When the dispatcher surprised him by mentioning his address (she could see the address on her 911 monitor), the caller slipped out of modulation:

Dispatcher:	*"Just calm down, I need you to calm down. That's what I want you to do, calm down."*
Guilty Caller:	*"Should I touch her? Should I, or, I don't think so. (crying) Oh my God! There's blood all over. You want me to touch her (crying)"?*
Dispatcher:	*OK, just stay on the phone with me 'till the first officer gets there. It's 204 Castle Lane, right?, the Newton residence, right?"*

At this point the crying immediately stopped, and the caller challenged the dispatcher with the following question, delivered in a controlled voice without inflection:

Guilty Caller:	*"How do you know that?"*
Dispatcher:	*"When you dial 911 it comes up on the screen, sir."*
Guilty Caller:	*"Oh my God! (crying resumed)."*

The investigation revealed that the caller killed his wife and staged the scene to resemble an accident. During the 911 call, he did not like the fact that the dispatcher knew more about him than he had volunteered, even if it meant that help would arrive at the correct location sooner. Because he was momentarily caught off guard, his contrived modulation temporarily disappeared. The caller was convicted of the homicide.

In the following case, a son called 911 to report that his father had committed suicide by shooting himself in the head. The son wailed and cried throughout the call, and it was often very difficult for the dispatcher to understand the caller's words. The caller's voice was so high pitched that the dispatcher mistakenly thought the caller was female. The call lasted several minutes and the son continued to sound distraught, sobbing as he answered the dispatcher's questions. However, the crying stopped abruptly when the dispatcher insulted him by calling him "Ma'am":

Guilty Caller:	*(Sobbing) "HE'S, HE, HE'S SHOT HIMSELF!"*
Dispatcher:	*"Is he alive?"*
Guilty Caller:	*(Sobbing) "I DON'T KNOW!"*
Dispatcher:	*"OK, Calm down."*
Guilty Caller:	*(Sobbing) "WHAT CAN I DO, WHAT CAN I DO?"*
Dispatcher:	*"What's your name?"*
Guilty Caller:	*(Sobbing) "MY NAME'S THOMAS!"*
Dispatcher:	*"Thomas, what's your last name?"*
Guilty Caller:	*(Sobbing) "CRAWFORD."*
Dispatcher:	*"I'm sorry, what?"*
Guilty Caller:	*(Sobbing) "CRAWFORD!"*
Dispatcher:	*"Ma'am?"*
Guilty Caller:	<u>*"It's Crawford, and I'm a sir."*</u>
Dispatcher:	*"OK, OK, do you know if he is breathing?"*
Guilty Caller:	*(Sobbing) "HUH?"*
Dispatcher:	*"Is he breathing?*"
Guilty Caller:	*(Sobbing) "SHOULD I TRY AND HELP HIM?"*

The caller's indignation at being called *"Ma'am"* and the dispatcher's confusion with his last name caused him to momentarily slip out of his contrived modulation and reply in a calm, terse manner. In addition to focusing on himself, the caller exhibited a "Huh?" Factor. The caller, who was a professional actor, had planned the homicide and he eventually confessed.

In cases of premeditated murders, No Modulation was often evident in the 911 calls because the deaths were not a shock and the callers were not desperate to save lives. Additionally, in these situations, the greatest stress was that which led up to the confrontations and it ended with the murders. The 911 call was placed during a period of relative calm.

For example, in a call in which a husband very calmly reported that his wife was dead, investigators discovered that he had been under inordinate stress long before the murder. He had learned that his wife was having an affair with his coworker and she refused to end the new relationship. When the husband threatened divorce, the wife informed him that she had already spoken to a lawyer and she would receive one-half of his pension, the house, and even the dog. The husband's stress level was extremely high for an extended period of time. The stress continued to escalate when his coworkers learned of the affair and began to mock him about the situation. The husband was further humiliated by his wife's boyfriend, his own coworker and former friend, whom he encountered each day at work. As the stress grew, the husband decided he had no way out and began to form a strategy to kill his wife. He thought about the plan for several weeks and then finally put it into action by killing her and staging her suicide. At the moment of her death, his stress was released. All the pressure of losing his marriage, his pension, his house, his dog, and all of the anxiety created by his work environment instantly evaporated with the act of killing his wife. With the stress removed, his voice was calm and robotic while communicating with the 911 dispatcher. The husband later confessed to the crime and explained why he had to kill his wife.

The 911 data and case histories studied included different ages, genders, education levels, and professions, and the modulation principles were found to apply to all groups except one—individuals with a background in theater. In the cases analyzed, guilty theater majors and professional actors exhibited more modulation than did other guilty callers.

Innocent police officers, dispatchers, and military veterans who routinely dealt with high-stress conditions exhibited modulation during their off-duty 911 calls. However, when callers in these same professions were guilty and under the stress created by their own premeditated actions, they often communicated with the dispatchers without modulation.

Considerations
Drugs and alcohol may have an effect on the No Modulation indicator. Individuals intoxicated on barbiturates, opiates (heroin), and other depressants often develop slurred speech, memory impairment, and decreased mental capabilities (Scott, 2015).

During crimes of passion, individuals might commit serious assaults without intent to kill. In such cases, the offenders may truly want to save the lives of the victims, and modulation would be expected in the 911 call.

Many callers in the 911 study (71%) exhibited some degree of modulation. It was the absence of modulation, more than its presence, which was more insightful in analyzing 911 calls.

MR. AND MRS. HUNT CASE

Jake's call revealed voice modulation.

<u>Guilty Indicators</u>
___ No Modulation

Reference

Scott, C. (2015), *Downside of Drugs, Dangerous Depressants and Sedatives*, Harvard Medical School, Boston.

Unexplained Knowledge

26

"No man's knowledge here can go beyond his experience."

John Locke

Occasionally, guilty 911 callers in the 911 study revealed details about the victims that innocent callers could not possibly have known. This Unexplained Knowledge is information that only the murderer, or someone who witnessed the act, could possess.

Unexplained Knowledge was present in 14% of the calls in the 911 study, and all of these calls were made by guilty callers. See Figure 26.1.

As an example of Unexplained Knowledge, a husband made the following statement to the dispatcher during his 911 call:

Guilty Caller: *"My wife has been <u>stabbed thirteen times</u>!"*

Since the husband advised that he was not present during the assault, it would have been nearly impossible to know with certainty the number of times his wife had been stabbed, especially since she was fully clothed. Observation of a single external wound may lead one to assume that the victim had been stabbed only once. However, an autopsy may later reveal multiple stab wounds that entered the body at the same location. Conversely, a single stabbing action might cause multiple external wounds. Consider the case of a woman who was stabbed at an angle with the blade entering one side of her breast, exiting the opposite side and then entering her shoulder. The three separate wounds would give the appearance of three thrusts of the attacker's knife. However, a single stabbing motion caused all three wounds. In the case of the 13 stab wounds, the husband had, in fact, been present for his wife's murder. He was accurate about the number of stab wounds because he had inflicted them. The husband was convicted of his wife's murder.

The following exchange occurred between a dispatcher and a caller who claimed he came home and discovered a "break-in" at his residence:

Dispatcher: *"911, where is your emergency?"*
Guilty Caller: *"1921 Henderson Street. I need an ambulance, my dad and mom have both been <u>hit across the head</u> with something."*

Unexplained Knowledge

100%

Innocent Callers

Guilty Callers

Figure 26.1 Percentages of Innocent vs. Guilty Callers in "Unexplained Knowledge."

A hit across the head could be one explanation for the victims' injuries. However, because the injuries were so severe, an experienced firearms instructor examined the victims' photographs and asked, "What type of shotgun was used?" The autopsy revealed that the victims had been assaulted with a baseball bat, and the caller's Unexplained Knowledge made him a person of interest. The caller eventually confessed and was convicted of the offense.

In another case, a man claimed that he discovered his wife in the upstairs bathroom, in the bathtub:

Dispatcher: *"911, what's the emergency?"*
Guilty Caller: *"Ah, my <u>my wife fell asleep in the bathtub</u> and I think she's dead."*
Dispatcher: *"What's the address?"*
Guilty Caller: *"221 Morningstar Court, Dayton, Ohio."*
Dispatcher: *"And what's going on?"*
Guilty Caller: *"Ah, <u>she fell asleep in the bathtub</u> I think, I was downstairs I just came up here and she was lying face down in the bathtub."*

Within the first few seconds of his 911 call, the husband stated twice that his wife had fallen asleep in the bathtub.* Then he added that he was actually downstairs when the event occurred and he *"just came up"* and discovered his wife *"lying face down in the bathtub."* How could he have known that his wife fell asleep in the bathtub and drowned? Further, since the victim was alleged to have been face down in the bathtub, it would have appeared that she slipped in the tub or had a medical event that caused her to lose consciousness and drown. The husband ignored those likely scenarios and offered the least logical explanation by sharing Unexplained Knowledge. He was eventually convicted of her murder.

---

* Dr. Michael M. Baden, forensic pathologist, describes the bathtub as a killing zone and recommends that investigators consider homicide as a possible cause of death in bathtub cases.

A careful examination of the previous call also reveals No Immediate Plea for Help for the Victim, Inappropriate Order (he commented that she fell asleep in the bathtub before explaining her condition), and Minimizing ("I just came up here."). The call contained Acceptance of Death, even though individuals can survive being under water for lengthy periods of time and the caller should have fought for his wife's survival.

In the following investigation, a dispatcher was instrumental in explaining indicators of guilt to her supervisor after receiving the following call:

Dispatcher:	*"911. What is your emergency?"*
Caller:	*"My house has been burglarized. I just walked in. I think my husband has been shot."*
Dispatcher:	*"Okay. What is the address there, ma'am?"*
Caller:	*"It's 491 Loraine."*
Dispatcher:	*"OK, we have help on the way. Have you checked his pulse?"*
Caller:	*"Yes, I checked his pulse and tried CPR. I think he's dead."*
Dispatcher:	*"Where is he shot at?"*
Caller:	*"I don't know."*
Dispatcher:	*"Stay on the phone. Do you know who did this?"*
Caller:	*"It looks like a burglary. It's been trashed in here. Are you guys coming?"*

As soon as the dispatcher ended the call and made sure that the officers and medics were en route, she consulted her supervisor. The dispatcher advised that she had been trained in 911 Call Analysis and found the call to be troublesome. The supervisor asked her to replay the audio of the call for her. As they listened, the dispatcher explained "She never asked for help for him, not once during the entire call!"

The supervisor agreed and was surprised at the caller's composed demeanor on the phone. She commented, "She seems really calm on the phone, I don't get that—I would be frantic." The dispatcher explained that the caller had No Modulation and that was one of the indicators of guilt that murderers sometimes exhibit.

She told the supervisor, "Look, she started off talking about the burglary. To her that was more important than her husband's condition." She explained that all callers reporting a death, whether innocent or guilty, were under great stress. A person under this type of stress might first state what is foremost in their mind, even when this was not the most important point of the situation. The dispatcher told her supervisor that when the caller quickly accepted her husband's death it raised a red flag. She explained, "Innocent people don't want to believe that their loved one is dying or dead…they won't give up hope. Guilty people accept the death because they know the person is dead, because they are the killers!"

The dispatcher went over the call with her supervisor and pointed out that the caller also used a Lack of Contraction and Minimizing. The supervisor asked the dispatcher to explain the minimizing concept. The dispatcher stated, "At the beginning of the first line the caller said, 'I just walked in.'" The dispatcher explained that guilty callers often minimized their own involvement in situations by using the term "just" to distance themselves from the events. She added "Innocent callers don't think like that…they don't focus on themselves, they focus on help for their loved ones and that's all that matters to them."

The supervisor was convinced that the dispatcher was right and asked, "Before I call the officers, is there anything else about this call that bothers you?" The dispatcher thought for a moment and then replied, "Yes. One more thing—if you came home and found your husband shot to death, wouldn't you be scared? Wouldn't you be terrified because there's a killer on the loose? You wouldn't be standing around, till the cops got there, would you? How did she know the killer was gone? The supervisor understood and began to smile. As she walked over to the phone in the next cubicle, she looked back and said, "Great job young lady, great job."

When the first two officers arrived at the scene, they found the caller standing in front of the house. They questioned her about what happened and she stated, "Someone shot my husband, he's dead, he's on the floor in the house." One officer asked her if she saw who did it and she replied, "No!" He asked if there was anyone else in the house and she stated, "No, just my husband." The wife did not explain how she knew with certainty that no one else was in the house, an example of Unexplained Knowledge.

Both officers drew their weapons and cautiously approached the open front door. They entered the house and observed an elderly male lying 15 feet from them, on the living room floor. He was lying face down, totally surrounded by a large pool of blood. The victim was wearing a white, long-sleeved sweatshirt and black sweat pants. They both could see the lividity beginning to settle on the lower portion of his hands and face and knew he was dead. With guns drawn, they searched the home and found no one else on the premises. When the scene was secure, one of the officers called it in over the radio and requested that the investigators respond. He confirmed that they did, in fact, have a dead victim. Both officers noted that the house was in neat order. However, the desk drawers in the master bedroom had been pulled open, as seen in Figure 26.2. It did not look right to them and one officer commented, "The only way those drawers could be opened like that is if the thief opened the very bottom drawer first, then the next bottom drawer and up 'till the top…who does that?" See Figure 26.2.

Figure 26.2 The scene of the crime.

The scene seemed staged to the officer. As he began to share his thoughts with his partner, his cell phone rang and he looked at the caller ID—it was the 911 Dispatch Center. The Dispatch Supervisor excitedly explained everything she had learned from the 911 call. She read over her notes and pointed out each guilty indicator the wife had made to the 911 dispatcher. The officer was especially interested in the supervisor's point that the wife stated there had been a burglary before she mentioned her husband's condition. The supervisor added that the caller said the house had been *"trashed."* That really bothered the officer because it simply was not true. Other than the drawers being open, the house was tidy and clean; it certainly wasn't *"trashed."*

The officer asked the supervisor to replay the 911 audio over the phone so he could hear the call. As he listened, the officer heard the caller say she checked her husband's pulse and tried CPR. "NO WAY!" the officer shouted into the phone. "There is no way she could have checked his pulse or done CPR on this guy—that just doesn't make sense." The officer explained that the victim was surrounded by a pool of blood, a pool of blood that had no footprints, no knee prints, in fact, no disturbances of any kind. If the wife had been close enough to check her husband's pulse or perform CPR, she would have had to kneel in that blood and she would have blood all over her white sweatshirt, which she did not. "Hell," he added "the guy is laying on his stomach—there's no way she did CPR on him!" The crime scene was illogical based on the account provided by the caller.

The 911 call in this case had numerous guilty indicators, and the dispatcher did an excellent job of identifying them and sharing that knowledge.

The officers compared the 911 call with their observations. The investigators later commented that when they arrived at the scene, they were provided with more information in this case than in any other case they had worked. The subsequent investigation revealed that the wife had arranged for her husband's death, and she and the offenders were convicted of the homicide.

MR. AND MRS. HUNT CASE
Jake's call contained no Unexplained Knowledge.
Guilty Indicators ___ Unexplained Knowledge

Trending Indicators

VI

Indicators Trending Toward Guilty

27

The 911 study identified eight indicators that were trending toward guilt but were found in too few cases to use in predicting the likelihood of innocence or guilt. These infrequent but insightful indicators are included for informational purposes and will not be added to the COPS Scale© until additional cases can be studied. The trending indicators consist of Apology to Victim, Asking Permission, Calling Another, Dispatcher as Witness, Eyes Comments, Nervous Laughter Indicator, Possession of a Problem, and Recounting Dialogue. A description of each indicator follows.

Apology to Victim

> *"Never make a defense or an apology until you are accused."*
> King Charles I

Some homicides occurred when offenders lost their temper and assaulted victims in a state of rage. Many domestic violence cases and incidents of child abuse fit this profile. These offenders may immediately regret their actions and call 911 to get help for the victims. Although they sincerely want the victims to live, they cannot divulge the entire truth to the dispatchers because they are in self-preservation mode. Some of these callers could be heard apologizing to the victims while on the phone with the dispatchers. Callers would have no need to apologize unless they were involved in the offense.

In the following case, a 19-year-old man called 911 because an infant left in his care was unresponsive:

Dispatcher:	*"911, what is your emergency?"*
Guilty Caller:	*"Oh my God, my girl—my girlfriend's son ain't breathin.'"*
Dispatcher:	*"What happened?"*
Guilty Caller:	*(crying) "Oh my God, <u>I'm so sorry Devin</u>, I've been watchin' him. Help us."*
Dispatcher:	*"Where's the mom, put the mom on the phone."*
Guilty Caller:	*(crying) "She's at work. Oh my God, please."*

The boyfriend was babysitting his girlfriend's developmentally challenged three-year-old son. The child was difficult to care for, and the boyfriend lost his composure and assaulted the child, causing his death. The boyfriend expressed regret for his actions by apologizing to the young victim as he lay dying on the couch.

In the next case, a wife came home and found her husband on the floor. He had suffered a gunshot wound to the chest, and the wife immediately called 911:

Dispatcher:	*"911, what is your emergency?"*
Guilty Caller:	*"My husband's been shot, send an ambulance!"*
Dispatcher:	*"What happened to him?"*
Guilty Caller:	*"Oh Bobby, I'm sorry. God damn it, Bobby!"*
Dispatcher:	*"Where is he shot at?"*
Guilty Caller:	*"Send an ambulance."*

During her communication with the dispatcher, the caller unexpectedly apologized to her husband. Some guilty spouses who had convinced other persons to kill their partners experienced remorse after returning home and finding the injured or deceased victims. In this case, the wife solicited her boyfriend to kill her husband; however, after walking in the house and actually seeing him critically injured, she regretted her role.

The Apology Indicator only applied when it was directed to the victim. When callers directed the courteous "I'm sorry" comments to dispatchers, these were examples of Ingratiating Remarks. The Apology to Victim was present in only 2% of the calls in the 911 study, but all of these calls were made by guilty callers.

Asking Permission

"When you ask permission, you give someone else veto power over your life."
Geoffrey F. Abert

Innocent 911 callers rarely sought the dispatchers' permission to complete basic, lifesaving measures. Most innocent callers focused on the victims and took immediate actions to comfort and stabilize them. Some guilty callers, however, asked dispatchers for consent before providing aid to victims. The Asking Permission indicator was present in 5% of the calls in the 911 study. Guilty callers made 89% of these calls and innocent callers made 11%.

Some guilty callers in the 911 study were passive when interacting with their critically injured loved ones. They timidly asked the dispatcher for permission to aid the victims. The defensive strategy of Asking Permission is illustrated in each of the following cases:

Dispatcher: *"Where is your father shot at?"*
Guilty Caller: *"<u>Should I touch him</u>? I don't know what to do."*

. . . .

Dispatcher: *"We have help coming, just hold on for a second."*
Guilty Caller: *"There's a pillow over her face, <u>should I take it off</u>?"*

. . . .

Dispatcher: *"Is she still breathing? Where's she at right now?"*
Guilty Caller: *"She's laying in the crib, <u>should I pick her up</u>?"*

In the previous cases, the callers asked the dispatchers for permission to complete simple tasks that could benefit the victims. Such tasks should have been accomplished without discussion or approval. This, of course, assumes that the callers had the victims' survival and best interests at heart.

Some guilty 911 callers asked permission to accomplish tasks that benefitted them but harmed the victims. As an example, callers might ask the dispatcher for permission to call someone else instead of focusing on the victim, as in the following case. A woman called 911 when her boyfriend allegedly committed suicide:

Dispatcher: *"Feel his wrist and tell me if he has a pulse."*
Guilty Caller: *"<u>Can I hang up and call his mother</u>?"*

The caller did not want to cooperate with the dispatcher by attending to the victim, and calling the boyfriend's mother would keep her from having to cooperate. She passively asked permission to make a telephone call instead of trying to save her boyfriend. The caller was found guilty of homicide.

Consideration
It is important to consider the context of the Asking Permission indicator. This indicator would not apply if the dispatcher gave explicit CPR instructions, but the caller had the need to adapt the instructions. For example, in the following case, a friend was instructed to give CPR to an overdose victim:

Dispatcher: *"Listen to me, lay him flat on his back."*
Innocent Caller: *"OK, I got him on the floor."*
Dispatcher: *"Is he on his back?"*
Innocent Caller: *"Yes."*

Dispatcher:	*"I want you to keep him like that and start doing chest compressions. Place the palm of your hand in the middle of his chest and push down fifteen times fast, let me hear you count."*
Innocent Caller:	*"One and two and three and four and five and—OH, he just threw up, should I turn him on his side?"*
Dispatcher:	*"He threw up? Yes, turn him on his side and use your fingers to sweep out his mouth. Do it now."*

During an earlier part of the 911 call, the dispatcher specifically directed the caller to keep the victim on his back. The dispatcher reiterated this instruction two more times. Therefore, when the caller needed to turn the victim onto his side to prevent aspiration after vomiting, he asked, *"should I turn him on his side?"* Because the caller was asking for consent in order to comply with the dispatcher's directives as much as possible, this request was not an Asking Permission Indicator.

Calling Another

"If I maintain my silence about my secret it is my prisoner...if I let it slip from my tongue I am ITS prisoner."

Arthur Schopenhauer

Innocent 911 callers understood that time was critical when seeking help for an injured person. Therefore, after assessing the situation as a life-threatening event, the first call should be to the 911 dispatcher. Some callers, however, made other phone calls before contacting 911. The Calling Another indicator appeared in 4% of the 911 study calls. All but one call with this indicator were made by guilty callers.

Calling Another before calling 911 wasted time and reduced the victims' chances of survival. A review of this practice revealed a twofold defensive strategy for the benefit of the callers at the expense of the victims. The callers could put their own spin on events by being first with the news of the incident. Additionally, callers could ensure that other persons were there to share responsibility when officers arrived.

In the 911 study, Calling Another was used most often when a nonbiological boyfriend or stepfather was babysitting while the biological mother was out. After assaulting the child and seeing the victim's health deteriorate, some guilty men panicked and called the mother before calling 911. This gave the guilty callers an opportunity to present an explanation to the mother before law enforcement provided the truth. In cases involving children, some guilty callers feared the parents of the victims as much, if not more, than they feared law enforcement.

In the second defensive strategy, the guilty callers sought the mothers' counsel and gave them time to return home before calling 911. When medics and officers then arrived, the guilty callers and the mothers were viewed as a team. The imminent scrutiny from first responders and eventually from investigators was therefore shared, thus easing the pressure on the offenders.

Investigators should always ask the callers' family members if other calls were made from the scene, and officers should obtain consent to review the 911 callers' and third parties' phones for communications prior to the 911 calls. In some cases, male offenders texted the biological mothers before calling 911, and in one extraordinary case, the 911 caller took the time to Facebook the biological mother about the victim's critical condition before calling 911.

Dispatcher as Witness

> "Don't let your ears witness what your eyes did not see."
> Anonymous

Some guilty callers deployed the strategy of bringing the Dispatcher as a Witness to the scene to support their feigned innocence. In this technique, the callers narrated each step as they walked through the scene with the dispatchers as if they were discovering the victim for the first time. The offenders also "discovered" points of entry, murder weapons, and other evidence while on the phone with the dispatchers, who had become the guilty 911 callers' witnesses. The Dispatcher as Witness indicator was present in 4% of the calls in the 911 study. All but one of these calls were made by guilty callers.

As an example of Dispatcher as Witness, a man called 911 regarding his partner:

Dispatcher:	*"911, what is the address of the emergency?"*
Guilty Caller:	*"216 Cindy Drive."*
Dispatcher:	*"Okay, tell me exactly what happened."*
Guilty Caller:	*"Um, I got over here and I came in the front door and <u>I see that the front room is destroyed</u>."*
Dispatcher:	*"Okay, so it looks like somebody may have broken in?"*
Guilty Caller:	*"Yes. Oh, <u>the side door looks like it's kicked in and the house has been destroyed</u> and <u>Dan is laying on the floor</u>."*
Dispatcher:	*"Who is Dan?"*
Guilty Caller:	*"Dan is my partner."*
Dispatcher:	*"OK, help is on the way."*
Guilty Caller:	*"<u>I'm going into the kitchen and the alarm has been ripped out of the wall</u>."*

Dispatcher:	"Okay but what's wrong with Dan?"
Guilty Caller:	"He's laying on the floor."
Dispatcher:	"Have you checked the whole house yet?"
Guilty Caller:	"*I'm walking upstairs now.*"
Dispatcher:	"So you just got in, saw him, and came out and called me?"
Guilty Caller:	"I'm upstairs now."
Dispatcher:	"Are you with Dan?"
Guilty Caller:	"Oh, he's not moving. He's got holes in him."
Dispatcher:	"Does it look like he's been shot or stabbed?"
Guilty Caller:	"Yes, it looks like he's got—*there's holes everywhere. There's a knife.*"
Dispatcher:	"There's a knife on the floor?"
Guilty Caller:	"Yeah, there's a knife on the floor."
Dispatcher:	"OK."

The caller brought the dispatcher along as a witness by giving a play-by-play narration as he entered the house, walked up the stairs, and searched the rooms. The dispatcher therefore "witnessed" his alleged discovery of the victim, the broken alarm, and the weapon. The caller's strategy failed, and he eventually confessed that his lover threw him out of the house and had been seeing another man. The caller was convicted of the murder.

In a variation on Dispatcher as Witness, some guilty callers convinced other people to physically enter the crime scene with them. After committing the murders, the offenders left the scenes to go to work or to establish other alibis. Upon their return, they invited others to enter the residence, sometimes under the guise of watching a ballgame on television or helping with a project. The unwitting witnesses could then corroborate the callers' stories and their distressed emotional states as they "discovered" the victims. Witnesses included friends, coworkers, neighbors, and family members, including the callers' children, as in the following example:

Dispatcher:	"911, what's your emergency?"
Guilty Caller:	"I just walked into the house *with my four-year-old daughter and my husband is on the floor. Looks like he's been shot. I'm taking my little one back outside.*"

Guilty callers might speculate that dispatchers would be more likely to believe a distraught caller with a young child. After all, only an innocent person would walk into a horrific crime scene with a child.

Having witnesses present not only helped conceal the offenders' role in the murders but also eased the stress of the dispatchers' questions. In the following case, an unwitting witness was used to share the burden of inquiry:

Dispatcher:	"911, what is your emergency?"
Guilty Caller:	"Yeah, this is Tim O'Shea, I just came home and my wife has committed suicide. I need to know what to do. I'm a doctor. <u>My neighbor</u> is a doctor and <u>we're here</u>. It looks like she's been here for hours."
Dispatcher:	"Have you started CPR?"
Guilty Caller:	"<u>We see</u> no reason to do it, she's cold."
Dispatcher:	"What's the address there?"
Guilty Caller:	"<u>We're at</u> 2901 Stanford Street."
Dispatcher:	"Okay 2901 Stanford?"
Guilty Caller:	"Yes, <u>we are</u> a block off 300 Street, just across from the school. <u>We came</u> in together."

The husband quickly introduced his "witness" and reiterated the witness' presence five more times during the 911 call. The neighbor later told police that he thought it odd when the husband asked him to come into the house with him. In the three years they had been neighbors, that had never happened before. The husband was subsequently convicted of his wife's murder.

The ultimate strategy for offenders bringing witnesses to the scenes of homicides was to convince the witnesses to make the 911 calls. With this approach, the offenders never had to answer the dispatchers' questions and thereby avoided incriminating themselves. Some offenders pretended to be too distraught to make the calls; others feigned preoccupation with other tasks and asked the unwitting witnesses to make the 911 calls. A few offenders made no excuses but simply directed witnesses to place the calls and the witnesses complied.

An employee of a landscaping crew arrived at his boss's house for work in the early morning hours. The boss's stepson was outside, and the stepson and the employee entered the house together to find the boss deceased in his bed:

Dispatcher:	"911, what is your emergency?"
Innocent Caller (employee):	"I think Mr. Ingram is having a heart attack or something. Send the medics here. (Speaking to another subject at the scene) What's the address? What's the address, Steve?"
Dispatcher:	"What is your address sir?"
Innocent Caller:	"I don't know, I don't live here. Speaking to another subject at the scene: Steve! What's the address?"
Dispatcher:	"What's going on there?"
Innocent Caller:	"I think Mr. Ingram has had a heart attack. He's cold and stiff. Steve, take the phone and give her the address."
Guilty Caller (stepson):	"<u>We're</u> at 546 Madison Road, it's back by the water tower."

Dispatcher:	*"What's going on there?"*
Guilty Caller:	*"Uhh, looks like blood's on his pillow. <u>We</u> just got here."*
Dispatcher:	*"Do you know the guy?"*
Guilty Caller:	*"Yeah, he's my mom's husband."*

When the police arrived at the scene, they saw that the victim had been shot in the back of his head as he slept. The officers interviewed the stepson and the employee and learned that they had entered the house together and discovered the body together. When the detective arrived, he separated the two "witnesses" and interviewed them individually. The employee stated that when he arrived for work, the stepson was waiting outside and wanted the employee to go inside the house with him to wake up the boss. The employee initially refused and the stepson cajoled him until he agreed to enter the home. Once inside, they called out to the boss and eventually located him in a bedroom. The stepson tossed his cell phone to the employee and yelled "Call 911!" The employee complied but was unable to give the dispatcher the address of the emergency and tried to get the information from the stepson. When that failed, the employee returned the phone to the stepson, forcing him to speak directly with the dispatcher. The stepson immediately referred to his "witness" and used the plural pronoun "we" twice. The investigation revealed that the stepson's mother had shot and killed her husband. The stepson helped cover up the crime by allowing his mother to leave the scene and using the employee as an unwitting witness. However, the detective broke the case and the wife was convicted of the murder; the stepson was convicted of being an accomplice after the fact.

Investigators who question witnesses to learn how they happened to be at the scene or how they happened to place the 911 calls can gain valuable insight. If dispatchers are used as witnesses, investigators will want to examine whether or not such contemporaneous "discoveries" are logical. Although witnesses were often present during the 911 conversations of innocent callers, these innocent callers felt no need to mention the witnesses, for their focus was on the victims.

Eyes Comments

"When I look into your eyes, there's nothing there to see, nothing but my own mistake staring back at me."

Linkin Park

Innocent callers focused on the victims' most serious injuries and quickly shared that crucial information with dispatchers. Some guilty callers failed to provide critical details and instead commented about the victim's eyes without being prompted by the dispatcher. In the 911 study, 6% of the calls contained Eyes Comments. Guilty callers made 82% of these calls and innocent callers made 18%.

In the following three cases, the "Eyes Comment" indicator was present:

Dispatcher:	*"Okay and he's down and layin' in the yard?"*
Guilty Caller:	*"Yeah, he's, um, <u>his eyes was wide open</u>."*

. . . .

Dispatcher:	*"Do you see any signs of forced entry?"*
Guilty Caller:	*"I don't know but her whole face is flaccid except for <u>these big white eyes</u>."*

. . . .

Dispatcher:	*"Okay, I need for you to get to your husband, can you go to him?"*
Guilty Caller:	*"He's layin' on his back with his arm over his head and <u>his eyes are staring up</u>."*

The previous three callers, who all had relationships with their victims, felt compelled to mention the victims' open eyes. Perhaps they were unnerved by the victims' eyes appearing to gaze back at them.

The following case is not an example of the "Eyes Comment" indicator because the 911 dispatcher prompted the caller to make the remark:

Dispatcher:	*"Is your wife conscious? Are her eyes open?"*
Innocent Caller:	*"Her eyes are open but she's not conscious!"*

Nervous Laughter

"God may forgive your sins, but your nervous system won't."
Alfred Korzybski

There is nothing humorous about potentially fatal situations. No innocent callers in the 911 study laughed when communicating with the 911 dispatchers as they sought help for dying victims. However, three percent of the callers in the 911 study laughed weakly when responding to the dispatchers' questions; all were guilty.

An unexpected phenomenon occurred during the well-known Milgram Obedience Studies. Subjects who believed they were administering increasing amounts of electric shocks to other individuals nervously laughed as they seemingly inflicted pain. Although no shocks were actually administered, the nervous laughter was a sign of the subjects' tension (Milgram, 1963). This type of nervous laughter comes from the throat, unlike hearty laughter at humor that involves the diaphragm and chest muscles, as air is forced out of the lungs. Such a nervous response is an expression of anxiety rather than true laughter. Similarly, the nervous response heard from guilty, anxious 911 callers was short, weak laughter that appeared at the middle or end of their comments.

In the following case, a woman cried during the first two lines of her 911 call, was unemotional during the next few lines, and ended the call with nervous laughter:

Dispatcher:	*"911, what is your emergency?"*
Guilty Caller:	*"My boyfriend overdosed (crying)."*
Dispatcher:	*"How do you know he overdosed?"*
Guilty Caller:	*"Um, because I—that's—that's—(crying) there's nothing else it could be."*
Dispatcher:	*"Okay."*
Guilty Caller:	*"I know that for a fact."*
Dispatcher:	*"Was this accidental or intentional?"*
Guilty Caller:	*"I think a—definitely accidental—accidental."*
Dispatcher:	*"Okay. What did he take?"*
Guilty Caller:	*"I'm not too sure. Pain killers? Like, um, pain killers."*
Dispatcher:	*"Okay. Was it his prescribed pain killers?"*
Guilty Caller:	*"Oh, I don't know (nervous laughter). You're asking the wrong person (nervous laughter)."*
Dispatcher:	*"Okay, not a problem. I'm sending the paramedics to help you now."*

The nervous laughter did not match the serious nature of the event. The caller eventually confessed to poisoning her boyfriend and was convicted of the offense.

The following case involves a woman who called 911 after she returned home to find her home burglarized:

Dispatcher:	*"911, what is your emergency?"*
Guilty Caller:	*"Um hi there. I just got home from taking my son to the doctor and my door was open and when I came inside there's stuff all over my house and my fiancé's home but I didn't see him just because I saw the stuff everywhere I walked back out (unintelligible)."*
Dispatcher:	*"What happened?"*
Guilty Caller:	*"I have my 5-year-old son with me."*
Dispatcher:	*"OK and tell me tell me what happened. I didn't quite hear what you had said."*
Guilty Caller:	*"Oh there is stuff everywhere and I don't see my fiancé but I didn't want to go further into the house."*

Dispatcher:	*"OK so you think somebody has broke in? OK and is your son safe? Is he outside?"*
Guilty Caller:	*"We're both sitting in the car, something's wrong, I'm worried about him in there."*
Dispatcher:	*"OK and when you left your fiancé was there at the house?"*
Guilty Caller:	*"Yeah, um, because the kids wanted him to come with us and they couldn't get him to wake up 'cause he was snoring so loud (<u>nervous laughter</u>).*"

The 911 caller nervously laughed at her own comment regarding her fiancée's snoring. When the first responders arrived, they located the husband lying in bed, shot in the head with a rifle. The investigators suspected the woman's involvement in the offense and analyzed her call, revealing several guilty indicators including Nervous Laughter. Two months after the call, the caller's sister, who lived three miles from the murder scene, noticed something unusual. The large snow bank in her own driveway began to melt and a rifle barrel protruded from the snow. The sister reported the discovery to the sheriff's department and cooperated with the police. She agreed to make a recorded call to her sister, the suspect, and explained that she found a rifle in the snow. During the call, the suspect told her sister not to touch the rifle or to discuss it with anyone. The suspect immediately drove to her sister's house, walked directly to the snow bank, and retrieved the murder weapon. As the suspect was driving home, she was arrested and charged with the murder of her fiancée. She was later convicted of the offense.

A day-care provider also displayed Nervous Laughter during a 911 call concerning a child in her care:

Dispatcher:	*"911, what is your emergency?"*
Guilty Caller:	*"Uh this is Sharon Peters and I have a daycare and the baby I was watching ate and then he burped and then he kind of just quit breathing."*
Dispatcher:	*"Okay what's the address that you are at please?"*
Guilty Caller:	*"1209 North Atchison Trail."*
Dispatcher:	*"Okay tell me exactly what happened."*
Guilty Caller:	*"Well he was um feeding and then he burped and then he just kind of seemed to go limp (<u>nervous laughter</u>)."*
Dispatcher:	*"Okay."*
Guilty Caller:	*"I'm very scared so I thought I better check and I um started giving him mouth to mouth."*
Dispatcher:	*"Okay."*
Guilty Caller:	*"And now he is just really sleeping and that's not normal."*
Dispatcher:	*"Okay."*
Guilty Caller:	*"And it's scaring me so."*

The day-care provider nervously laughed after making the deadly serious comment *"he just kind of seemed to go limp."* Her anxiety of having a limp child caused the Nervous Laughter. Additionally, the caller focused on her own condition by twice admitting that she was scared. The investigation revealed that the caller was guilty of homicide. In the 911 study, both male and female guilty callers exhibited this nervous reaction.

Possession of a Problem

> *"When you focus on problems, you get more problems."*
> Zig Zigler

Several guilty callers began their calls by taking personal possession of victims' conditions. These callers revealed their ownership of the problems by using the singular personal pronoun "I" and beginning their first turn to speak with "I have a..." as in the following cases:

Dispatcher: *"What is your emergency?"*
Guilty Caller: *"I have an infant, he's not breathing."*

....

Dispatcher: *"What is your emergency?"*
Guilty Caller: *"I have a stabbing."*

....

Dispatcher: *"What is your emergency?"*
Guilty Caller: *"I have a problem. My wife is missing."*

....

Dispatcher: *"What is your emergency?"*
Guilty Caller: *"I have an unconscious child who is breathing very shallowly."*

....

Dispatcher: *"What is your emergency?"*
Guilty Caller: *"I have a four-year-old little girl here who is not coherent."*

In the previous five cases, the callers focused on themselves and treated the victims' conditions as their own problems; all were convicted of the victim's deaths. Possession of a Problem was present in 6% of the calls in the 911 study. Sixty-four percent of these callers were guilty and 36% were innocent.

Considerations
Callers in the 911 study who used the words "We have" when describing victims' conditions were innocent rather than guilty. These callers were parts of

groups at the scenes, and they did not take singular possession of the problems. The following is an example of an innocent caller who shared ownership of the problem with other employees at a motel:

Dispatcher: *"911, what is your emergency?"*
Innocent Caller: *"We have a dead woman at the Ranch Inn Motel."*

The caller was a housekeeper at a motel known for narcotics use and prostitution. The cause of the death was unknown until toxicology reports identified it as a heroin overdose.

Recounting Dialogue

> *"Dialogue is used to reveal not what we want to say,*
> *but what we are trying to hide."*
> William Monahan

Place yourself in the shoes of one who walks into a death scene. The body is lifeless, possibly with massive injuries and severe bleeding. If the victim is a friend or family member, the stress would be severe, and the 911 call should convey this. An urgent demand for help and an intense focus on the victim is expected, and any information that delays the dispatcher from sending immediate aid is counterproductive. Some callers, however, took the time to recount previous dialogue with the victim. Recounting Dialogue was present in 6% of the calls in the 911 study. Guilty callers made 82% of these calls and innocent callers made 18% of the calls.

   Guilty callers in the 911 study used Recounting Dialogue for three main reasons:

   1. To incriminate the victim and gain sympathy:
      Guilty Caller: *"<u>I told her that I was worried and to stop doing the dope</u> and she said '<u>shut up and leave me alone</u>' and I said '<u>please stop for the kids.</u>'"*
   2. To present an alibi to the dispatcher:
      Guilty Caller: *"<u>I told her I was going to the movies and would be back in a couple hours</u> and she said '<u>bring me some Mountain Dew when you come back</u>' and I told her '<u>ok, see you in a while.</u>'"*
   3. To divert attention to a possible outside suspect:
      Guilty caller: *"She had friends over and she <u>told me they were suspicious.</u>"*

Considerations

If 911 callers recounted previous dialogue to the dispatchers that directly related to the victims' health condition, this did not qualify as the Recounting Dialogue indicator. Sharing previous comments made by victims regarding pain or illness benefited the victims by alerting dispatchers to the serious nature of the events. As an example, in the following case, a young lady called 911 regarding her grandmother:

Dispatcher:	*"911, state your emergency."*
Innocent Caller:	*"Hey I need a ambulance at 29 Carrie Drive, my grandma just passed out."*
Dispatcher:	*"Okay, and what happened?"*
Innocent Caller:	*"She doesn't feel really good, and she said she 'bout to fall out, she 'bout to fall out and she just fell out."*
Dispatcher:	*"Okay. What's your name?"*
Innocent Caller:	*"Stephanie Markey."*
Dispatcher:	*"Markey?"*
Innocent Caller:	*"Yes."*
Dispatcher:	*"Okay, how old is your grandmother?"*
Innocent Caller:	*"She's 83."*
Dispatcher:	*"How long has she felt this way?"*
Innocent Caller:	*"She—she hasn't been feelin' good all night, she doesn't want me to call but she hasn't been feelin' good all night and all mornin', and she hasn't been eatin' anything, and all of a sudden she was layin' to bed, and she was like 'I'm 'bout to fall out—I'm 'bout to fall out,' and we don't know what happened."*
Dispatcher:	*"Okay. I got a trauma unit en route, and I got a deputy en route also."*

The granddaughter immediately demanded medical help for the victim. She then recounted previous dialogue between the two to help the dispatcher understand the grandmother's condition. The sharing of dialogue in this case was of value because the dispatcher learned details that lead to the pertinent follow-up question, *"How long has she felt this way?"* The grandmother died at the scene, and the subsequent investigation revealed that she suffered a massive stroke.

In the following case, a son called 911 after finding his father lying on the bathroom floor:

Dispatcher:	*"911, where is your emergency?"*
Innocent Caller:	*"Can I get an ambulance at 322 Clive Street?"*
Dispatcher:	*"What's going on?"*

Innocent Caller:	*"My dad—he's—he fell on the floor with the mirror on him..." He said his back was hurting."*
Dispatcher:	*"Mm-hm."*
Innocent Caller:	*"Please get somebody please!"*
Dispatcher:	*"Hold on. Don't hang up, okay?"*
Innocent Caller:	*"Come on."*

The son recounted the dialogue with his father regarding his back pains. The son believed the information was relevant to the father's condition and shared it with the dispatcher because he knew back pain might be a precursor of a heart attack. The autopsy revealed that the father did suffer a fatal heart attack. An examination of the scene determined that the victim, who had been standing in front of the bathroom mirror, fell forward and knocked the large mirror onto him when they both fell.

Reference

Milgram, S. (1963), "Behavioral Study of Obedience," *The Journal of Abnormal and Social Psychology*, Vol. 67(4), 371–378.

Practical Applications VII

Does the Call Match the Scene?

28

"A clean call equals a clean scene; a dirty call equals a dirty scene."

S. Adams, T. Harpster

When investigators take time to analyze the 911 call before responding to the scene of a death, they can gain clearer understanding of the emergency, whether it is a homicide, suicide, accident, or medical event. There is a direct relationship between the 911 call and the crime scene. Cases in which 911 callers display innocent indicators correspond to crime scenes that are logical and make sense to the officers at the scene. Therefore, a "clean" 911 call predicts a "clean" scene.

Conversely, in cases involving callers who display guilty indicators, questionable issues often appear at the crime scene. Thus, a "dirty" call corresponds to a "dirty" scene. A "dirty" scene may include the following problems: illogical objects near the victim's body, implausible witness statements, inconsistencies with timelines, and impossibilities regarding the victim's physical condition and location at the scene.

A woman called 911 to report that an intruder had broken into her home and shot her husband. She stated there had been a robbery and advised that *"the house was trashed."* The responding officers discovered the husband deceased on the couch from multiple gunshot wounds. Just as the wife had explained, the house had been ransacked as if offenders were searching for valuables. Many of the husband's personal items (trophies, NASCAR items, photos, cigar boxes) were lying broken on the floor. However, the wife's valuables, including a Hummel collection and antique dishes in a hutch, were not disturbed. This "dirty" scene is an example of proprietary damage because only the husband's possessions were damaged.

Officers investigated the death of a four-year-old girl. The case developed as follows:

Dispatcher:	*"911, what is your emergency?"*
Caller:	*"MY DAUGHTER IS CHOKING! GET AN AMBULANCE NOW! HURRY!"*
Dispatcher:	*"Slow down, slow down...what is your address?"*
Caller:	*"VALLEY VIEW APARTMENTS, APARTMENT 3, HURRY, HURRY. SHE'S NOT BREATHING, OH MY GOD!"*

Dispatcher:	*"I'm sending an ambulance, what did she choke on?"*
Caller:	*"HURRY, I DON'T KNOW, I WAS IN MY ROOM, SHE WAS EATING A HOT DOG!"*
Dispatcher:	*"How old is your daughter?"*
Caller:	*"SHE'S FOUR YEARS OLD, I DON'T SEE ANYTHING IN HER MOUTH (sobbing), SHE'S NOT BREATHING NOW! SHE'S ALL LIMP! SHE'S TURNING BLUE! OH MY GOD HURRY!"*
Dispatcher:	*"She's not breathing? Do you know how to do CPR?"*
Caller:	*"NO, TELL ME HOW TO DO IT!"*

When officers arrived at the scene, they had to pull the mother away from her daughter to give first responders enough room to treat the little girl. The distraught mother, screaming and crying, told the officers *"My daughter was choking and I took her into the bathroom and she threw up in the toilet and then went limp."* The mother had to be helped into a neighbor's car because her legs could not support her, and she followed the ambulance to the hospital.

The officers spoke to the victim's grandfather who shared the unkempt and filthy apartment with the girl's family. He explained that he was with the little girl while the mother was in her bedroom. He added that the mother had the flu and had been throwing up all day. The grandfather, did not provide many details about the event and claimed that he had left to put clothes in the washing machine. The laundry room was on a different floor within the apartment building, and he advised that he was *"only gone for ten minutes."* He said that when he returned, he saw that the victim was choking and he yelled for the girl's mother to help. The mother came out, grabbed her daughter, and quickly called 911.

The officers were suspicious of the grandfather and feared that he may have shaken the girl, causing her condition. Both officers had responded to a "shaken baby" call two days earlier in the same apartment building, and both had seen numerous child fatalities in which a parent or a mother's boyfriend was the actual killer. There was a small abrasion on the girl's forehead and when questioned about the injury, the grandfather hesitated and then answered, *"She got that at school. She was playing on the playground."*

The officers observed a hot dog positioned on a napkin on the arm of an easy chair in front of the television in the living room. A very small bite had been taken from the end of the hot dog. The officers also noted an open bag of Gummy Bear candies on the armrest of a second easy chair in front of the television. One officer asked the grandfather if the girl could have choked on some of the candy, and the grandfather replied sternly, *"No way, she knows better than to touch my candy. She is not allowed to touch my stuff. I have yelled at her for that before."*

When the investigators arrived at the apartment, they spoke to the grandfather and he consented to allow them to search the apartment. The investigators noted that the small, two-bedroom apartment was extremely cluttered and smelled like urine. There were empty pizza boxes, soda pop bottles, and potato chip bags scattered on the floor. Soiled clothing was strewn over the furniture and floor. Officers searched the entire apartment, room to room, dresser to dresser. They even looked in the refrigerator, freezer, and stove (a common location used to hide illegal drugs). However, they found nothing of evidentiary value. Before they left, one detective checked the small, dirty bathroom one last time and noticed something she had not seen during the first search. Inside the toilet bowl was an inch long swirl of blue liquid on top of the clear water. The detective had no idea what the "swirl" was but ordered the evidence technician to photograph the material and then collect it. Per departmental protocol, the evidence technician also photographed the entire apartment, the contents of each room, and all the debris in the rooms.

Meanwhile, officers learned that the four-year-old girl was pronounced dead by the emergency room physicians. One investigator, who had not been to the apartment, stopped in dispatch and obtained a copy of the 911 call made by the victim's mother. Using his training in 911 Call Analysis, he examined the call for guilty and innocent indicators. The investigator noted all of the innocent indicators made by the mother and thought, "This is a clean call!"

When the investigators who were on scene and at the hospital finished with their duties, they all met at the police department and reviewed the case before interviewing the mother further. The autopsy would be performed the following day, and it would take at least eight weeks to get the toxicology report back from the coroner's office. The investigator who analyzed the mother's 911 call pointed out each innocent indicator and explained each one to the team. He played the audio for the other officers and shared his analysis with them:

> Look, the first thing I liked is that the mother made the 911 call while her daughter was still alive. If she intentionally killed her daughter, she could have just waited 'till after the little girl was dead to place the call. Also, the mom demanded immediate help for her daughter. Throughout the whole call mom exhibited great urgency and voice modulation. Her modulation was up and down and all over the place. There was no pattern to it. She focused on the child and the child's survival. I really like that the mom volunteered sensory details about the victim and didn't have to be prompted by the dispatcher for this critical information. I don't think she was faking it 'cause it sounded like the mom was under great stress.

The officer who arrived first on scene commented that the mother had advised him that she had the flu and was in bed all day. This comment was consistent with the grandfather's statement regarding her physical condition and location when the event was transpiring. The team discussed that issue and noted that the mother never mentioned her illness on the 911 call. Instead of focusing on her own problems, she focused solely on getting help for her daughter. The team agreed that the checks on the COPS Scale© were on the innocent side and the call was a "clean" call.

Next, the first responders discussed what they learned from the scene itself. The street officers advised that the mother had to be dragged away from her child so that medics could have room to work on her. All agreed that this type of behavior would be expected from an innocent mother. They discussed the fact that the mother had to be physically assisted into the neighbor's car in order to follow the ambulance to the hospital. One of the first responders mentioned that he saw the mother moving unsteadily on her feet. The team discussed this issue and agreed that the mother's physical response, weakness in her legs, was predictable for the level of stress that an innocent mother would be enduring. None of the team thought that the mother had assaulted her child. However, most team members were suspicious of the grandfather. They did not like his *"I was in the laundry room downstairs"* story, and they were wary about the grandfather's explanation of the child's injury. The detective who rechecked the bathroom then voiced her opinion:

> You know, the grandfather was cooperative with us. He never lawyered up and he answered all our questions. Remember, he wanted to go to the hospital with Mom but we held him there for a while...and he was mad as hell about that. I checked the laundry room downstairs and there was a pair of kid's jeans in the dryer. His story kinda checks out. But what the heck was that blue stuff in the toilet?

Nobody had an answer for that question so the team turned their focus to the hot dog and argued back and forth whether that small bite could have been enough to occlude the child's airway and cause death.

The detective who was still pondering the blue swirl in the toilet asked *"What about the Gummy Bears that the grandfather had sitting on his armrest? Maybe the little girl choked on them."*

The first officer on scene quickly negated her theory and advised that the grandfather had specifically stated that the little girl *"would never"* take any of his candy. The detective laughed out loud and asked *"You don't have kids, do you? What kid is not going to eat Gummy Bears from an open bag when her grandfather is out of the room?"* She added, *"I bet the kid grabbed some of those candies when he left and shoved them into her mouth before he got back and busted her. That's what my kids would do."* She then froze and said *"Let me see those crime scene photos again, the one of the grandfather's chair."*

Figure 28.1 The cup full of Gummy Bears.

She looked through the pictures and stopped when she came to the one she wanted. She held up the photo for the team to see; it was the picture of the grandfather's chair and the cup of Gummy Bears on the armrest. See Figure 28.1. The other officers looked at the picture but didn't see the relevancy, and finally one commented, *"So what?"*

The detective replied, *"How many blue Gummy Bears do you see?"* There was total silence; they all now knew what the blue swirl was in the toilet. Mom had said that the little girl threw up in the toilet before she lost consciousness and went limp. That blue swirl was the dissolved remains of blue Gummy Bears, that she had shoved into her mouth while her grandfather was out of the apartment. The detectives later learned that the girl's favorite candy was blue Gummy Bears. She was warned to stay away from her grandfather's candy and she was afraid she would be in trouble if he returned and caught her.

The 911 call was determined to be "clean" and a "clean" call predicts a "clean" scene. An evaluation of the scene revealed that the witness statements were consistent with the evidence. It was a "clean" scene. The autopsy revealed that the child was not assaulted or abused, and the toxicology report did not indicate any drugs in the child's system. The coroner concluded that the cause of death was suffocation from an occluded airway. The child choked to death on blue Gummy Bears.

Create a Timeline: Murder Does Not Happen in a Vacuum

29

"Oh dear, I never realized what a terrible lot of explaining one has to do in a murder!"

Agatha Christie

Murder does not happen in a vacuum. Therefore, valuable insight can be gained by visualizing the act of murder as one of numerous events on a timeline, with the 911 call as the midpoint. Numerous offense-related events occur before and after the murder, and each of these significant points can be identified by the investigator. Sometimes relevant events occurred years before the date of the murder. Prior acts of criminal behavior or violence, previous suspicious deaths, financial issues, infidelity, new marriages, recent insurance purchases, arguments between the caller and the victim, and calls made by the caller before placing the 911 call are all examples of previous actions that should be identified on the timeline. The murder and the corresponding 911 call, made by an innocent or guilty caller, are also scored on the timeline. The 911 call provides insight to the caller's mindset. The points on the timeline prior to the 911 call often bring into focus the rationale for the caller's choice of words during the call.

The timeline continues after the 911 call, with the caller's actions continually added, until the court has rendered a verdict. In some cases, the timeline continues even after adjudication, including the caller's new romantic interests, insurance payoffs, moving out of the community, spending habits, and job changes. Emotional distancing by family members, up to the point of disowning the caller, should also be marked on the timeline.

After the timeline is completed, the investigator will have a detailed chain of events leading to the victim's death and following the death. To build a successful case, the investigator must scrutinize every point on the timeline. Further, the prosecutor can use the timeline during the trial to illustrate why and how the offense occurred.

In the following case, a father called 911 concerning his 18-year-old son:

Dispatcher:	*"911, what is your emergency?"*
Innocent Caller:	*"Send the ambulance to 793 Holman Street! My son shot himself!"*
Dispatcher:	*"Your son what?"*

Innocent Caller: *"Oh God….what have I done?"* (sobbing)
Dispatcher: "What happened?"
Innocent Caller: *"He came downstairs"* (sobbing).
Dispatcher: *"Calm down and tell me what happened."*
Innocent Caller: *"My son came downstairs and he, he shot himself in the head."*
Dispatcher: *"Sir, the ambulance is on the way."*
Innocent Caller: (crying) *"Oh my God, it's all my fault."*
Dispatcher: *"Where is the gun, sir?"*
Innocent Caller: *"It's here, it's on the floor,* *please hurry!"*
Dispatcher: *"Sir, tell me—"*
Innocent Caller: *"Oh Chris, my boy, my boy!"* (sobbing).
Dispatcher: *"Who is there with you?"*
Innocent Caller: *"My son and my wife"* (sobbing).
Dispatcher: *"Where is she?"*
Innocent Caller: *"She's here with us, she's holding him"* (crying).
Dispatcher: *"They're almost there, can you hear the sirens?"*
Innocent Caller: *"No—I can't hear them!* *Please hurry!"*
Dispatcher: *"They're almost there."*

Innocent Caller: *"Tell them it's the yellow house with white shutters…I'm going to turn the porch lights on for them, tell them the door's open so they can just come in."*

Dispatcher: *"OK, sir."*

Note the events in the following timeline in Figure 29.1 regarding the death of the caller's son.

In this case, the caller and his wife adopted a young boy who had come from a family with a history of mental illness. The parents were well educated, had good jobs, had a very nice home, and were excellent role models for their son. As the boy grew up, the family loved and supported him while setting boundaries and being fair and firm with discipline. They encouraged him to succeed in school and attended all of the boy's sporting events and school functions. The parents had no criminal record and were very disappointed when their son began getting into trouble during his teenage years. The boy was arrested several times and spent time in a psychiatric unit. Despite their support and encouragement, the boy began using cocaine and spiraled further downward. The family took him to drug counselors and clinics to no avail. Finally, the parents forced their son to leave the home, although they relented after three weeks and allowed him to move back into the residence. This cycle continued for a year, and the father told the son that he had to leave again. The son went upstairs and then returned to the dining room and confronted his father. He stated, *"Hey Dad, this is what you are making me do"* and shot himself in the head. The father immediately called

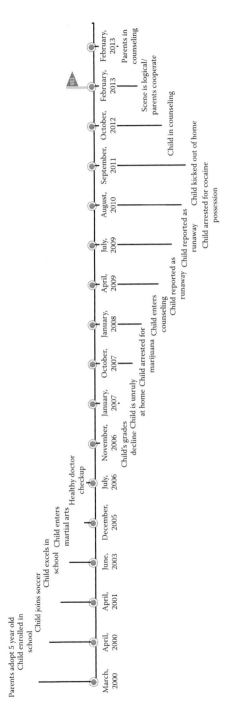

Figure 29.1 Timeline of events.

911, and the parents attempted CPR on their son. Despite their efforts, the son was pronounced dead at the scene and both parents were devastated. They told the investigators that they felt responsible for their son's actions because they were throwing him out again. The case was ruled a suicide, and the crime scene, autopsy, and statements were all consistent with the ruling. The parents went to grief counseling for a year and have never fully recovered.

The father's 911 call contained many indicators of innocence. The Defendant Mentality guilty indicators ("...*what have I done?*" and "...*it's all my fault*") are explained by the fact that the father believed his actions led to his son's suicide. The timeline brought the case into perspective with the son's long and troubled history.

In another case, a mother getting ready to leave for work at 7 a.m. fed her three-year-old son a cupcake for breakfast. As usual, her unemployed boyfriend was responsible for the care of her child while she was at work. The child was developmentally slow and still in diapers. Six hours later, the boyfriend called the child's mother and advised her that the child was unresponsive. Panicked, she told him to call 911 and sped home, pulling in as the medics were arriving on scene. The child was lying on the wood floor near the front door, and the medics immediately began to assess and treat the child. When asked, the boyfriend stated that the child was watching TV and "*fell off the couch onto the floor.*" The TV was located in the carpeted living room.

The child was not breathing and had no pulse; the medics began CPR and quickly transported the baby to the hospital. The child's mother rode in the ambulance with the victim, and the boyfriend advised that he would follow in his car. The child was pronounced dead at the hospital and the mother was inconsolable. However, the boyfriend never showed up at the hospital. He called the mother while she was still at the hospital to check on the victim, and she told him that her son had died. While in the emergency room, the police requested to speak to the boyfriend about the event; however, the mother would not cooperate with the investigators and refused to give his location to the police. Investigators later learned that he was at his aunt's house during this time period.

When investigators finally found the boyfriend, he stated that he was driving to the hospital when he called his girlfriend to check on the child's condition. He added that when his girlfriend told him that the child had died, he was so distraught that he lost control of his car and struck a guardrail. He further stated that during the collision, he was not buckled in and struck his head on the windshield, which caused "*a complete memory loss for that whole day.*" As investigators questioned him further, he immediately lawyered up and refused to answer any further questions regarding the child, the event at the house, or the car accident.

Investigators obtained a search warrant and seized the boyfriend's car. A professional mechanical analysis of the vehicle was completed, and the results conflicted with the boyfriend's version of the *"accident."* The mechanics' report was based on the data provided by the vehicle's Black Box, which was removed and forensically examined. The Black Box computer indicated that the driver was wearing a seat belt when the collision occurred. Further, it indicated that the driver decreased the speed of his vehicle before the collision by taking his foot off of the accelerator and tapping the breaks. When the vehicle reached a speed of 10 mph, the accelerator was pushed until the vehicle's speed reached 15 mph, and a collision occurred without braking.

The autopsy of the victim revealed that the three-year-old had a previously broken leg, healed compression fractures of the spine, a subdural hematoma, and several bruises in various stages of healing, and was suffering from malnutrition. Examination of the stomach contents showed no food other than the partially digested cupcake, which was given to him in the early morning by his mother.

The boyfriend's 911 call was retrieved and analyzed by the investigators:

Dispatcher:	*"911, what is the address of your emergency?"*
Guilty Caller:	*"Ah, 501 Eastern Avenue, <u>I have a</u> 3-year-old baby that, that is recovering from—umm—a seizure. He went unresponsive and he is barely breathing. <u>I need someone here really quick</u>."*
Dispatcher:	*"And how old is the baby?"*
Guilty Caller:	*"<u>Do what?</u>"*
Dispatcher:	*"How old is the baby?"*
Guilty Caller:	*"3 years old (<u>long pause</u>)"*
Dispatcher:	*"Hang on the line. I'm gonna page out an ambulance, OK?"*
Guilty Caller:	*"OK."*
Dispatcher:	*"Is he teething right now hun?"*
Guilty Caller:	*"He's not doing anything right now, he's like, he's like, barely, (stutter) it's like he takes a breath once every minute, he's <u>not—he</u> won't do anything he's <u>completely</u>—I don't know what's wrong with him. He tries, he tries to breathe and then he can't, he can't cough or nothing and <u>he's—and</u> his eyes are messed up. <u>Please!</u>"*
Dispatcher:	*"I do have an ambulance en route, OK?"*
Guilty Caller:	*"OK" (pause).*
Dispatcher:	*"Is there a defibulater available?"*
Guilty Caller:	*"I don't even know what that is" (<u>nervous laugh</u>).*
Dispatcher:	*"It's kinda like a shock box."*
Guilty Caller:	*"No, uh, ah, I can feel his heart, his heart is beating like crazy but he's not breathing."*

Dispatcher:	*"OK, listen carefully, lay him on the floor, flat on his back."*
Guilty Caller:	*"He's laying on the floor."*
Dispatcher:	*"Kneel down next to him and look in the mouth for food or vomit, is there anything in the mouth?"*
Guilty Caller:	*"No there isn't."*
Dispatcher:	*"OK, I'm going to help with CPR, are you ready?"*
Guilty Caller:	*"The ambulance is here."*

Caller terminates the call.

The investigators examined the actions of the mother, the child, and the suspect previous to the child's death. They gained critical insight from analyzing the 911 call. Indicators of both innocence and guilt were present, as indicated on the transcript, but the preponderance of check marks on the COPS Scale© was on the guilty side. The detectives learned that the victim's grandparents suspected that the boyfriend had killed the child, and the grandparents refused to speak with the boyfriend after the child's death. The grandparents cooperated with the police throughout the investigation and later alerted the detectives when the boyfriend left the state two months after the death of the child. The lead investigator completed the timeline, shown in Figure 29.2, which proved to be revealing.

The timeline enabled analysis of all the relevant events before and after the death and the 911 call. The events provided insight regarding the caller, the crime, and the call. By establishing this type of graphic, the case came into focus and was a valuable tool for investigators and prosecutors. The caller was convicted of the child's homicide. Timelines can also be presented to the jury on a PowerPoint or charts, impressing upon the jury members the case-relevant events and educating them that murder does not happen in a vacuum.

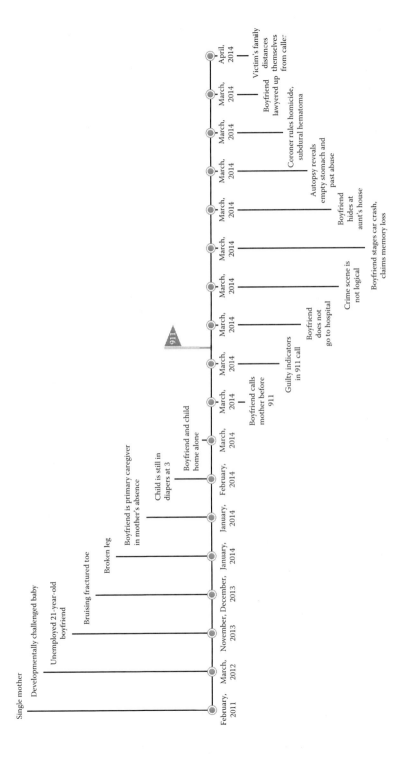

Figure 29.2 Timeline of events.

911 Analysis Tips for the Law Enforcement Team

VIII

911 Analysis Tips for the Law Enforcement Team: Dispatchers

30

Dispatchers have unique skills that enable them to talk with hysterical callers in emotionally charged situations and still gain critical information to save lives. After listening to hundreds of dispatchers in life-and-death cases, patterns emerged that were shared by the most effective ones. These dispatchers had perfected the ability to gain maximum information during 911 homicide calls, while providing optimum care and assistance. The following tips were gained from these exceptional dispatchers, some of the unsung heroes of law enforcement.

1. Stay Calm

Dispatchers handle a constant flow of routine calls that flood into the dispatch center. Because 911 homicide calls are rare, dispatchers themselves can experience initial shock as they process the magnitude of the events. Most dispatchers remember their first homicide call and the flood of adrenaline they felt as they fought to remain in control. With experience they learned that taking a deep breath and staying calm helps them to think through the necessary steps in providing aid. This calm demeanor was contagious and helped to calm the callers. Experienced dispatchers coached frantic callers to *"Take a breath, slow down, and tell me what's going on."* Dispatchers are often described as the true first responders. They are the callers' first contact with law enforcement, and their approach to the call can shape the course of events. Skilled dispatchers not only save lives but also elicit key investigative details that may never be repeated. In fact, some callers may later refuse to be interviewed. If the caller is the offender, the dispatcher thus acquires the only subject statement in the entire investigation. Remaining calm and nonthreatening allows the dispatchers to gain as much information as possible while the caller is still willing to talk. Because the dispatcher is the lifeline for officer safety, calm dispatchers can also stay alert for any threats to their responding officers.

2. Tell Callers That Help Is on the Way

Experienced dispatchers inform the callers that help is on the way, so the callers can then focus on answering questions. In some

instances, frantic callers repeatedly asked, *"Are they coming?"* and
"Where are they?" The sooner the dispatchers inform callers that help
has already been sent, the sooner callers can provide valuable information instead of worrying about whether help is coming or not.

The following exchange is from a dispatcher who realized the
caller was panic-stricken and needed to be reassured that help was
en route:

Dispatcher:	*"Okay. I've got the address. What's goin' on there?"*
Innocent Caller:	*"My husband passed out and fell flat on his face and he can't breathe now. He's having trouble breathing! He's, begging for air! HE CAN'T BREATHE!!"*
Dispatcher:	*"Okay. Just to let you know, the ambulance is on the way, so the questions..."*
Innocent Caller:	*"Okay."*
Dispatcher:	*"...that I'm gonna ask are not gonna delay us from getting there, okay?"*
Innocent Caller:	*"Okay."*

3. Show Compassion

In the calls studied, dispatchers who showed compassion gained
the callers' confidence, which resulted in more information shared.
When faced with violent deaths, callers needed a supportive human
voice to guide them through the tragedy. Some empathetic dispatchers sounded like parents comforting their children. Whether innocent or guilty, callers provided more information when speaking to
compassionate dispatchers.

Because callers may not think of dispatchers as law enforcement,
they often revealed more than they intended. The dispatcher is usually the first person the callers communicate with during the emergency, and the callers may need to vent their emotions. Offenders
blurted out their resentment and jealousy toward the victims, even
insulting and blaming their dying spouses and friends. Guilty callers
begged for help for themselves instead of help for the victims, and
the dispatchers who responded with compassion encouraged open
communication from the callers.

4. Learn and Use the Callers' Names

When dispatchers learned and used the callers' names, a bond
was more apt to develop between the dispatchers and callers. Skilled
dispatchers, who developed a first-name basis with callers, worked

collaboratively with them, addressing the emergency together. These dispatchers complimented callers on their assistance and addressed them personally: *"Sara, you're doing a good job describing what's going on."* If the callers became distracted, dispatchers repeated the callers' names, thus refocusing the callers' attention on the task of communicating key details.

Addressing guilty callers by their first names directly contributed to solving cases. When guilty callers felt support from the dispatchers, they provided more information than they originally intended. Some revealed the motivation for the murder; some even confessed.

5. Perfect the Art of Open-Ended Questioning

During the first few seconds of the call, dispatchers sought answers to the basic questions: who? what? where? and when? Once help was dispatched, experienced dispatchers asked open-ended questions to gain additional information. Open-ended questions are invaluable tools for they "invite an open, unrestricted response" (Watkins et al., 2011). The nearly universal open-ended question initially asked in the 911 calls was, *"What happened?"* This key question elicited a flood of information.

Some of the most effective open-ended questions asked by dispatchers in the examined calls were *"What's going on there?"* and *"How did this all start?"* Other questions that elicited valuable information included *"Describe exactly what happened"* and *"Tell me what you see."* Dispatchers who asked such open-ended questions dramatically increased the chances of successful case resolutions.

In contrast to open-ended questions, early use of closed-ended questions often elicited one- or two-word answers. A series of closed-ended questions such as *"How long were you married?"* or *"Do you have any children?"* created a pattern of short and limited answers. After necessary closed-ended questions like, *"Where is the gun now?"* skilled dispatchers shifted almost entirely to open-ended questions.

As an example of an effective open-ended question, a man called 911 to report that his girlfriend committed suicide, and the dispatcher's question uncovered valuable details:

> Dispatcher: *"What happened?"*
> Guilty Caller: *"We're havin' an argument and I—I been (unintelligible) mean, she grabbed my gun and then—then I—I."*

The caller likely did not intend to place himself at the scene of the crime, but the dispatcher asked an open-ended question that prompted the caller to release his emotions. The caller also provided a clue to his motivation by mentioning the argument; he later confessed to killing his girlfriend.

When experienced dispatchers were confused by the information provided by callers, they asked open-ended follow-up questions for clarification. Dispatchers are professionals at extracting information from emotional callers, and if these professionals remained confused after repeated questioning, it was probably because the callers did not want to be understood. Innocent callers aimed to make the emergency situation crystal clear, but some guilty callers preferred to obfuscate. Innocent callers also wanted to aid the victims, but not all guilty callers had the same intention. If dispatchers sensed resistance to performing CPR, for example, they used open-ended questions to learn what made the callers so hesitant. There may be logical reasons, such as severe damage to the victim's face. Open-ended questions revealed this type of information. Conversely, some guilty callers had no desire to revive the victims. Through open-ended questions, dispatchers identified callers' reluctance to providing relevant details and continued the questioning to draw out the withheld information.

6. Persevere When Caller Is Resistant

When guilty callers resisted answering crucial questions, experienced dispatchers persevered. If open-ended questioning failed to uncover the key facts, dispatchers shifted to closed-ended questioning such as, *"Did he...?"* or *"Did you...?"* These closed-ended questions had only two possible answers, *"Yes"* or *"No."* Any other answer was a form of resistance and needed to be professionally overcome. When asked in a supportive tone using the caller's name, closed-ended questions often uncovered the truth. Once the resistance was overcome, the dispatchers returned to their open-ended questions to gain the full depth of information.

In the following case, a woman called 911 regarding her husband's condition. When she resisted a key question, the dispatcher professionally persevered by repeating a closed-ended question:

> Dispatcher: *"911, what is your emergency?"*
> Guilty Caller: *"Oh my God, oh my God. Gunshot wound."*
> Dispatcher: *"Where at?"*
> Guilty Caller: *"At 1010 Westminster. Oh my God, oh my God, oh my God."*
> Dispatcher: *"How was it shot?"*
> Guilty Caller: *"Oh my God. Himself."*
> Dispatcher: *"Did he do it on purpose?"*

> Guilty Caller: *(to husband) "Baby—baby, are you with me?"*
> Dispatcher: *"Did he do it on purpose?"*
> Guilty Caller: *(to husband) "Can you hear me? Can you hear me?"*
> Dispatcher: *"Sarah?"*
> Guilty Caller: *"Yes."*
> Dispatcher: *"Did he do it on purpose?"*
> Guilty Caller: *"Um, he—we were—we were struggling."*

Throughout the call, the caller appeared to hear the dispatcher's questions, but whenever the caller heard a question she did not want to answer, she resisted. She did not want to tell the dispatcher the truth—that this was not a suicide but a homicide. Accusatory or aggressive questioning could cause the caller to take the ultimate form of resistance—hanging up. Instead, this dispatcher's gentle perseverance by repeating *"Did he do it on purpose?"* revealed additional information and kept the caller on the line. The dispatcher later returned to open-ended questions to learn the caller's full involvement. This persevering approach helped solve the case and the caller confessed to homicide.

7. Use Reflection

Talented dispatchers used reflection to gain additional information. They simply repeated the callers' last phrase in a calm manner, without judgment. This was the optimum open-ended question, because it originated from the caller and was not influenced by the dispatcher.

As an example of a dispatcher's use of reflection, a young distraught wife called 911. After describing her husband's lack of breathing and the large amount of blood under his body, she told the dispatcher:

> Guilty Caller: *"I shot him."*
> Dispatcher: *"You shot him?"*

Without hesitating or reacting emotionally, the dispatcher calmly repeated what the wife said. This low-key approach of using the wife's words instead of asking the judgmental question, *"Why?"* allowed the wife to feel safe. Sensing the dispatcher's support, the wife released her frustrations about her husband and answered the very question that she was <u>not</u> asked—why she shot him. She explained that her husband was planning to leave her and she refused to accept his decision.

In another example of the use of reflection, a caller reported that his baby was not breathing:

> Guilty Caller: *"The baby was fussy all day and wouldn't stop crying."*
>
> Dispatcher: *"The baby wouldn't stop crying?"*
>
> Guilty Caller: *"No, I picked him up but didn't shake him that hard."*

The caller did not realize he had just confessed. The dispatcher showed compassion through gentle reflection, and the caller provided key information. The caller was found guilty of the baby's death.

8. Avoid Leading Questions

Inexperienced dispatchers sometimes asked leading questions such as, *"Did you see any men leaving the house?"* This question could lead the caller to agree with the suggestion that more than one male intruder left the house. In contrast, experienced dispatchers phrased the same questions more objectively, as in *"What exactly did you see?"*

The most effective dispatchers obtained pure statements from callers by not inserting their own ideas into the conversation. They carefully avoided contaminating the information by asking *"What?"* and *"How?"* questions and then waited for complete replies before continuing.

As an example of ineffective questioning, examine the use of a leading question during a husband's 911 call:

> Dispatcher: *"911, what is your emergency?"*
>
> Guilty Caller: *"My wife's been shot."*
>
> Dispatcher: *"Did you see the person who did this?"*
>
> Guilty Caller: *(pause) "Ah, no."*

A nonleading question such as *"What happened?"* would have allowed the caller to say whatever he wished. In fact, the caller appeared ready to confess at several points during the 911 call, but the dispatcher missed this opportunity by focusing so intently on an "intruder offender" that no other possibility was considered. In a subsequent face-to-face interview, the caller confessed that he shot his wife.

In another call, a husband confessed to killing his wife, but the dispatcher then asked a contaminating leading question:

> Dispatcher: *"911, what is your emergency?"*
>
> Guilty Caller: *"My wife's been shot!"*

Dispatcher: *"Who shot her?"*
Guilty Caller: *"I did!"*
Dispatcher: *"Oh! Was it an accident?"*
Guilty Caller: *"Uh...uh...yes, it was an accident."*

The caller seemed confused by the dispatcher's third question and paused before he responded. When he realized, however, that the dispatcher was offering him an "accident" theme, the caller suddenly agreed that the shooting was indeed an accident. The husband had called 911 to confess, but he was not allowed to fully confess during the call. He later told investigators that he planned and carried out his wife's murder.

Negatively phrased questions can also be leading questions by causing the caller to avoid providing details. The question, *"You didn't see who did this, did you?"* invited the negative response, *"No."* A grateful guilty caller just dodged the role of witness, which would have necessitated further inquiry. Another negative question, *"You weren't home when this happened?"* removed the caller from the scene and therefore from culpability. The guilty caller was relieved to answer this question with *"No."* Callers who were rescued in this way seemed to gain strength. Their previously whimpering voices became louder and more confident as they realized they were not seen as suspects. Unfortunately, when officers arrived to question the callers face-to-face, those previously ready to confess responded with more confidence as they delivered their "story." At a minimum, this delays the investigators from reaching the truth; at the worst, it can mean a guilty party walks away free.

Skilled dispatchers avoided asking questions such as, *"You didn't see who did this, did you?"* and instead asked, *"Who did this?"* Likewise, they did not ask, *"You weren't home when this happened?"* They directed callers to *"Walk me through what happened from the beginning."* Exceptional dispatchers kept the questioning neutral and avoided leading questions and negative leading questions.

Negative questions asked when verifying information, however, were necessary. Their effect was not to end communication but to verify accuracy. For example, when callers told dispatchers they could not find the victims' pulse, the dispatchers verified, *"You can't find a pulse?"* Because verifying questions simply repeated previously provided details, they did not influence the callers' information.

9. Be an Active Listener

Dispatchers with active listening skills encouraged callers to talk, while withholding judgment. One caller stated, *"I killed my wife,"* and the dispatcher continued calmly, asking open-ended questions such as, *"How did this happen?"* Active listening required prompting by dispatchers, who encouraged callers to continue talking with phrases like, *"Go on,"* or short questions like, *"What happened next, Tom?"* These prompts also assured the callers that the dispatchers were paying attention.

Effective dispatchers let callers answer questions completely without interrupting. Dispatchers who interrupted did not learn what the caller was about to say. Perhaps the caller was ready to identify the assailant or to confess. Repeated interruptions frustrated callers and reduced responses to one-word answers. Through patient listening, however, dispatchers learned key information about weapons, drug use, and intended suicides—details that could save an officer's life.

The rhythm of outstanding dispatchers was slightly different from that of inexperienced dispatchers. After gaining critical information and dispatching help, experienced dispatchers typically slowed their pace. They often paused briefly after the caller's responses because they realized that callers might offer more information if given the chance. During this pause, additional information flowed from highly emotional callers. For some offenders, the opportunity to talk provided a much needed stress release. The callers' spontaneous, unedited responses revealed their frustrations and occasionally their motivations for the homicides.

Another attribute of skilled dispatchers was the ability to listen without jumping to conclusions. If the caller said, *"My wife has been shot,"* the dispatchers did not assume that a third person shot the wife. Instead, the dispatchers use open-ended questions to ask, *"What happened?"* or *"What's going on there?"* If the caller said, *"I shot her,"* experienced dispatchers did not assume that the death was either intentional or accidental. They responded in calm voices with, *"How did it happen?"* The exceptional dispatchers were neutral listeners with the intent to learn as much as possible.

Many innocent callers provided information promptly and clearly. Guilty callers, however, were less forthcoming. The dispatchers' guidance through the use of open-ended questioning and active, nonjudgmental listening elicited relevant facts from resistant callers.

10. Remain on the Line

Dispatchers kept callers on the lines long after the callers wanted to stop talking. With gentle prodding, the dispatchers continued with their open-ended questions such as, *"What do you think happened here?"* *"How is your wife doing now?"* and *"Tell me every time she takes a breath."*

	10 Tips for Dispatchers **Tips Learned from Exceptional Dispatchers**
1	**Stay Calm.** Homicide calls are infrequent and shocking. Dispatchers who remain calm provide maximum assistance to callers and gain maximum information from callers.
2	**Tell Callers that Help Is on the Way.** Callers who know help is en route can focus on dispatchers' questions instead of worrying about whether help is coming or not.
3	**Show Compassion.** Be the supportive human voice to guide callers through their tragedy.
4	**Learn and Use the Callers' Names.** Ask for the callers' names and use them often to personalize the interaction and refocus the callers' attention.
5	**Perfect the Art of Open-ended Questioning.** Use questions like *"What happened?"* to elicit a flood of information. Keep callers talking with follow up open-ended questions: *"What caused this?"* and *"Tell me what you see…"*
6	**Persevere when Callers are Resistant.** Gentle perseverance such as repeating key questions can overcome callers' resistance.
7	**Use Reflection.** Gain additional information by repeating the callers' last phrase in a calm, nonjudgmental manner.
8	**Avoid Leading Questions.** Carefully avoid contaminating the callers' information. Do not ask: *"Did you see any men leaving the house?"* Instead, ask: *"What did you see?"*
9	**Be an Active Listener.** Encourage callers to talk. Let them speak without interruptions, negative judgment, or assumptions to learn as much as possible about the event.
10	**Remain on the Line.** Never hang up on an opportunity for providing continued support and for gaining further information.

Figure 30.1 Ten Tips for Dispatchers.

There were many reasons why dispatchers remained on the lines even though callers wanted to hang up. Some dispatchers aided callers in providing CPR and other aid to the victims. Other dispatchers gained additional directions to help responding units locate the house. Dispatchers also learned key details later in the calls that changed the course of the investigation. For example, burglary calls were actually death scenes, although callers were reluctant to initially share this information. Additionally, dispatchers who kept the callers on the lines gained insight from the callers' reactions when the first responders arrived. Most innocent callers expressed genuine relief for any type of help, while some guilty callers were not pleased to see police cruisers in front of their houses.

Skilled dispatchers never dismissed opportunities for gaining additional information. The single most important attribute of exceptional dispatchers was their ability to keep the callers talking. Figure 30.1 shows ten tips for dispatchers.

Reference

Watkins, K., Turtle, J., and Euale, J. (2011), *Interviewing and Investigation*, Emond Montgomery Publications, Toronto. p. 40.

911 Analysis Tips for the Law Enforcement Team: Patrol Officers

31

Patrol officers who listen to 911 calls on the way to equivocal death scenes arrive on location with a distinct advantage. Whether the death is a result of a homicide, an alleged suicide, or an accidental death, the 911 call provides vital insight for investigative leads and interviewing strategies. Officers can analyze the calls in depth later, with the aid of a transcript, but hearing the callers' own words and voice en route to the scene, or as soon as practical, can pay immediate dividends in gaining a more complete picture of events.

Officers trained in analyzing 911 calls will recognize guilty indicators such as No Immediate Plea for Help for the Victim, Acceptance of Death, Extraneous Information, and No Urgency. There are also 10 additional tips to help officers determine if the callers are involved in the crime:

1. Arrival at scene: Are officers' welcomed?

    Did the 911 callers genuinely demand help while on the phone, and are they eager to see officers and medics arrive? Do they assist with an expedient arrival by directing officers to the correct location and yelling for them to hurry? Innocent callers in the 911 study were enthusiastic when officers and medics arrived, but many guilty callers were not.

2. Medical assistance: Are there any signs that medical aid was provided?

    While on the phone, did the callers agree to perform CPR? If so, does the scene support such actions? Are the victims found in a bathtub, lying partially off a bed, or in any other position that would make CPR difficult? Is there a pristine pool of blood surrounding the victims, with no knee prints or footprints in the blood? Are the victims in a prone position or in an awkward position that would make checking for breathing and pulse difficult? Are any bleeding victims found without signs of efforts to stop the bleeding, such as towels pressed against the wounds? Innocent callers made desperate efforts to save the victims; most guilty callers did not.

3. Voluntary details

    Is the caller forthcoming or resistant concerning details about the victim's condition and the incident? During the 911 call, did the callers provide relevant information to dispatchers or did the callers

239

resist giving specific details? At the scene, does the caller provide a flood of information about the victim or withhold details? Innocent callers in the 911 study were on the offense, demanding help and providing help. Guilty callers were more defensive, answering only the questions asked.

4. Dynamics between caller and victim

While on the phone, did the caller claim to be in the vicinity of the victim? At the scene, is the caller positioned near the victim? Is the parent holding a distressed child or a husband touching an injured wife? Do medics need to pry babies away from parents' arms, or remove spouses from their partner's side in order to provide aid? Conversely, does the caller stand away from the victim, as if distancing oneself from the events? During the call, did the caller cast the victim in a negative light by insulting, blaming, or verbalizing anger toward the victim? At the scene, does the caller continue the negative characterization or appear to be supportive of the victim?

5. Dynamics between caller and offender

If an offender was mentioned in the 911 call, does the caller volunteer a detailed description of the offender? Is the caller helpful in trying to identify the offender? During the 911 call, did the caller reveal fear of the offender or was fear lacking? After observing the scene, should the caller have logically been fearful that the offender might cause further harm?

6. Defendant mentality

Does the caller make self-preservation comments such as, "I didn't touch the knife" or "I got some blood on me?" Do the patrol officers notice the caller's overexaggerated attempts to convince them of exculpatory actions such as "I just got home"? Innocent callers in the 911 study were focused on the victims' survival, but many guilty callers were focused on their own survival and how to avoid culpability in the crime.

7. Third-person dynamics

During the 911 call, were persons other than the caller or the victim heard in the background or mentioned in the call? If other persons were heard during the call or are at the scene when patrol officers arrive, it is important to identify them and ask how they happened to be present. Did the caller personally bring them to the scene or telephone them? If they were contacted by phone, was this call placed before calling 911? From observations made at the scene, would it have been logical to delay the 911 call until after placing a nonemergency call? What is the relationship of the third person—neighbor, friend, family member? If children are present, do they appear to trust the caller or fear the caller? Does the caller hinder the officers' efforts to speak with the children by explaining, *"They don't know anything— they were sleeping"*? Patrol officer interviews with extra persons at the scene can provide valuable insight. Third-person dynamics can reveal much about the caller and the caller's state of mind.

8. Voice modulation

Does the caller's voice modulation at the scene match that during the 911 call? Did the caller lack modulation while talking with the dispatcher and as patrol officers approached the door, yet suddenly employ modulated tones when the officers enter the premises? Conversely, does the caller's ample modulation during the 911 call contrast with a lack of modulation at the scene? If there is a clear difference in the level of the caller's modulation in the 911 call and at the scene, one of the two modulation levels may be contrived.

9. Noteworthy features at the scene

Innocent callers in the 911 study told the dispatchers about noteworthy features such as knives protruding from victims' chests or zip ties binding victims' wrists and ankles. These were such remarkable sights that innocent callers spontaneously volunteered their descriptions. Guilty callers, however, rarely reported conspicuous features in their conversations with dispatchers. The guilty callers were not surprised by objects at the scene because they placed them there. They therefore did not deem the features to be noteworthy. Patrol officers who observe noteworthy features at the scene that were not mentioned in the 911 call should question why the caller omitted such key details. Conversely, 911 callers may have advised dispatchers of actions that would result in specific features being present at the scenes, such as evidence of forced entry. Patrol officers gain additional clues when such expected aspects of the scene are missing. Listening to the 911 calls will alert patrol officers to look for not only the presence of key features but also their absence.

10. The scene: Does the scene match the 911 call?

Patrol officers who listen to 911 calls en route to the scene have a picture in their mind of how they expect the scene to appear. Guilty callers in the 911 study, however, rarely painted a clear picture of the crime scene. If the call and the scene do not match, patrol officers should scrutinize any discrepancies.

The following case that began as a vehicle accident reveals the importance of 911 analysis and patrol officer tips:

A young man called 911 and advised that he was involved in an accident
on a country road. He told the dispatcher that he lost control of his truck,
which swerved and then crashed into a lake. The caller seemed to have a difficult time speaking with the dispatcher and repeatedly coughed during the
call. He explained that he and his mother had been under water for a long
period of time:

Dispatcher:	*"911, what is your emergency?"*
Guilty Caller:	*(coughing) "My vehicle went into the lake."*
Dispatcher:	*"Are you in the water?"*
Guilty Caller:	*(coughing) "No, I got out, my Mom's in the water."*
Dispatcher:	*"Where are you right now?"*
Guilty Caller:	*(coughing) "Right next to shore, the vehicle went into the lake, but I got out, I pulled her out, her foot got stuck on the door. It's pretty deep."*
Dispatcher:	*"Where is your mother now?"*
Guilty caller:	*(coughing) "I'm cold, Oh God."*

Later in the call, the caller explained that he held his breath for as long as possible, but he had to let go of his mother and swim up to get air. The dispatcher,
concerned for the mother's well-being, asked the 911 caller to return and
pull his mother to safety, but he replied "I'm exhausted (coughing) I almost
drowned." The mother was pronounced dead at the scene.

Unfortunately, the patrol officers were not familiar with 911 call analysis
and did not listen to the 911 call en route to the scene. If they had, the call
analysis and the tips for patrol officers would have revealed a more complete
version of the events:

1. Arrival at scene: Are officers' welcomed?

    The officers were not welcomed with enthusiasm or gratitude at
    the scene of the accident. The caller did not appear to be comfortable
    talking with the dispatcher and was not comfortable in the officers'
    presence.

2. Medical assistance: Are there any signs that medical aid was
    provided?

    Although the dispatcher specifically directed the caller to perform
    CPR three times during the call, there was no evidence of the caller's
    knee prints in the dirt beside the victim. In fact, the victim was lying
    face down when officers arrived.

3. Explanation of events and victim's condition: Forthcoming or reticent?

The caller was reticent and defensive during the 911 call. At the scene, the caller volunteered no information and only answered the specific questions asked. The caller resisted cooperating with the patrol officers.

4. Dynamics between caller and victim:

The caller had walked away from his mother, who was lying on the lake's shore. He was standing in the street an eighth of a mile from the accident when the patrol officers arrived. The caller appeared to be emotionally distant from his mother as well as physically distant.

5. Dynamics between caller and offender:

(This tip is not applicable in this case, as no offender was mentioned in the 911 call.)

6. Defendant mentality:

During the 911 call, the caller repeatedly told the dispatcher that the car swerved into the lake. He repeated this theme to the patrol officers. The caller was more focused on convincing the officers of the legitimacy of the accident than on his mother's survival.

7. Third-person dynamics:

(This tip is not applicable, as no other person was present at the scene.)

8. Voice modulation:

The caller displayed voice modulation during the 911 call, but at the scene, patrol officers noted a distinct lack of emotion during the caller's calm, robotic communication.

9. Noteworthy features at the scene:

The caller described a truck accident, yet no brake marks were evident in the dirt.

10. The scene: Does the scene match the 911 call?

If the patrol officers had listened to the call, they would have envisioned a serious accident scene in a deep lake, with a drowning victim in a sinking vehicle. Figure 31.1 is a photograph of the vehicle accident.

The scene did not align with the caller's description of the event during the 911 call. The mother in the passenger's seat could have safely exited the

Figure 31.1 A photo of the crime scene.

truck and walked to shore. If she chose to remain in the truck until help arrived, her upper body would have remained dry. Because all four of the truck's wheels were still making contact with the ground at the shoreline, it would have been logical to attempt to simply back the truck out of the water. However, the shore showed no signs of an effort to reverse the wheels, and no dirt spray was observed in the wheel wells or behind the truck.

If the patrol officers on scene had heard the 911 caller describe the accident to the dispatcher, they would have recognized the implausibility of the caller's story. They also would have realized that the caller provided Conflicting Facts with a Focus on the Caller rather than on his mother's critical condition. With knowledge of the guilty indicators in the 911 call and the contrast between the version of events presented in the 911 call and the evidence at the scene, the fictitious accident story would have unraveled. The patrol officers might also have questioned how the son's cell phone could still be operable after allegedly being submerged in the lake.

When the veracity of the driver's account was later questioned, investigators then analyzed the 911 call and recognized the discrepancies. If the patrol officers had heard the 911 call, the investigation could have been quite different. The case would have been initiated as a possible homicide with the caller as the suspect.

The autopsy revealed that the victim died from a hypoxic brain injury from being suffocated at least two hours prior to the 911 call. The caller was convicted in the homicide of his mother.

Patrol officers who listen to 911 calls on their way to death scenes and use the Tips for Patrol Officers can uncover critical evidence and conduct effective interviews to help identify whether callers are innocent or guilty.

911 Analysis Tips for the Law Enforcement Team: Investigators

32

Investigators who listen to 911 calls before arriving at the scene will be alert to conflicts between the information in the call and the conditions at the scene. During further study of the 911 call transcript and audio, investigators will gain insight to use during the interview of the caller. The following 10 tips can help guide investigators in determining the likelihood of the caller's guilt in the homicide.

1. Be alert for discrepancies between the 911 call and the scene.

   Investigators will have the benefit of the patrol officers' insight regarding any features of the scene that do not match the 911 call. These discrepancies, added to the investigators' observations, can be fully explored during the interview of the caller. For example, a woman informed the 911 dispatcher that her house was ransacked. She repeated this information two more times in an attempt to convince the dispatcher of her version of events. She mentioned her injured husband only once. The house showed very little disruption and certainly did not appear to be ransacked. The husband, however, was dead. Knowledge of the 911 call made the condition of the house noteworthy for its contrast to the information in the call.

2. Note any improbabilities regarding the victim's physical condition or location and the 911 call.

   Some 911 callers advised that they were performing CPR as they spoke with dispatchers. The callers' relaxed breathing recorded on the 911 audio is a clue that CPR might not have been administered. A pristine circle of blood surrounding a victim would also refute the caller's claim of kneeling beside the victim to perform CPR.

   Any confusing aspects of the victim's condition or location need further explanation, particularly if the scene conflicts with information in the 911 call. For example, there may be a valid reason for a victim to be doubled over in a bedroom closet instead of lying supine on the bedroom floor by the time help arrives. It is possible that an object became wedged under the closet door and attempts to release it were unsuccessful. However, if no obstruction prevented pulling the victim into an open space, the investigator will want to learn why the caller felt the need to preserve the scene instead of aiding the victim.

All puzzling aspects of crime scenes need further clarification, and the contents of the 911 call can serve as a starting point to identify such discrepancies.

3. Explore unexplained knowledge.

Examine the scene with the specifics of the 911 call in mind to identify any Unexplained Knowledge. For example, if the caller said he arrived home to find his wife shot three times, does the scene support the fact that an observer could see three bullet holes? If not, explore how the caller could have learned this information.

4. Interview all witnesses and determine why they were present.

In-depth interviews with all people at the scene can reveal valuable insight not only about the caller but also about the witnesses' presence at the scene. Guilty callers in the 911 study sometimes brought neighbors into their homes to "discover" victims together. These witnesses often found it strange that they would be invited to the callers' home without a clear purpose or a previous pattern of visiting the home.

5. Use information from the 911 call in a search warrant affidavit.

To add to the probable cause to search the scene, investigators can include their training in 911 Call Analysis and the results of the COPS Scale© in the affidavit section of the search warrant. Search teams will want to examine all locations mentioned in the 911 call. Callers may inadvertently refer to a significant area because it is on their mind, without realizing that they have disclosed pertinent information.

6. Search phone calls, texts, and photos before and after 911 call.

Communications prior to a homicide can reveal an offender's motivation. This is particularly relevant in spousal homicides, when electronic communications reveal relationships outside the marriage. After the homicide, the communications show what effect the homicide had on the 911 caller. If there is no shock, outrage, or sense of loss, investigators will want to learn why such natural reactions are missing.

7. Create a timeline.

Because murder does not happen in a vacuum, prior events affect the final act of taking another's life. Carefully constructed timelines can show patterns of financial stress, violence, infidelity, and other life stressors. Activities after the homicide, such as cashing in life insurance policies or an immediate remarriage, can shed additional light on a suspect's reaction to the death.

8. Explore the possibility of multiple offenses.

    Several guilty callers in the 911 study were repeat offenders. Husbands had killed previous wives, and mothers had killed multiple children. The earlier deaths were originally thought to be from natural causes or Sudden Infant Death Syndrome, until the investigators in the final deaths decided to research the offenders' history.

9. Conduct a thorough analysis of the 911 call.

    Although the investigator initially reviewed the 911 call en route to the scene, it is important to study the call in-depth with an accurate transcript. A triple-spaced transcript will allow room to write comments and questions for use during the interview. Mark the indicators of innocence and guilt on a COPS Scale and enlist a second investigator to do the same. Walk away from the transcript and return later to reread the transcript while listening to the call. The investigators will likely see indicators that were missed during the first analysis. Discuss the results with the second investigator, as two people will add more accuracy to the analysis.

10. Interview the caller with insight from 911 call analysis.

    Obtain a full narrative from the caller without interruption from the interviewer. Instruct the caller to "Start from the beginning and tell me what happened." Allow the caller to determine the start, because this point may be well before the actual homicide, and may reveal the motivation for the offense. If the caller needs prompting, the interviewer can ask, "What led up to this?" After the caller has provided a complete version of the events, ask specifically what type of aid was given to the victim.

    Use the COPS Scale and the notes written on the transcript to develop questions and clarify discrepancies among the 911 call, the narrative provided by the caller, and the scene. If most of the indicators are on the guilty side of the COPS Scale, closely examine the location of the guilty indicators and incorporate them into an effective interview strategy. Guilty indicators such as Extraneous Information and Mental Miscues can often reveal the motivation and the method of the homicide.

    Study all areas of resistance in the 911 call to learn where the caller omits information. For example, note where a caller resists when asked to describe the intruder in a burglary/homicide. If the caller also possesses Unexplained Knowledge about the victim's injuries, the investigator can focus on these specific areas. The caller should be alerted about discrepancies, advised that the story is implausible, and offered the chance to provide an accurate statement. One technique used successfully by investigators is to explain to the caller that his 911 call has been carefully analyzed using a structured method and the analysis revealed deception. In some cases, detectives showed the 911 analysis articles and COPS Scale to callers so they realized that the officers were not bluffing.

911 Analysis Tips for the Law Enforcement Team: Prosecutors

33

Prosecutors frequently play 911 calls in court to allow juries to hear the defendants' tone of voice as well as their words as defendants gave their initial statement to law enforcement. The voice and words provide insight to juries. However, when prosecutors who are trained in 911 Call Analysis guide juries through both the audio and the transcript of the calls, they create lasting impressions of this critical evidence. Unlike complex and intimidating DNA evidence, 911 Call Analysis is logical and straightforward. Jurors can understand the basic principles of the analysis because many of them have placed 911 calls themselves.

Homicide prosecutors who have used 911 Homicide Call Analysis in court contributed the following 10 tips:

1. Obtain a copy of the 911 call audio and transcript as soon as possible.
   Examine the call thoroughly and ensure that the transcript is accurate. Know the call word for word.

2. Review 911 Call Analysis and the related COPS Scale©.
   Apply this insight to the 911 call in the case.

3. Provide a copy of the audio call and transcript to all witnesses.
   In addition to the dispatcher and officers, ensure that subject matter experts can review the call to offer greater insight related to their field. Because the knowledge and experience of expert witnesses is unique to them, they may hear something significant in the 911 call that went unnoticed by the dispatcher, officers, or prosecutor.

   a. Medical examiners
      The caller might describe actions before or after the victim was attacked. Medical examiners may be able to provide analysis of the relative positioning of the victim.

   b. Blood spatter experts
      In addition to providing testimony regarding the positioning of the victim, blood spatter experts can also provide information regarding the movement of the people involved. They can use

249

the stain patterns to recreate the event to determine if the stains match the statements in the defendant's call.

c. DNA analysts

Without specific directions, DNA analysts often swab entire items for any DNA evidence. For example, if analysts receive a hat for potential evidence collection, they will swab the entire inside and the bill as one collection of evidence. Consider a situation where it is important to determine who touched the bill of a hat but did not wear it. Instead of taking a single swab of the whole hat, the lab analyst could swab the bill separately from the inside. Similarly, analysts will often take a single swab of the handle, hammer, and trigger of a firearm. Again, hypothetically, it may be important to determine whether the hammer had been pulled back, and this point might only become apparent upon review of the 911 statement. A DNA analyst with knowledge of the 911 call might decide to take separate swabs from the three areas of the firearm. In reviewing the 911 call, analysts can determine which areas to test in a way that will be most meaningful to answer the questions that actually matter.

4. Talk to all witnesses regarding the 911 call.

Prepare witnesses for questions regarding the 911 call and their knowledge of 911 analysis. Incorporate portions of the 911 call into the questions and give the questions to the witnesses in advance.

5. Insert a 911 analysis brief into the affidavit.

If assisting in the completion of a search warrant for a murder scene, recognize the value of adding a 911 analysis brief to the affidavit.

6. Ask relevant questions in Voir Dire.

Begin weaving the 911 research throughout the case by asking the jury pool relevant questions such as:

"*How many of you have ever been in a stressful situation that required you call 911?*"

"*Juror 45—thank you for answering my question—why did you call, sir?*"

"*What did you say during the call?*"

"*What was your demeanor like?*"

"*Your daughter had just fallen down the stairs and she was unconscious? Did you tell the dispatcher where you had been before you got home?*"

"*Why not?*"

Exchange dialogue with jurors, letting them point out how illogi-cal it would be to say some of the things that guilty callers say and specifically what the defendant said. Use hypothetical scenarios in Voir Dire with specific jurors to make some of the points that will later be made during trial. The goal is to educate the jury so they understand ahead of time what they should look for before they learn about the case specifics. When they later hear the defendant's 911 call, it will be an *"Ah Ha!"* moment.

7. In opening statement, continue weaving in the 911 research.

    Remind the jurors about what they heard in jury selection and then tell them what they will hear the defendant say during his 911 call. Continue introducing the 911 research by focusing on the cues picked up from the 911 analysis and from the expert witnesses.

8. Through witness testimony in the case-in-chief, directly address the anomalies in the 911 call.

    Introduce the call and distribute transcripts to each jury member so they can follow along visually. Have the dispatcher walk through the call with the jury, contrasting elements in the call with other calls, such as No Modulation or No Urgency.

    Guide the detectives through discrepancies between the 911 call and the scene. Talk about why it was remarkable that the defendant had no fear of remaining at the house where an assailant recently killed someone and where officers drew their own weapons for safety when searching the house for the offender. Go through the COPS Scale with the detectives and have them explain how their training and experience investigating homicides differentiates this 911 call from other calls. Highlight key points of the call in a PowerPoint presentation, identifying indicators of guilt. Reinforce the incriminating sections of the call and the failure to act appropri-ately, such as No Immediate Plea for Help, Extraneous Information, and Acceptance of Death of the victim. Argue to the jury that the cues are just common sense, and they are one more piece of the guilty puzzle.

    Present a visual timeline, impressing upon the jury that murder does not happen in a vacuum. Events prior to and following the homicide can be significant when considering motivation.

    Enter the 911 recording and transcript into evidence so the jury can review them during their deliberations. The jury will be alert for inconsistencies and incriminating information in the call because of their earlier introduction to 911 calls.

9. Cross-examine the defendant.

If the defendant takes the stand, the cross-examination should focus on specific areas related to the 911 call. Perhaps the defendant never asked for help for a dying spouse, was not willing to give CPR, and instead immediately accepted her husband's death. The goal is to guide the jury to start thinking the same thought the detectives and prosecutors are thinking: *"That's not how I would sound if I was calling 911."* Information stated in a 911 call can also be refuted and used to argue consciousness of guilt.

10. Bring it all together in the closing argument.

Remind the jury of Voir Dire, each witness statement, and specifically what the defendant said during the call. Remind the jury again of the father whose daughter fell down the steps and how illogical the jury pool thought it was to suggest that the father would tell the dispatcher where he had been prior to his daughter falling down the steps. Compare each analogy to that of the real 911 call in the case. Hit all of the key points again in closing argument, reminding the jury what each witness said and what the defendant said and did. Also include what the defendant did not say and do.

As an example of weaving the 911 Call Analysis throughout the trial, consider the following case of a woman who shot her husband while he was sleeping in bed. After the murder, the defendant drove her young children to school and returned home alone. She then called 911 to report that her house had been burglarized. She explained that she had been at school, came home, and allegedly found the house in disarray. She went outside without checking on her husband, who she said had the day off from work and was sleeping when she initially left the house.

After mentioning a few incriminating factors about the 911 call in opening, the prosecutor played the tape during the case-in-chief, while the jury followed the dialogue with typed transcripts.

During the closing argument, the prosecutor walked the jury through a summary of the call:

Let's look at just a few of the highly incriminating aspects of the 911 call.

First, listen to how hysterical the defendant's voice is on the tape, as though she already knows her husband is dead, although she supposedly hasn't even gone into the bedroom yet. The hysterics are clearly an act for the dispatcher.

Second, if the defendant is so convinced that someone's broken in, why wouldn't she ever go in and check on the welfare of her husband? Wouldn't that be *your* first priority? She was on the phone with 911 for 15 minutes, and never went back into the house to check on her husband. This is extremely strange behavior.

Third, the whole time she was on the phone, the defendant was standing at the front door at the top of her driveway. If she was so afraid the "burglars" were still there that she wouldn't even go in and check on her husband, why was she staying at the front door? Why didn't she run or drive away to wait for the police? This makes no sense. The "burglars" could have easily come out and killed her if they were still there. She knew that no one was there; otherwise she wouldn't have remained in harm's way.

Fourth, there was no sense of urgency for her husband's safety, even though the defendant was putting on a show of hysteria to cover up her own involvement in the case. Not once did she ever say she was concerned about her husband, not once during the 15-minute call. She even laughed a few times.

Fifth, at one point she asked, *"Should I go back in?"* Asking whether she should go in and check on the welfare of the man who supposedly means more to her than anyone else is irrational. Most wives would do this without asking anyone for permission.

Sixth, look at the inconsistencies in her statement. She has trouble keeping her stories straight.*

The prosecutor continued summarizing the call. After deliberating on the totality of the evidence, including the 911 Call Analysis, the jury returned a verdict of guilty.

In another case, a caller was babysitting his girlfriend's two-year-old daughter when the child became unresponsive and he called 911. The prosecutor studied the caller's guilty indicators and wove them throughout the trial for the presiding judge. The judge ruled that the defendant was guilty of murder, and in the written judgment, he noted several guilty indicators regarding the 911 call. The judge's ruling stated:

The defendant's demeanor during the 911 call was abnormal. When asked what was wrong, his first statement to the operator was that he placed the child in the car seat. He did not advise the dispatcher that the child was not breathing and he did not ask for help. The defendant seemed focused on something other than reviving the child. In contrast to the lack of modulation in the defendant's voice, the child's mother arrived home and screamed hysterically for help. She began CPR and demanded that the ambulance hurry. The child was life-flighted to Children's Hospital where she died from complications resulting from an acute blunt force injury to the abdomen.†

---

* Prosecutor Stuart L. Fenton, Emmet County, Michigan.
† Sioux City, Iowa.

The boyfriend was convicted of homicide. He had violently struck the child when he became impatient trying to placing her into the car seat.

Prosecutors who weave the 911 calls into their cases allow juries and judges to walk through the events to gain firsthand knowledge of the callers and their reactions to the homicides.

Case Studies  IX

Case Studies

34

CASE STUDIES

Each case study consists of a numbered transcript and a blank COPS Scale© to be used to mark any indicators of innocence and guilt that are present in the call.

- If an indicator is present, check the appropriate line.
- If an indicator is not present, leave the indicator unchecked. Some calls will have many indicators, and others will have only a few.
- If an indicator is not applicable to the case, circle the n/a.

Many calls will have checks on both the innocent and guilty sides of the COPS Scale©.

No single indicator can determine innocence or guilt, but a majority of checks on either side of the COPS Scale© inform investigators that the call was consistent with innocent or guilty calls in the 911 study.

Option: If numerous instances of the same indicators are present in a call, additional checks can be added for each occurrence.

A completed analysis of each case, followed by a completed COPS Scale©, can be found in Appendix A.

CASE STUDY #1   MR. AND MRS. HUNT CASE

1. Dispatcher: *"911, what is your emergency?"*
2. Caller: *"I just got to my in-laws house, they didn't come to church this morning and my wife and I were worried. I found them in the—there's been a break-in, I think!"*
3. Dispatcher: *"Slow down—I can't understand you."*
4. Caller: *"Somebody broke in and tore up their house. There is stuff everywhere. My wife's parents are dead!"*
5. Dispatcher: *"Did…Did you say somebody is dead? Who is dead?"*
6. Caller: *"Please, oh my God…please!"*
7. Dispatcher: *"Who did you say is dead?"*
8. Caller: *"Someone broke in!"*
9. Dispatcher: *"Give me your address, give me your address. What happened to them, sir?"*
10. Caller: *"Oh my God, oh my God, oh my God."*
11. Dispatcher: *"Sir! What is your address, give me your address right now, sir."*
12. Caller: *"It's East Kennedy Street, 2322 East Kennedy Street. Hurry."*
13. Dispatcher: *"OK, hold on a second (three-second pause). Sir, what's your name?"*
14. Caller: *"My name is, Jake."*
15. Dispatcher: *"Jake, are you sure it's too late? Do you want me to help you with CPR?"*
16. Caller: *"There is blood everywhere it's all over the floor."*
17. Dispatcher: *"Can you check for pulses?"*
18. Caller: *"I don't want to move them."*
19. Dispatcher: *"Jake, was this an accident or did somebody hurt them?"*
20. Caller: *"This was not an accident!"*
21. Dispatcher: *"Are you sure they're both gone, are they breathing…do they have pulses?"*
22. Caller: *"Oh my God, oh my God, oh my God what am I going to do? Help me."*
23. Dispatcher: *"Take deep breaths, Jake, help is on the way. Are you hurt?"*
24. Caller: *"Huh?"*
25. Dispatcher: *"Does it look like someone broke in?"*
26. Caller: *"I don't know what's going on here!"*
27. Dispatcher: *"Jake, go outside and wait there for the police."*

28. Caller:	*"I am outside. I'm in the driveway, there's blood all over the floor."*
29. Dispatcher:	*"You're doing a great job, Jake. They're almost there."*
30. Caller:	*"I can see them, here they are."*
31. Dispatcher:	*"Ok, Jake you can hang up now."*

911 COPS Scale ©

Considering Offender Probability in Statements

Place a check mark for any indicator that applies or circle n/a for not applicable

Innocent Indicators		Guilty Indicators

WHO is the call about?

Immediate Plea for Help for Victim ____	n/a	____ No Immediate Plea for Help for Victim
Immediate Assessment of Victim ____	n/a	____ No Immediate Assessment of Victim
Focus on Victim ____	n/a	____ Focus on Caller
No Acceptance of Victim's Death ____	n/a	____ Acceptance of Victim's Death
Aid Provided to Victim ____	n/a	____ No Aid Provided to Victim

WHAT is the call about?

Relevant Information ____	n/a	____ Extraneous Information
Sensory Details ____	n/a	____ Lack of Sensory Details
Prioritized Order ____	n/a	____ Inappropriate Order
Bleeding Comments ____	n/a	____ Blood/Brains Comments

HOW is the call made?

Urgency ____	n/a	____ No Urgency
Fear for Caller's Safety ____	n/a	____ No Fear for Caller's Safety
Proximity to Victim ____	n/a	____ No Proximity to Victim
Initial Sounds or Comments ____	n/a	____ Initial Delays

Aggressive Demands ____   n/a   Passive Defenses:

____ Defendant Mentality   ____ Ingratiating Remarks
____ Insults or Blames Victim ____ Mental Miscues
____ Minimizes

Cooperation with Dispatcher ____   n/a   Resistance to Dispatcher:

____ Dispatcher Confusion   ____ Diversion ____ Equivocation
____ Evasion ____ Hangs Up ____ Only Answers What's Asked
____ Pauses ____ Repetition ____ Self-Interruption
____ Short Answers   ____ Unintelligible Comments

Additional Guilty Indicators:

____ Attempts to Convince ____ Awkward Phrases ____ Conflicting Facts ____ "Huh?" Factor ____ I Don't Know
____ Isolated "Please"   ____ Lack of Contractions ____ No Modulation ____ Unexplained Knowledge

Deputy Chief Tracy Harpster (Tracy.Harpster@gmail.com) **and Susan H. Adams, Ph.D.**

CASE STUDY #2

1. Dispatcher:	*"911?"*
2. Caller:	*"Help me, help."*
3. Dispatcher:	*"What's going on?"*
4. Caller:	*"This is Bob Tuggs in Trenton, a log just fell on my wife and she's bleeding all over."*
5. Dispatcher:	*"What fell on her?"*
6. Caller:	*"A log."*
7. Dispatcher:	*"Okay, what is your address?"*
8. Caller:	*(no answer) (caller begins to cry)*
9. Dispatcher:	*"Is it 105?"*
10. Caller:	*"Yes"*
11. Dispatcher:	*"Highway 73?"*
12. Caller:	*"Yes (four-second pause). Please."*
13. Dispatcher:	*"And where is she bleeding from?"*
14. Caller:	*"I don't know, there's a lot...(crying) oh God, I don't wanna look at her." (crying)*
15. Dispatcher:	*"How big of a log is it?"*
16. Caller:	*"It's huge. Please."*
17. Dispatcher:	*"Okay, we got help, help is coming."*
18. Caller:	*"What do I do?"*
19. Dispatcher:	*"You need to check and see if she's breathing; how big of a log is it? How big around?"*
20. Caller:	*"It's twenty inches, it's big."*
21. Dispatcher:	*"It's a big log; where did it land on her?"*
22. Caller:	*"Oh God, her neck's crushed, oh God (crying)."*
23. Dispatcher:	*"Stay on the phone with me, you need to, did you check and see if she's breathing?"*
24. Caller:	*"Help me."*
25. Dispatcher:	*"We got help coming okay, take a deep breath and-"*
26. Caller:	*"I can't hear you (crying)."*
27. Dispatcher:	*"Is she conscious?"*
28. Caller:	*"No."*
29. Dispatcher:	*"Can you check and can you get close enough to her to see if she's breathing?"*
30. Caller:	*"She's not."*
31. Dispatcher:	*"Okay, are you able to get close enough to give her some breaths?"*
32. Caller:	*"Oh God, no, no, no, no, no (crying) there's blood all over the floor."*

33. Dispatcher: *"Okay."*
34. Caller: *"Oh honey (crying) oh God."*
35. Dispatcher: *"Okay, we got help coming, is, is there any...can you get...wipe some of the blood off and start giving her rescue breaths?"*
36. Caller: *"(crying) I can't get close to her."*
37. Dispatcher: *"You can't get close to her? You can't get to her face at all?"*
38. Caller: *"I just can't look at her."*
39. Dispatcher: *"Okay, is there any way you can get the log off of her?"*
40. Caller: *"Oh God, it's big, I don't know."*
41. Dispatcher: *"Is there any way you can try and get something to, ah, lift it up just a little bit to take some of the pressure off?"*
42. Caller: *"Oh."*
43. Dispatcher: *"Can you pry the log up off of her?"*
44. Caller: *"Oh (crying) I can't get that close to her."*
45. Dispatcher: *"You're gonna have to try and help her."*
46. Caller: *"I'll try I can't do it by myself, I have to use equipment."*
47. Dispatcher: *"Is it your wife?"*
48. Caller: *"Yes."*
49. Dispatcher: *"Okay. Can you go near her, are you able to do that and maybe try and get the snow out from underneath her?"*
50. Caller: *"No, we're in the shop, she's landed on the concrete floor."*
51. Dispatcher: *"Is there a way you can put a, a, chain around the log and try and lift it up a little bit on one side?"*
52. Caller: *"I'd have to use a piece of equipment and I don't wanna touch it. I don't wanna touch it. I don't know what to do."*
53. Dispatcher: *"The only thing you can do is try and get close to her and try and give her rescue breaths, ok?"*
54. Caller: *"She's not moving at all."*
55. Dispatcher: *"Is the log right on her neck, is it on her chest?"*
56. Caller: *"Oh God, the brace, (unintelligible) that we put the log on is on top of her neck."*
57. Dispatcher: *"Oh."*
58. Caller: *"Somebody's coming, oh God here they are."*
59. Dispatcher: *"You got help?"*
60. Caller: *"(crying) HELP ME! (crying)."*
61. Dispatcher: *"Are they in the shop? I wanna know when they're in the shop."*
62. Caller: *"Help me (crying)." (Caller hangs up)*

911 COPS Scale ©

Considering Offender Probability in Statements

Place a check mark for any indicator that applies or circle n/a for not applicable

Innocent Indicators		Guilty Indicators

WHO is the call about?

Innocent Indicators		Guilty Indicators
Immediate Plea for Help for Victim ____	n/a	____ No Immediate Plea for Help for Victim
Immediate Assessment of Victim ____	n/a	____ No Immediate Assessment of Victim
Focus on Victim ____	n/a	____ Focus on Caller
No Acceptance of Victim's Death ____	n/a	____ Acceptance of Victim's Death
Aid Provided to Victim ____	n/a	____ No Aid Provided to Victim

WHAT is the call about?

Relevant Information ____	n/a	____ Extraneous Information
Sensory Details ____	n/a	____ Lack of Sensory Details
Prioritized Order ____	n/a	____ Inappropriate Order
Bleeding Comments ____	n/a	____ Blood/Brains Comments

HOW is the call made?

Urgency ____	n/a	____ No Urgency
Fear for Caller's Safety ____	n/a	____ No Fear for Caller's Safety
Proximity to Victim ____	n/a	____ No Proximity to Victim
Initial Sounds or Comments ____	n/a	____ Initial Delays

Aggressive Demands ____   n/a   Passive Defenses:

____ Defendant Mentality   ____ Ingratiating Remarks
____ Insults or Blames Victim ____ Mental Miscues
____ Minimizes

Cooperation with Dispatcher ____   n/a   Resistance to Dispatcher:

____ Dispatcher Confusion   ____ Diversion ____ Equivocation
____ Evasion ____ Hangs Up ____ Only Answers What's Asked
____ Pauses ____ Repetition ____ Self-Interruption
____ Short Answers   ____ Unintelligible Comments

Additional Guilty Indicators:

____ Attempts to Convince ____ Awkward Phrases ____ Conflicting Facts ____ "Huh?" Factor ____ I Don't Know
____ Isolated "Please" ____ Lack of Contractions ____ No Modulation ____ Unexplained Knowledge

Deputy Chief Tracy Harpster (Tracy.Harpster@gmail.com) **and Susan H. Adams, Ph.D.**

CASE STUDY #3

1. Dispatcher:	*"911."*	
2. Caller:	*"I need a, an ambulance to 220 Court Street."*	
3. Dispatcher:	*"What's goin' on?"*	
4. Caller:	*"Uh, we got a girl, she fell down the stairs."*	
5. Dispatcher:	*"How old is she?"*	
6. Caller:	*"Uh, she's about 36?"*	
7. Dispatcher:	*"Is she breathing?"*	
8. Caller:	*"I don't know. I can't tell."*	
9. Dispatcher:	*"Okay. Can you check for me?"*	
10. Caller:	*"Yeah, my buddy's here. He's tryin' to check for a pulse and he say he don't feel it."*	
11. Dispatcher:	*"Okay."*	
12. Caller:	*"But we just picked her up and carried her home and she pissed all the way, all the way home here and, uh…"*	
13. Dispatcher:	*"Where did she fall at?"*	
14. Caller:	*"Down the street at the neighbor's house."*	
15. Dispatcher:	*"Okay. Has she been drinking?"*	
16. Caller:	*"Yeah, she's drunk as fuck."*	
17. Dispatcher:	*"Okay. Do you have her inside the house right now?"*	
18. Caller:	*"Yeah, I have her inside the doorway of the house right now."*	
19. Dispatcher:	*"Okay. Can you put your ear up to her, see if you can hear her breathing?"*	
20. Caller:	*"I don't hear her breathing, lady!"*	
21. Dispatcher:	*"You don't hear her breathing and she doesn't have a pulse?"*	
22. Caller:	*"NO AND HE DOESN'T FEEL A PULSE!"*	
23. Dispatcher:	*"Okay."*	
24. Caller:	*"And I'm call—I don't know what's goin' on here."*	
25. Dispatcher:	*"Okay. Are you comfortable doin' CPR until the ambulance gets there?"*	
26. Caller:	(yells to male in background) *"DO CPR THEY SAID ERIC!"*	
27. Dispatcher:	*"This is, is he, why don't you hand the phone to him and if he's willing to do CPR, I can walk him through it."*	
28. Caller:	(talking to male in background) *"Here. She's willing to do CPR to you."*	
29. (Phone disconnects. Sound of Dispatcher redialing phone number.)		
30. Dispatcher:	*"Hold on. Just disconnected. He tried to give it to his buddy…"*	
	(sound of phone ringing)	

31. *Automated voice mail states: "I'm sorry, but the person you called has a voicemail box that is…"*

32. Dispatcher:	*"911."*
33. Caller:	*"Yeah, I just called—"*
34. Dispatcher:	*"Oh, okay."*
35. Caller:	*"—and I accidentally hung up."*
36. Dispatcher:	*"Okay. What's your name?"*
37. Caller:	*"My name is Rick O'Neil."*
38. Dispatcher:	*"All right. Is your friend willing to do CPR?"*
39. Caller:	*"He's doing it right now."*
40. Dispatcher:	*"Okay. I want you to put him on the phone. I'm gonna walk him through this."*
41. Caller:	(talking to male in background) *"Here, she's gonna walk you through it, Eric."*
42. Male #2:	*"No, I know what I'm doin'."*
43. Caller:	*"He says he knows what he's doin'."*
44. Dispatcher:	*"Okay. How does he know? Is he certified in CPR?"*
45. Caller:	*"DO YOU HAVE AN AMBULANCE?"*
46. Dispatcher:	*"There, yes. Sir, they're already on their way, okay?"*
47. Caller:	*"Okay, because she's got blood comin' out of her nose and her mouth."*
48. Dispatcher:	*"Okay."*
49. Caller:	*"And, I seen when he was blowing in her mouth. Her, her stomach was blowing up."*
50. Dispatcher:	*"Okay. That's that's good. We want."*
51. Caller:	*"Yeah, I don't know what's goin' on here. I-"*
52. Dispatcher:	*"Okay. Just-"*
53. Caller:	*"-was home."*
54. Dispatcher:	*"Is anyone else home with you at that address?"*
55. Caller:	*"Her son is home but he's in bed."*
56. Dispatcher:	*"Okay. How old is the son?"*
57. Caller:	*"He's eighteen. YOU GUYS GOTTA GET HERE QUICK!"*
58. Dispatcher:	*"They're, they're coming and we have law enforcement on the way, I want you to stay on the phone with me."*
59. Caller:	*"You, can you tell 'em to come to the back door?"*
60. Dispatcher:	*"Come to the back door? Okay."*
61. Caller:	*"Yeah, 'cause she's in the back, at the back door."*
62. Dispatcher:	*"Okay. He's doing chest compressions and he's breathing for her?"*
63. Caller:	*"Yes, he's givin' her three breaths and OH, THE AMBULANCE IS HERE!"*
64. Dispatcher:	*"The ambulance is there?"*
65. Caller:	*"Should I get off the phone with you?"*

66. Dispatcher:	*"Well, just, I think it's, uh, it's gonna be law enforcement that's there. Just go open the door and let them in, okay?"*
67. Caller:	*"The door's open."*
68. Dispatcher:	*"You, you can disconnect with me."*
69. Caller:	*"All right. Thank you."*

911 COPS Scale ©

Considering Offender Probability in Statements

Place a check mark for any indicator that applies or circle n/a for not applicable

Innocent Indicators   ### Guilty Indicators

WHO is the call about?

Innocent Indicators	n/a	Guilty Indicators
Immediate Plea for Help for Victim ____	n/a	____ No Immediate Plea for Help for Victim
Immediate Assessment of Victim ____	n/a	____ No Immediate Assessment of Victim
Focus on Victim ____	n/a	____ Focus on Caller
No Acceptance of Victim's Death ____	n/a	____ Acceptance of Victim's Death
Aid Provided to Victim ____	n/a	____ No Aid Provided to Victim

WHAT is the call about?

	n/a	
Relevant Information ____	n/a	____ Extraneous Information
Sensory Details ____	n/a	____ Lack of Sensory Details
Prioritized Order ____	n/a	____ Inappropriate Order
Bleeding Comments ____	n/a	____ Blood/Brains Comments

HOW is the call made?

	n/a	
Urgency ____	n/a	____ No Urgency
Fear for Caller's Safety ____	n/a	____ No Fear for Caller's Safety
Proximity to Victim ____	n/a	____ No Proximity to Victim
Initial Sounds or Comments ____	n/a	____ Initial Delays

Aggressive Demands ____   n/a   Passive Defenses:

____ Defendant Mentality   ____ Ingratiating Remarks
____ Insults or Blames Victim ____ Mental Miscues
____ Minimizes

Cooperation with Dispatcher ____   n/a   Resistance to Dispatcher:

____ Dispatcher Confusion   ____ Diversion ____ Equivocation
____ Evasion ____ Hangs Up ____ Only Answers What's Asked
____ Pauses ____ Repetition ____ Self-Interruption
____ Short Answers   ____ Unintelligible Comments

Additional Guilty Indicators:

____ Attempts to Convince ____ Awkward Phrases ____ Conflicting Facts ____ "Huh?" Factor ____ I Don't Know
____ Isolated "Please"   ____ Lack of Contractions ____ No Modulation ____ Unexplained Knowledge

Deputy Chief Tracy Harpster (Tracy.Harpster@gmail.com) **and Susan H. Adams, Ph.D.**

CASE STUDY #4

1. Dispatcher:	*"911, what is the emergency?"*	
2. Caller:	*"He's dead!"*	
3. Dispatcher:	*"Hello."*	
4. Caller:	*"I came home."*	
5. Dispatcher:	*"Ma'am, where are you?"*	
6. Caller:	*"99 Center Road."* (crying)	
7. Dispatcher:	*"Ma'am, you need to calm down. What happened?"*	
8. Caller:	*"I came home my husband is dead."* (crying)	
9. Dispatcher:	*"You what?"*	
10. Caller:	*"My husband is dead."* (crying)	
11. Dispatcher:	*"OK. Ma'am. I'm going to have to ask you a couple questions, OK?"*	
12. Caller:	*"OK."*	
13. Dispatcher:	*"What's the problem? Tell me exactly what happened."*	
14. Caller:	*"He's on the floor and it looks like somebody came in and robbed us. There's stuff everywhere. He has blood under his head."* (crying)	
15. Dispatcher:	*"OK. Are you with him right now? Ma'am?"*	
16. Caller:	*"I'm in the hallway."*	
17. Dispatcher:	*"OK. How old is he?"*	
18. Caller:	*"He's 72."*	
19. Dispatcher:	*"Is he conscious?"*	
20. Caller:	*"No."* (sobbing)	
21. Dispatcher:	*"Is he breathing?"*	
22. Caller:	*"No (crying). God, who would do this?"*	
23. Dispatcher:	*"Ma'am. We're gonna get you some help. Hold on, OK?"*	
24. Caller:	*"OK."*	
25. Dispatcher:	*"Did you see what happened?"*	
26. Caller:	*"No, I didn't. I just got home from shopping."*	
27. Dispatcher:	*"OK. Are you right by him now? Ma'am?"*	
28. Caller:	*"I can go back."*	
29. Dispatcher:	*"Let me know when you're by him."*	
30. Caller:	*"OK."*	
31. Dispatcher:	*"OK. Are you right by him now?"*	
32. Caller:	*"Yes."*	
33. Dispatcher:	*"OK, ma'am. Listen carefully. I need you to lay him flat on his back on the ground and remove any pillows."*	
34. Caller:	*"He's on his back."*	
35. Dispatcher:	*"OK. Is there anything in his mouth?"*	
36. Caller:	*"No. He-"*	

37. Dispatcher:	*"I need you to place your hand on his forehead and your other hand under his neck and then tilt his head back."*
38. Caller:	*"He's all bloody."*
39. Dispatcher:	*"He's all bloody?"*
40. Caller:	*"Yeah."*
41. Dispatcher:	*"Where is he bleeding from?"*
42. Caller:	*"It looks like the back of his head."*
43. Dispatcher:	*"He's bleeding from the back of his head. Ma'am, hold on, OK. Did you say everything is thrown around?"*
44. Caller:	*"Yeah, it looks like somebody's been through here."* (crying)
45. Dispatcher:	(over the radio) *"She said it looks like someone was in the house. Maybe a robbery."*
46. Dispatcher:	*"OK. Ma'am? We're gonna try to do CPR, OK?"*
47. Caller:	*"OK."*
48. Dispatcher:	*"Can you feel or hear any breathing?"*
49. Caller:	*"He's not, I checked he's not breathing at all. He's gray."*
50. Dispatcher:	*"We're gonna try to help him, OK?"*
51. Caller:	*"OK."*
52. Dispatcher:	*"OK. We're gonna try to do compressions, all right?"*
53. Caller:	*"OK."*
54. Dispatcher:	*"If you need to put the phone down, it's OK. But just listen carefully. I'm gonna try to tell you how to do chest compressions."*
55. Caller:	*"OK."* (crying)
56. Dispatcher:	*"Place the heel of your hand on the breastbone in the center of his chest right between the nipples, then put your other hand on top of that hand."*
57. Caller:	*"Uh-huh."*
58. Dispatcher:	*"OK. I need you to push down firmly two inches with only the heel of your lower hand touching the chest."*
59. Caller:	*"OK."*
60. Dispatcher:	*"Pump the chest hard and fast at least twice per second. You need to do this 400 times. That's only three and a half minutes."*
61. Caller:	*"OK."* (ten-second pause)
62. Caller:	(crying) *"It's not working."*
63. Dispatcher:	*"Ma'am, you just need to keep going, OK? They're on their way there, ma'am. Did you do this 400 times?"*
64. Caller:	*"I'm working on it. It isn't working."* (crying)
65. Dispatcher:	*"The chest should rise with each breath."*
66. Caller:	*"OK. I'm sorry. Hold on."*
67. Dispatcher:	*"Did you feel the air going in and out?"*
68. Caller:	*"What?"*

69. Dispatcher:	*"Did you feel any air going in and out?"*	
70. Caller:	*"He's cold." (crying)*	
71. Dispatcher:	*"OK. We've got to keep trying, ma'am."*	
72. Caller:	*"OK."*	
73. Dispatcher:	*"Is there anyone else there with you?"*	
74. Caller:	*"No. His mouth has—it's full of blood."*	
75. Dispatcher:	*"His mouth is full of blood?"*	
76. Caller:	*"Yes."*	
77. Dispatcher:	*"We just need to continue to help him until they get there, ma'am."*	
78. Caller:	*"I'm working. I'm trying."*	
79. Dispatcher:	*"I know. You might have to blow through some of the blood, ma'am."*	
80. Caller:	*"Do what?"*	
81. Dispatcher:	*"You might have to, just clean out his mouth as best you can, but we might have to blow through some of the blood to get air into his body. Ma'am?"*	
82. Caller:	*"Yes."*	
83. Dispatcher:	*"OK, ma'am, what does it look like inside the house? You said there's stuff thrown around?"*	
84. Caller:	*"I haven't checked the other rooms, but in the kitchen, it looks like somebody's gone through the drawers and stuff and his wallet's on the floor and (crying) and I haven't gone in any other rooms."*	
85. Dispatcher:	*"Is he in the kitchen?"*	
86. Caller:	*"Yes."*	
87. Dispatcher:	*"OK. What's your name?"*	
88. Caller:	*"Isabelle."*	
89. Dispatcher:	*"What's your last name, Isabelle?"*	
90. Caller:	*"Laird. L-A-I-R-D."*	
91. Dispatcher:	*"Ma'am. You want to try to keep doing CPR?"*	
92. Caller:	*"Yes."*	
93. Dispatcher:	*"OK. Keep going til they get there, ma'am. Don't give up."*	
94. Caller:	*(noises of CPR) (crying)*	
95. Caller:	*"Yes."*	
96. Dispatcher:	*"Ma'am? What color is your house?"*	
97. Caller:	*"Um, there is (crying) ... They're here."*	
98. Dispatcher:	*"They're there?"*	
99. Caller:	*"They're here." (crying)*	
100. Dispatcher:	*"Somebody's there with her. Is it an officer?"*	
101. Caller:	*"Yes."*	
102. Dispatcher:	*"OK. I'm gonna let you go, ma'am. OK? Bye."*	

911 COPS Scale ©

Considering Offender Probability in Statements

Place a check mark for any indicator that applies or circle n/a for not applicable

Innocent Indicators		Guilty Indicators

WHO is the call about?

Innocent Indicators	n/a	Guilty Indicators
Immediate Plea for Help for Victim ____	n/a	____ No Immediate Plea for Help for Victim
Immediate Assessment of Victim ____	n/a	____ No Immediate Assessment of Victim
Focus on Victim ____	n/a	____ Focus on Caller
No Acceptance of Victim's Death ____	n/a	____ Acceptance of Victim's Death
Aid Provided to Victim ____	n/a	____ No Aid Provided to Victim

WHAT is the call about?

	n/a	
Relevant Information ____	n/a	____ Extraneous Information
Sensory Details ____	n/a	____ Lack of Sensory Details
Prioritized Order ____	n/a	____ Inappropriate Order
Bleeding Comments ____	n/a	____ Blood/Brains Comments

HOW is the call made?

	n/a	
Urgency ____	n/a	____ No Urgency
Fear for Caller's Safety ____	n/a	____ No Fear for Caller's Safety
Proximity to Victim ____	n/a	____ No Proximity to Victim
Initial Sounds or Comments ____	n/a	____ Initial Delays

Aggressive Demands ____   n/a   Passive Defenses:

____ Defendant Mentality   ____ Ingratiating Remarks
____ Insults or Blames Victim ____ Mental Miscues
____ Minimizes

Cooperation with Dispatcher ____   n/a   Resistance to Dispatcher:

____ Dispatcher Confusion   ____ Diversion ____ Equivocation
____ Evasion ____ Hangs Up ____ Only Answers What's Asked
____ Pauses ____ Repetition ____ Self-Interruption
____ Short Answers   ____ Unintelligible Comments

Additional Guilty Indicators:

____ Attempts to Convince ____ Awkward Phrases ____ Conflicting Facts ____ "Huh?" Factor ____ I Don't Know
____ Isolated "Please" ____ Lack of Contractions ____ No Modulation ____ Unexplained Knowledge

Deputy Chief Tracy Harpster (Tracy.Harpster@gmail.com) **and Susan H. Adams, Ph.D.**

CASE STUDY #5

1. Dispatcher:	*"911?"*	
2. Caller:	*(simultaneously yelling at another subject) "I don't know what's happened, she's gone!"*	
3. Dispatcher:	*"Can I help you?"*	
4. Caller:	*"Yes! We need, we need help at 3616 Sussex!"*	
5. Dispatcher:	*"3616 what street?"*	
6. Caller:	*"SUSSEX!"*	
7. Dispatcher:	*"What's the problem?"*	
8. Caller:	*"My, my daughter's gone! She's due in two weeks and my grandson's here alone and this whole house has been ransacked!"*	
9. Dispatcher:	*"How old is your-"*	
10. Caller:	*"My grandson is two."*	
11. Dispatcher:	*"...and he's gone?"*	
12. Caller:	*"He's here alone!"*	
13. Dispatcher:	*"OK, you need to calm down so I can understand you!"*	
14. Caller:	*"I'm trying!"*	
15. Dispatcher:	*"OK."*	
16. Caller:	*"He's here alone and she's gone, her car's here..."*	
17. Dispatcher:	*"Who's gone?"*	
18. Caller:	*"MY DAUGHTER!"*	
19. Dispatcher:	*"OK, how old is she?"*	
20. Caller:	*"She's twenty-seven years old."*	
21. Dispatcher:	*"OK, and how old is the child who was left alone?"*	
22. Caller:	*"She didn't leave him alone! My God! Something is wrong! She's due, she's due in two weeks! And she's just missing! Her car's here, her purse and her house is trashed and she's not here!"*	
23. Dispatcher:	*"OK, what's your name Ma'am?"*	
24. Caller:	*"My name is Tami Carter."*	
25. Dispatcher:	*"Tami what?"*	
26. Caller:	*"CARTER! JUST GET SOMEBODY HERE NOW!" (sobbing)*	

---

911 COPS Scale ©

Considering Offender Probability in Statements

Place a check mark for any indicator that applies or circle n/a for not applicable

Innocent Indicators		Guilty Indicators
WHO is the call about?		
Immediate Plea for Help for Victim ____	n/a	____ No Immediate Plea for Help for Victim
Immediate Assessment of Victim ____	n/a	____ No Immediate Assessment of Victim
Focus on Victim ____	n/a	____ Focus on Caller
No Acceptance of Victim's Death ____	n/a	____ Acceptance of Victim's Death
Aid Provided to Victim ____	n/a	____ No Aid Provided to Victim

WHAT is the call about?

Relevant Information ____	n/a	____ Extraneous Information
Sensory Details ____	n/a	____ Lack of Sensory Details
Prioritized Order ____	n/a	____ Inappropriate Order
Bleeding Comments ____	n/a	____ Blood/Brains Comments

HOW is the call made?

Urgency ____	n/a	____ No Urgency
Fear for Caller's Safety ____	n/a	____ No Fear for Caller's Safety
Proximity to Victim ____	n/a	____ No Proximity to Victim
Initial Sounds or Comments ____	n/a	____ Initial Delays

Aggressive Demands ____   n/a   Passive Defenses:

____ Defendant Mentality   ____ Ingratiating Remarks
____ Insults or Blames Victim ____ Mental Miscues
____ Minimizes

Cooperation with Dispatcher ____   n/a   Resistance to Dispatcher:

____ Dispatcher Confusion   ____ Diversion ____ Equivocation
____ Evasion ____ Hangs Up ____ Only Answers What's Asked
____ Pauses ____ Repetition ____ Self-Interruption
____ Short Answers   ____ Unintelligible Comments

Additional Guilty Indicators:

____ Attempts to Convince ____ Awkward Phrases   ____ Conflicting Facts ____"Huh?" Factor ____ I Don't Know
____ Isolated "Please"   ____ Lack of Contractions ____ No Modulation   ____ Unexplained Knowledge

Deputy Chief Tracy Harpster (Tracy.Harpster@gmail.com) **and Susan H. Adams, Ph.D.**

CASE STUDY #6

1. Dispatcher:	*"911, what is your emergency?"*
2. Caller:	*"Yes, ma'am, I've just been shot; so have my parents."*
3. Dispatcher:	*"Where have you been shot at?"*
4. Caller:	*"My leg..."*
5. Dispatcher:	*"Who shot you?"*
6. Caller:	*"I don't know."*
7. Dispatcher:	*"You don't know who shot you? What kind of gun was it?"*
8. Caller:	*"Oh my God!" (moaning)*
9. Dispatcher:	*"Where were you shot at?"*
10. Caller:	*"In my leg, in my groin."*
11. Dispatcher:	*"Okay, where were your parents shot at?"*
12. Caller:	*"Possibly in the head... I don't know. I'm sitting downstairs trying—I don't know, they're not moving, I think they're dead."*
13. Dispatcher:	*"You have no idea who shot them?"*
14. Caller:	*"No, Ma'am." (moaning)*
15. Dispatcher:	*"How old are you?"*
16. Caller:	*"I'm 38! Hurry."*
17. Dispatcher:	*"They're hurrying. Is somebody inside your house? Where were they?"*
18. Caller:	*"Yes, they came in."*
19. Dispatcher:	*"You're at 1101 Cherokee Hill? Right?"*
20. Caller:	*"Yes, Ma'am." (moaning)*
21. Dispatcher:	*"What did they look like?"*
22. Caller:	*"One person with a gun, mask, I don't know. I didn't see him, I just heard shots and went upstairs and I got shot and I turned around and ran. Oh my god!" (moaning)*
23. Dispatcher:	*"OK, is anybody else in the house?"*
24. Caller:	*"No Ma'am."*
25. Dispatcher:	*"Have you been having any kind of problems with anybody?"*
26. Caller:	*"Not that I'm aware of...(moaning) Oh God! Please!"*
27. Dispatcher:	*"Where is your mom and dad at?"*
28. Caller:	*"My mom was upstairs and my dad's on the stairs."*
29. Dispatcher:	*"They're both on the stairs?"*
30. Caller:	*"Oh...God."*
31. Dispatcher:	*"Your mom and dad were both shot in the head?"*
32. Caller:	*"I'm sorry, what?"*
33. Dispatcher:	*"They're both shot in the head?"*

34. Caller:	"My dad was shot in the head, I don't know where my mom is."
35. Dispatcher:	"OK."
36. Caller:	"I can't walk."
37. Dispatcher:	"What room are you in?"
38. Caller:	"I'm downstairs in the den."
39. Dispatcher:	"This just happened, right?"
40. Caller:	"I'm sorry, what?"
41. Dispatcher:	"This just happened?"
42. Caller:	"Yes, Ma'am."
43. Dispatcher:	"And how did they get into the house?"
44. Caller:	"All the doors are unlocked, I guess, I don't know."
45. Dispatcher:	"When did you discover that they were shot? Did you hear it?"
46. Caller:	"I heard a shot upstairs, he and I both got up, I saw him go down and I got shot and I turned around and ran down here." (moaning)
47. Dispatcher:	"You have no description of what he looked like, if he was a male?"
48. Caller:	"I have no idea. I'm guessing it was a man...." (moaning)
49. Dispatcher:	"Was he wearing a mask or anything?"
50. Caller:	"Yes, Ma'am, all I saw was the back. It looked like a hat."
51. Dispatcher:	"A mask or a hat?"
52. Caller:	"Like a mask." (moaning)
53. Dispatcher:	"Was it black?"
54. Caller:	"Yes, Ma'am. I don't know what color."
55. Dispatcher:	"Was he a heavy build, thin build?"
56. Caller:	"I'm sorry, what?"
57. Dispatcher:	"Heavy build?"
58. Caller:	"No, not fat."
59. Dispatcher:	Was he like an average build?"
60. Caller:	"Ma'am, I don't know." (moaning)
61. Dispatcher:	"OK."
62. Caller:	(moaning) "Please hurry!"
63. Dispatcher:	"Are you sure no one else is in the house?"
64. Caller:	"There's no one that I know of."
65. Dispatcher:	"Did he run back out the door?"
66. Caller:	"I don't know Ma'am." (moaning)
67. Dispatcher:	"Will there be any cars in the driveway?"
68. Caller:	"I'm sorry, what?"
69. Dispatcher:	"Do you know if it was like a shotgun or handgun?"

70. Caller:	*"I don't know, Ma'am, I ran."* (moaning)
71. Dispatcher:	*"Have you checked your mom and dad or are you not able to get to them?"*
72. Caller:	*"Oh God."*
73. Dispatcher:	*"We have an officer there. Is he inside?"*
74. Caller:	*"He is, I think."*
75. Dispatcher:	*"They are there, I'm going to let you go now."*
76. Caller:	*"OK, bye Ma'am."*

911 COPS Scale ©

Considering Offender Probability in Statements

Place a check mark for any indicator that applies or circle n/a for not applicable

Innocent Indicators		Guilty Indicators

WHO is the call about?

Innocent	n/a	Guilty
Immediate Plea for Help for Victim ____	n/a	____ No Immediate Plea for Help for Victim
Immediate Assessment of Victim ____	n/a	____ No Immediate Assessment of Victim
Focus on Victim ____	n/a	____ Focus on Caller
No Acceptance of Victim's Death ____	n/a	____ Acceptance of Victim's Death
Aid Provided to Victim ____	n/a	____ No Aid Provided to Victim

WHAT is the call about?

Innocent	n/a	Guilty
Relevant Information ____	n/a	____ Extraneous Information
Sensory Details ____	n/a	____ Lack of Sensory Details
Prioritized Order ____	n/a	____ Inappropriate Order
Bleeding Comments ____	n/a	____ Blood/Brains Comments

HOW is the call made?

Innocent	n/a	Guilty
Urgency ____	n/a	____ No Urgency
Fear for Caller's Safety ____	n/a	____ No Fear for Caller's Safety
Proximity to Victim ____	n/a	____ No Proximity to Victim
Initial Sounds or Comments ____	n/a	____ Initial Delays

Aggressive Demands ____   n/a   Passive Defenses:

____ Defendant Mentality   ____ Ingratiating Remarks
____ Insults or Blames Victim ____ Mental Miscues
____ Minimizes

Cooperation with Dispatcher ____   n/a   Resistance to Dispatcher:

____ Dispatcher Confusion   ____ Diversion ____ Equivocation
____ Evasion ____ Hangs Up ____ Only Answers What's Asked
____ Pauses ____ Repetition ____ Self-Interruption
____ Short Answers   ____ Unintelligible Comments

Additional Guilty Indicators:

____ Attempts to Convince ____ Awkward Phrases   ____ Conflicting Facts ____"Huh?" Factor ____I Don't Know
____ Isolated "Please"   ____ Lack of Contractions ____ No Modulation   ____ Unexplained Knowledge

Deputy Chief Tracy Harpster (Tracy.Harpster@gmail.com) **and Susan H. Adams, Ph.D.**

CASE STUDY #7

1. Caller: *(heavy breathing)*
2. Dispatcher: "911, What is-"
3. Caller: "PLEASE COME QUICK. MY WIFE SHOT HERSELF!"
4. Dispatcher: "Where are you at?"
5. Caller: "41 CRAIN. SHE'S STILL BREATHING. PLEASE HELP!"
6. Dispatcher: "Okay, hold on, hold on. It's your wife?"
7. Caller: "YES YES! (crying) She's still breathing, please help her." *(sobbing)*
8. Dispatcher: "Attention Ambulance Crew, please respond to 41 Crain, have a report of a female that has shot herself; she is still breathing."
9. Caller: "Please hurry, please, please help."
10. Dispatcher: "Is she breathing fine?"
11. Caller: "Hardly, she's just gurgling. Please help!"
12. Dispatcher: "Okay, as long as she is still breathing, then we won't need to do CPR."
13. Caller: *(crying).*
14. Dispatcher: "Where did she shoot herself at?"
15. Caller: *(crying)* "In the head. *(sobbing)* Oh, God."
16. Dispatcher: "Okay, okay, the officers should be there in just one moment, okay."
17. Caller: *(sobbing)* "Oh, my God. Oh, my God."
18. Dispatcher: "Okay, did she shoot herself like in the front of the head or in the back of the head?"
19. Caller: "I can't tell, it's not in the front, I can see her face."
20. Dispatcher: "Okay. Do you maybe want to step out of the room?"
21. Caller: "NOOO I can't leave her!"
22. Dispatcher: "Okay, hold on."
23. Caller: "I can't leave her. *(crying)* God, oh my God, please get help."
24. Dispatcher: "Attention Ambulance Crew, please respond to 41 Crain, report of a female who has shot herself. She is still breathing."
25. Caller: "HURRY!"
26. Dispatcher: "Do you see an officer? Is your front door open?"
27. Caller: "No it's not, it's locked."
28. Dispatcher: "Okay, can you go to the front door and unlock it."
29. Caller: "Yes. Yes. IS SOMEBODY HERE?"
30. Dispatcher: "Do you got the front door unlocked?"
31. Caller: "Yes, the front door's unlocked."
32. Dispatcher: "Okay. What is your name?"

33. Caller:	*"Kevin Springer."*
34. Dispatcher:	*"What?"*
35. Caller:	*"SPRINGER!"*
36. Dispatcher:	*"And they should be coming just shortly, okay. Do you see the officers outside the door?"*
37. Caller:	*(crying) "Noooo. Nobody. There's nobody here!"*
38. Dispatcher:	*"Okay, I am going to set the phone down for one moment, okay?"*
39. Caller:	*"All right (sobbing). Please help!"*
40. Dispatcher:	*"Kevin, Kevin, Kevin, do you see the officers at the front door?"*
41. Caller:	*(directed to dispatcher) "YES! (sobbing). (directed towards first responder) Please help her, she's not moving, I came in here and grabbed her."*
42. Officer:	*"Were you here?"*
43. Caller:	*"No, she sent me to the store. Please help." (crying)*

911 Operator disconnected the call.

911 COPS Scale ©

Considering Offender Probability in Statements

Place a check mark for any indicator that applies or circle n/a for not applicable

Innocent Indicators		Guilty Indicators

WHO is the call about?

Innocent	n/a	Guilty
Immediate Plea for Help for Victim ____	n/a	____ No Immediate Plea for Help for Victim
Immediate Assessment of Victim ____	n/a	____ No Immediate Assessment of Victim
Focus on Victim ____	n/a	____ Focus on Caller
No Acceptance of Victim's Death ____	n/a	____ Acceptance of Victim's Death
Aid Provided to Victim ____	n/a	____ No Aid Provided to Victim

WHAT is the call about?

Innocent	n/a	Guilty
Relevant Information ____	n/a	____ Extraneous Information
Sensory Details ____	n/a	____ Lack of Sensory Details
Prioritized Order ____	n/a	____ Inappropriate Order
Bleeding Comments ____	n/a	____ Blood/Brains Comments

HOW is the call made?

Innocent	n/a	Guilty
Urgency ____	n/a	____ No Urgency
Fear for Caller's Safety ____	n/a	____ No Fear for Caller's Safety
Proximity to Victim ____	n/a	____ No Proximity to Victim
Initial Sounds or Comments ____	n/a	____ Initial Delays

Aggressive Demands ____   n/a   Passive Defenses:

____ Defendant Mentality   ____ Ingratiating Remarks
____ Insults or Blames Victim ____ Mental Miscues
____ Minimizes

Cooperation with Dispatcher ____   n/a   Resistance to Dispatcher:

____ Dispatcher Confusion   ____ Diversion ____ Equivocation
____ Evasion ____ Hangs Up   ____ Only Answers What's Asked
____ Pauses ____ Repetition ____ Self-Interruption
____ Short Answers   ____ Unintelligible Comments

Additional Guilty Indicators:

____ Attempts to Convince ____ Awkward Phrases ____ Conflicting Facts ____ "Huh?" Factor ____ I Don't Know
____ Isolated "Please"   ____ Lack of Contractions ____ No Modulation ____ Unexplained Knowledge

Deputy Chief Tracy Harpster (Tracy.Harpster@gmail.com) **and Susan H. Adams, Ph.D.**

Epilogue

Investigator Karen Blake responded to a suicide call in rural Louisiana. Upon arrival, she learned that a suicidal man argued with his wife, put a rifle in his mouth, and pulled the trigger. The scene was horrific, and the victim's wife was inconsolable. While still on scene, Investigator Blake received another dispatch regarding a homicide that had occurred 20 miles away in another section of the Parish. She quickly left the suicide and drove toward the homicide scene.

Investigator Blake had read the literature on analyzing 911 calls published by Dr. Adams and Deputy Chief Harpster and later attended their training. She was taught the value of reviewing the 911 call en route to the scene, and she knew the call would contain crucial information. The investigator called dispatch and asked to listen to the 911 audio as she drove toward the homicide. She noted several guilty indicators in the call and immediately called the authors and asked if they would analyze the call. The investigator mentioned that she was leaving a suicide scene and advised that her agency would email the homicide audio as soon as possible. When asked if she had listened to the 911 call regarding the suicide, the investigator admitted that she had not. She told the authors that the case was not suspicious and that the victim's wife witnessed the event, called 911 to report it, and cooperated fully with law enforcement. After being reminded that she had been taught to listen to ALL death calls, Investigator Blake advised that her office would send both calls to be analyzed.

An hour later, both 911 calls were sent to the authors, and surprisingly, both 911 calls contained guilty indicators. The homicide caller was arrested at the scene but the suicide caller was presumed to be innocent. Frantic phone messages to Investigator Blake revealed that the suicide victim's body was sent directly to the funeral home and was soon to be embalmed. Investigator Blake immediately called the funeral home and stopped the process. She picked up the body and transported it to the medical examiner for an autopsy.

The next day, Investigator Blake got the call from the medical examiner; the victim had been shot in the head with a rifle—from behind. The wife had lied and was arrested for the murder of her husband.

Appendix A:
Case Study Analyses

CASE STUDY #1   ANALYSIS

1. Dispatcher: *"911, what is your emergency?"*
2. Caller: *"<u>I just got to my in-laws house</u>, they didn't come to church this morning and my wife and I were worried... <u>I found them in the—there's been</u> a break-in, <u>I think!</u>"*

Jake gave no Immediate Assessment of the Victims and did not exhibit an Immediate Plea for Help for the Victims. Instead, he began the call with Minimizing and ended the sentence with Equivocation. Jake used Self-interruption so he would not have to complete the explanation of where he found his in-laws: *"<u>I found them in the—there's been a</u> break-in, <u>I think!</u>"*

3. Dispatcher: *"Slow down—I can't understand you,"*
4. Caller: *"<u>Somebody broke in and tore up their house. There is stuff everywhere. My wife's parents are dead!</u>"*

Jake revealed Inappropriate Order by prioritizing the burglary before stating that two people were dead, the Acceptance of Death Indicator. Jake Attempted to Convince by referring to a burglary three times ("break-in," "broke in," and "stuff everywhere"). Throughout the call, Jake expressed No Urgency and used Lack of Contractions, as in "There is," which slowed down the communication.

283

5. Dispatcher: *"Did...Did you say somebody is dead? Who is dead?"*
6. Caller: *"Please, oh my God...please!"*

Jake used Evasion to avoid answering the question asked. He also added Isolated Pleases.

7. Dispatcher: *"Who did you say is dead?"*
8. Caller: *"Someone broke in!"*

Jake again used Evasion to avoid answering the question.

9. Dispatcher: *"Give me your address, give me your address. What happened to them, sir?"*
10. Caller: *"Oh my God, oh my God, oh my God!"*

Jake continued using Evasion to resist answering and he also inserted Repetition.

11. Dispatcher: *"Sir! What is your address, give me your address right now, sir"*
12. Caller: *"It's East Kennedy Street....2322 East Kennedy Street."*
13. Dispatcher: *"OK, hold on a second. Sir, what's your name?"*
14. Caller: *"My name is... Jake."*

Note that Jake hesitated when providing his name to the dispatcher and he only offered his first name.

15. Dispatcher: *"Jake, are you sure it's too late? Do you want me to help you with CPR?"*
16. Caller: *"There is blood everywhere...it's all over the floor."*

Jake's pattern of Evasion continued as he resisted the dispatcher's question. He added a Blood/Brains Comment by describing the scene instead of the victims. The Lack of Contractions continued in "There is."

17. Dispatcher: *"Can you check for pulses?"*
18. Caller: *"I don't want to move them."*

The dispatcher made a second attempt to assist Jake in aiding the victims but Jake Provided No Aid to the Victims.

19. Dispatcher: *"Jake, was this an accident or did somebody hurt them?"*
20. Caller: *"This was not an accident!"*

Jake provided No Sensory Details about the victims.

21. Dispatcher: *"Are you sure they're both gone, are they breathing...do they have pulses?"*
22. Caller: *"<u>Oh my God, oh my God, oh my God...what am I going to do</u>? <u>Help me</u>."*

Jake had provided no Immediate Assessment of the Victims, and through Evasion he resisted the dispatcher's request for assessment at this point in the call. He used Repetition again and the Focus on Caller indicator. Jake finally asked for help; however, the plea was for himself, not the victims.

23. Dispatcher: *"Take deep breaths, Jake, help is on the way. Are you hurt?"*
24. Caller: *"<u>Huh?</u>"*

The dispatcher was worried about Jake's safety, but since Jake had No Fear for his own safety, he failed to track the dispatcher's question and responded with the "Huh?" Factor.

25. Dispatcher: *"Does it look like someone broke in?"*
26. Caller: *"I don't know what's going on here!"*
27. Dispatcher: *"Jake, go outside and wait there for the police."*
28. Caller: *"I am outside. I'm in the driveway... <u>there's blood all over the floor!</u>"*

Jake again provided a Blood/Brains Comment.

29. Dispatcher: *"You're doing a great job, Jake. They're almost there."*
30. Caller: *"I can see them...here they are."*
31. Dispatcher: *"OK, Jake you can hang up now."*

Jake continued to express No Fear for his Safety. He remained standing in the driveway until the officers arrived.

CASE STUDY #1   SUMMARY

All of the checks on the COPS Scale© were on the guilty side.

Jake's 911 call is an example of a case in which 911 analysis was not initially used. Despite the street officers' belief that the killer or killers were members of a cult, the detectives knew better. They realized that the scene was staged to resemble a satanic cult offense. The victims were severely beaten to death, overkill was present, and nothing had been stolen. The lead detective believed the killer or killers were passionate, in a rage, and probably had a relationship with the victims.

On the surface, Jake appeared to be a model citizen and a pillar in his church. Although distraught, he cooperated at the crime scene and at the police department. He provided verbal and written statements and agreed to meet with the detectives the next day for further interviews. Initially, Jake was not a suspect in the murders. After investigators examined tips from the department's "hot line" and chased down false leads, the case went cold.

The investigators took a closer look at Jake's 911 call after the lead detective attended training in 911 Homicide Call Analysis at the National Homicide Conference. Investigators identified numerous indicators of guilt in the call. They also learned that Jake had a serious gambling addiction and was in desperate financial straits. The death of Jake's in-laws resulted in an economic windfall for Jake, and he became the prime suspect in the case.

The following COPS Scale reflects the indicators that are present in this call.

911 COPS Scale©

Considering Offender Probability in Statements

Place a check mark for any indicator that applies or circle n/a for not applicable

Innocent Indicators   ### Guilty Indicators

WHO is the call about?

Innocent		n/a		Guilty
Immediate Plea for Help for Victim	___	n/a	✓	No Immediate Plea for Help for Victim
Immediate Assessment of Victim	___	n/a	✓	No Immediate Assessment of Victim
Focus on Victim	___	n/a	✓	Focus on Caller
No Acceptance of Victim's Death	___	n/a	✓	Acceptance of Victim's Death
Aid Provided to Victim	___	n/a	✓	No Aid Provided to Victim

WHAT is the call about?

Relevant Information	___	n/a	___	Extraneous Information
Sensory Details	___	n/a	✓	Lack of Sensory Details
Prioritized Order	___	n/a	✓	Inappropriate Order
Bleeding Comments	___	n/a	✓	Blood/Brains Comments

HOW is the call made?

Urgency	___	n/a	✓	No Urgency
Fear for Caller's Safety	___	n/a	✓	No Fear for Caller's Safety
Proximity to Victim	___	(n/a)	___	No Proximity to Victim
Initial Sounds or Comments	___	n/a	___	Initial Delays

Aggressive Demands ___   n/a   Passive Defenses:

___	Defendant Mentality	___	Ingratiating Remarks
___	Insults or Blames Victim	___	Mental Miscues
✓	Minimizes		

Cooperation with Dispatcher ___   n/a   Resistance to Dispatcher:

___	Dispatcher Confusion	___ Diversion	✓ Equivocation
✓	Evasion	___ Hangs Up	___ Only Answers What's Asked
___	Pauses	✓ Repetition	✓ Self-Interruption
___	Short Answers	___	Unintelligible Comments

Additional Guilty Indicators:

✓ Attempts to Convince	___ Awkward Phrases	___ Conflicting Facts	✓ "Huh?" Factor	___ I Don't Know		
✓ Isolated "Please"	✓ Lack of Contractions	___ No Modulation	___ Unexplained Knowledge			

Deputy Chief Tracy Harpster (Tracy.Harpster@gmail.com) **and Susan H. Adams, Ph.D.**

CASE STUDY #2   ANALYSIS

1. Dispatcher: *"911?"*
2. Caller: *"Help <u>me</u>, help."*

Although the caller made an immediate plea for help, the plea was for the caller and not for the victim, as would be expected. The caller had to be asked "What's going on?" before he mentioned his wife.

3. Dispatcher: *"What's going on?"*
4. Caller: *"<u>This is Bob Tuggs</u> in Trenton, a <u>log just fell on my wife</u>.*

Instead of prioritizing his wife and her circumstances, the caller relayed information in an Inappropriate Order. He first focused on himself again instead of the victim, using the Focus on Caller indicator. He did not provide an Immediate Assessment of the Victim ("she has a head/neck injury," "she is not breathing," "she has no pulse," "she is unconscious," "the log is still on her," etc.). The caller spoke in a soft, slow voice and exhibited No Modulation throughout the entire 911 call.

5. Dispatcher: *"What fell on her?"*
6. Caller: *"<u>A log</u>."*

The two-word response, *"A log,"* is the beginning of a Short Answer pattern. The caller offered no additional information.

7. Dispatcher: *"Okay, what is your address?"*
8. Caller: *(crying).*

The caller displayed Evasion by ignoring the dispatcher's critical question. This strategy delayed the arrival of medical aid.

9. Dispatcher: *"Is it 105?"*
10. Caller: *"...yes..."*
11. Dispatcher: *"Highway 73?"*
12. Caller: *"Yes (<u>four-second pause</u>). <u>Please</u>."*

The caller answered the dispatcher's question with a Short Answer and then used the Pause indicator followed by an Isolated Please. The caller displayed No Urgency.

| 13. Dispatcher: | *"And where is she bleeding from?"* |
| 14. Caller: | *"I don't know, there's a lot…(crying) oh God, I don't wanna look at her"* (crying). |

The caller used the I Don't Know Indicator, later providing information proving that he did know the source of the victim's bleeding.

| 15. Dispatcher: | *"How big of a log is it?"* |
| 16. Caller: | *"It's huge. Please."* |

The caller used another Isolated Please and continued with his Short Answers.

17. Dispatcher:	*"Okay, we got help, help is coming."*
18. Caller:	*"…what do I do?"*
19. Dispatcher:	*"You need to check and see if she's breathing, how big of a log is it? How big around?"*
20. Caller:	*"It's twenty inches, it's big."*
21. Dispatcher:	*"It's a big log, where did it land on her?"*
22. Caller:	*"Oh God, her neck's crushed, oh God (crying)…"*

The caller had provided No Immediate Assessment of the Victim's Condition. At the prompting of the dispatcher, he now revealed that he did know the location of the injury and therefore the source of the bleeding.

| 23. Dispatcher: | *"Stay on the phone with me, you need to, did you check and see if she's breathing."* |
| 24. Caller: | *"…help me."* |

The caller again gave a plea for help for himself and provided No Plea for Help for the Victim. His brief response was a continuation of the Short Answer indicator.

25. Dispatcher:	*"We got help coming okay, take a deep breath and-"*
26. Caller:	*"I can't hear you"* (crying).
27. Dispatcher:	*"Is she conscious?"*
28. Caller:	*"No."*

The caller used another Short Answer. After this answer, the caller could have expressed a demand for urgent help and added important victim details, which he did not.

29. Dispatcher: *"Can you check and can you get close enough to her to see if she's breathing?"*
30. Caller: *"<u>She's not</u>."*

The caller continued with his pattern of Short Answers.

31. Dispatcher: *"Okay, are you able to get close enough to give her some breaths?"*
32. Caller: *"Oh God, <u>no, no, no, no, no</u> (crying) <u>there's blood all over the floor</u>."*

The caller used the Repetition Indicator by stating the word *"no"* three or more times. He then added a trending indicator, Non Sequitur, when advising the dispatcher that he could not get close to the victim because *"there's blood all over the floor."* His illogical statement does not support his false contention because he could have easily stepped onto the blood to aid his dying wife. He also included a Blood/Brains Indicator.

33. Dispatcher: *"Okay."*
34. Caller: *"....Oh honey (crying) oh God."*
35. Dispatcher: *"Okay, we got help coming, is, is there any...can you get...wipe some of the blood off and start giving her rescue breaths?"*
36. Caller: (crying) *"<u>I can't get close to her...</u>"*
37. Dispatcher: *"You can't get close to her? You can't get to her face at all?"*
38. Caller: *"<u>I just can't look at her</u>."*
39. Dispatcher: *"Okay, is there any way you can get the log off of her?"*
40. Caller: *"Oh God, <u>it's big, I don't know</u>..."*
41. Dispatcher: *"Is there any way you can try and get something to ah lift it up just a little bit to take some of the pressure off?"*
42. Caller: *"<u>Oh</u>."*
43. Dispatcher: *"Can you pry the log up off of her?"*
44. Caller: *"Oh (crying) <u>I can't get that close to her</u>."*
45. Dispatcher: *"You're gonna have to try and help her."*
46. Caller: *"...<u>I'll try</u>...<u>I can't do it by myself, I'll have to use equipment</u>."*

The caller repeatedly Provided No Aid to the Victim and resisted the dispatcher's attempts to have him initiate CPR. The caller advised that he would "try" to aid the victim, which indicated that he had not made any attempts to help his wife to this point. Also, the caller informed the dispatcher that he would have to use equipment to help his wife. If the caller had access to equipment that could assist in aiding the victim he should have immediately used the machinery without being prompted. The caller used another Short Answer.

47. Dispatcher: *"Is it your wife?"*
48. Caller: *"Yes."*

The caller used the Short Answer indicator by providing answers of three words or less during more than 25% of the call.

49. Dispatcher: *"Okay. Can you go near her, are you able to do that and maybe try and get the snow out from underneath her?"*
50. Caller: *"No, we're in the shop, she's landed on the concrete floor."*

The caller chose the word "landed" during this exchange, which provided insight into what happened before the 911 call. "Landed" implied the victim was upright before the event and not lying on her stomach underneath a log on a brace as the caller later claimed.

51. Dispatcher: *"Is there a way you can put a, a, chain around the log and try and lift it up a little bit on one side?"*
52. Caller: *"I'd have to use a piece of equipment and I don't wanna touch it. I don't wanna touch it. I don't know what to do."*

For the second time, the caller advised that he had access to equipment that could be used to aid the victim; however, he resisted using the apparatus.

53. Dispatcher: *"The only thing you can do is try and get close to her and try and give her rescue breaths, OK?"*
54. Caller: *"She's not moving at all."*
55. Dispatcher: *"Is the log right on her neck, is it on her chest?"*
56. Caller: *"Oh God, the brace, (unintelligible) that we put the log on is on top of her neck."*

The caller repeated the No Aid Provided to Victim indicator by resisting the dispatcher's efforts to have him initiate CPR. The assertion that the victim was "not moving" should not preclude medical assistance. The caller previously stated that a log was on his wife. When asked a second time, he stated that a "brace" was on his wife, a Conflicting Fact. Further, the caller, who had spoken clearly up to this point in the 911 call, displayed the Unintelligible indicator midsentence on line 56.

Note that the caller shared the blame by including the victim as a participant of the event when stating "we" put the log on the brace.

57. Dispatcher: *"Oh."*
58. Caller: *"...somebody's coming, oh God...here they are..."*
59. Dispatcher: *"You got help?"*
60. Caller: *(crying) "<u>Help me</u>!" (crying).*
61. Dispatcher: *"Are they in the shop? I wanna know when they're in the shop."*
62. Caller: *"<u>Help me</u>" (crying). (Caller hangs up.)*

Although the caller cried for help there was no specific plea for help for the victim at this point or throughout the entire six minutes of the call. This call also Lacked Sensory Details.

The caller never stated that his wife had died; therefore, No Acceptance of Death was present in this call.

CASE STUDY #2   SUMMARY

One indicator of innocence and numerous indicators of guilt were present in this call.

When officers arrived at the scene, they observed the victim lying on the concrete floor, under the end of a 30-foot totem pole carved from a log. The caller and victim carved and painted totem poles and then sold them as a family business. The totem pole weighed approximately 700 pounds and had been resting on two braces that held the log 18 inches above the floor. The pole was held in place by a large chain that was attached to a Bob Cat, a heavy equipment machine used for lifting. The caller advised that his wife lay on the floor and "scooted" her head under the totem pole, when the chain slipped, causing the log to crush her head and neck. The caller showed great emotion at the scene when the officers arrived, and he screamed and yelled in apparent agony at what had occurred. This display was in contrast to the lack of modulation in his 911 call as the event transpired in real time. The caller could have simply used the heavy equipment already attached to the totem pole to aid his wife, but he resisted. He could have also lifted the end of the pole. A face was carved at the end of the totem pole with two protruding ears that the detective used as handles to raise the end of the totem pole; the weight of the entire pole did not need to be lifted. An autopsy revealed that the victim died of a skull fracture and brain trauma. X-rays of the skull revealed Mosaic (Spider Web) Fractures, which were not consistent with a crushing event. Mosaic Fractures are consistent with injuries from swinging weapons such as baseball bats.

The caller was initially cooperative but quickly obtained counsel when the detective's questions began to focus on him. He left the state and moved across the country. A search of the residence and the husband's computer revealed that the husband was meeting with prostitutes and had been emailing love letters to a sex worker, whom he later married. A year after the incident, the caller was arrested for murder and transported back to his home state. Eight months later, he was convicted of the victim's homicide.

Note: The caller did not remove the totem pole from the victim because he had gone to great lengths to stage the scene to resemble an accident. It benefited him to have the first responders observe, photograph, and articulate in the written police report their observations at the scene. If the husband had followed the dispatcher's directions and removed the pole, the alleged accident would have been supported only by his words.

The following COPS Scale reflects the indicators that are present in this call:

911 COPS Scale©

Considering Offender Probability in Statements

Place a check mark for any indicator that applies or circle n/a for not applicable

Innocent Indicators   Guilty Indicators

WHO is the call about?

Innocent		n/a		Guilty
Immediate Plea for Help for Victim	____	n/a	✓	No Immediate Plea for Help for Victim
Immediate Assessment of Victim	____	n/a	✓	No Immediate Assessment of Victim
Focus on Victim	____	n/a	✓	Focus on Caller
No Acceptance of Victim's Death	✓	n/a	____	Acceptance of Victim's Death
Aid Provided to Victim	____	n/a	✓	No Aid Provided to Victim

WHAT is the call about?

Relevant Information	____	n/a	____	Extraneous Information
Sensory Details	____	n/a	✓	Lack of Sensory Details
Prioritized Order	____	n/a	✓	Inappropriate Order
Bleeding Comments	____	n/a	✓	Blood/Brains Comments

HOW is the call made?

Urgency	____	n/a	✓	No Urgency
Fear for Caller's Safety	____	(n/a)	____	No Fear for Caller's Safety
Proximity to Victim	____	n/a	____	No Proximity to Victim
Initial Sounds or Comments	____	n/a	____	Initial Delays

Aggressive Demands n/a Passive Defenses:

____ Defendant Mentality ____ Ingratiating Remarks
____ Insults or Blames Victim ____ Mental Miscues
____ Minimizes

Cooperation with Dispatcher ____ n/a Resistance to Dispatcher:

____ Dispatcher Confusion ____ Diversion ____ Equivocation
✓ Evasion ____ Hangs Up ____ Only Answers What's Asked
✓ Pauses ____ Repetition ____ Self-Interruption
✓ Short Answers ✓ Unintelligible Comments

Additional Guilty Indicators:

____ Attempts to Convince ____ Awkward Phrases ✓ Conflicting Facts ____ "Huh?" Factor ✓ I Don't Know
✓ Isolated "Please" ____ Lack of Contractions ✓ No Modulation ____ Unexplained Knowledge

Deputy Chief Tracy Harpster (Tracy.Harpster@gmail.com) **and Susan H. Adams, Ph.D.**

CASE STUDY #3   ANALYSIS

1. Dispatcher: *"911."*
2. Caller: *"I need a, an ambulance* to 220 Court Street."

The caller stated an Immediate Plea for Help for the Victim.

3. Dispatcher: *"What's goin' on?"*
4. Caller: *"Uh, we got a girl, she fell down the stairs."*

The caller answered the dispatcher's question without resistance. It is interesting to note that the caller curiously referred to the victim with the generic word "girl," which does not clarify if the victim is a child, a teenager, or a woman, or if the relationship is with a friend, a girlfriend, or a stranger.

5. Dispatcher: *"How old is she?"*
6. Caller: *"Uh, she's about 36."*
7. Dispatcher: *"Is she breathing?"*
8. Caller: *"I don't know. I can't tell."*
9. Dispatcher: *"Okay. Can you check for me?"*
10. Caller: *"Yeah, my buddy's here. He's tryin' to check for a pulse and he says he don't feel it."*

The caller Focused on the Victim, Cooperated with the Dispatcher, and assisted in Aid Provided to the Victim.

11. Dispatcher: *"Okay."*
12. Caller: *"But we just picked her up and carried her home and she pissed all the way, all the way home here and, uh..."*

The caller volunteered Sensory Information regarding the victim's condition. Many victims of sudden trauma lose bladder control, and this information was pertinent and not an example of Insult or Blame.

13. Dispatcher: *"Where did she fall at?"*
14. Caller: *"Down the street at the neighbor's house."*
15. Dispatcher: *"Okay. Has she been drinking?"*
16. Caller: *"Yeah, she's drunk as fuck."*

The caller Cooperated with the Dispatcher by answering questions without delay, pauses, or resistance. The expression "drunk as fuck" is not an insult but a direct answer to the dispatcher's question that provided additional information about the level of intoxication.

17. Dispatcher: "Okay. Do you have her inside the house right now?"
18. Caller: "Yeah, I have her inside the doorway of the house right now."
19. Dispatcher: "Okay. Can you put your ear up to her, see if you can hear her breathing?"
20. Caller: "I don't hear her breathing, lady!"
21. Dispatcher: "You don't hear her breathing and she doesn't have a pulse?"
22. Caller: "NO AND HE DOESN'T FEEL A PULSE!"

The caller and the friend continued to Focus on the Victim and Cooperate with the Dispatcher. In addition, because the caller was near the victim, the Proximity Indicator was present. Despite the fact that the caller did not hear the victim breathing and did not feel a pulse, he expressed No Acceptance of Death.

23. Dispatcher: "Okay."
24. Caller: "And I'm call—I don't know what's goin' on here."

The caller used Self-interruption.

25. Dispatcher: "Okay. Are you comfortable doin' CPR until the ambulance gets there?"
26. Caller: (yells to male in background) "DO CPR THEY SAID ERIC!"
27. Dispatcher: "This is, is he, why don't you hand the phone to him and if he's willing to do CPR, I can walk him through it."
28. Caller: (talking to male in background) "Here. She's willing to do CPR to you."
29. (Phone disconnects. Sound of Dispatcher redialing phone number.)
30. Dispatcher: "Hold on. Just disconnected. He tried to give it to his buddy..." (sound of phone ringing).
31. Automated voice mail states: I'm sorry, but the person you called has a voicemail box that is..."
32. Dispatcher: "911."
33. Caller: "Yeah, I just called-"
34. Dispatcher: "Oh, okay."
35. Caller: "—and I accidentally hung up."

The caller was acting as a conduit between the dispatcher and the friend who was giving CPR. The dispatcher directed the caller to hand the phone to the friend doing the CPR, and as a result, the call was disconnected. The caller immediately called the dispatcher back, revealing that the disconnection was unintentional and not an example of the Hangs Up indicator.

36. Dispatcher: *"Okay. What's your name?"*
37. Caller: *"My name is Rick O'Neil."*

The caller did not hesitate to provide his full name to the dispatcher.

38. Dispatcher: *"All right. Is your friend willing to do CPR?"*
39. Caller: *"He's doing it right now."*
40. Dispatcher: *"Okay. I want you to put him on the phone. I'm gonna walk him through this."*
41. Caller: *(talking to male in background)* *"Here, she's gonna walk you through it, ERIC."*
42. Male #2:   *"No, I know what I'm doin'."*
43. Caller: *"He says he knows what he's doin'."*
44. Dispatcher: *"Okay. How does he know? Is he certified in CPR?"*
45. Caller: *"DO YOU HAVE AN AMBULANCE?"*

The caller continued to answer questions without resistance. He also continued to Focus on the Victim by yelling "DO YOU HAVE AN AMBULANCE?"

46. Dispatcher: *"There, yes. Sir, they're already on their way, okay?"*
47. Caller: *"Okay, because she's got blood comin' out of her nose and her mouth."*

The caller volunteered additional information and Sensory Details about the victim by alerting the dispatcher that the victim was "bleeding" from her nose and mouth. The caller's comment is a Condition of Victim Indicator/Bleeding Comments.

48. Dispatcher: *"Okay."*
49. Caller: *"And, I seen when he was blowing in her mouth. Her, her stomach was blowing up."*
50. Dispatcher: *"Okay. That's, that's good. We want…"*

In most cases, it is difficult to be certain if the caller (or other subjects at the scene) are actually doing CPR or faking the procedure to appear innocent. However, in this case, the caller's words added credibility to his assertion. When CPR is done correctly, the victim's chest rises and falls with each breath. When done incorrectly and air is forced into the abdomen, the stomach rises and falls. The caller voluntarily described what he was observing—CPR being done incorrectly. However, the fact that CPR was attempted at all is an innocent indicator. The caller provided Relevant Information throughout the call.

51. Caller: *"Yeah, I don't know what's goin' on here. I-"*
52. Dispatcher: *"Okay. Just..."*
53. Caller: *"-was home."*
54. Dispatcher: *"Is anyone else home with you at that address?"*
55. Caller: *"Her son is home but he's in bed."*
56. Dispatcher: *"Okay. How old is the son?"*
57. Caller: *"He's eighteen.* YOU GUYS GOTTA GET HERE QUICK!*"*

The caller answered the questions about the victim's son, and he Urgently and Aggressively Demanded help.

58. Dispatcher: *"They're...they're coming and we have law enforcement on the way, I want you to stay on the phone with me."*
59. Caller: *"You...can you tell 'em to come to the back door?"*
60. Dispatcher: *"Come to the back door? Okay."*
61. Caller: *"Yeah, 'cause she's in the back, at the back door."*

The caller asked the dispatcher to direct the first responders to the "back door," indicating that the caller was focused on getting aid to the victim as quickly as possible.

62. Dispatcher: *"Okay. He's doing chest compressions and he's breathing for her?"*
63. Caller: *"Yes, he's givin' her three breaths and OH, THE AMBULANCE IS HERE!"*
64. Dispatcher: *"The ambulance is there?"*
65. Caller: *"Should I get off the phone with you?"*
66. Dispatcher: *"Well, just...I think it's, uh...it's gonna be law enforcement that's there. Just go open the door and let them in, okay?"*
67. Caller: *"The door's open."*

The caller already had opened the door for the responders without being prompted, and he showed enthusiasm when help arrived.

| 68. Dispatcher: | *"You...you can disconnect with me."* |
| 69. Caller: | *"All right. Thank you."* |

The caller was provided a service from the dispatcher, and the "Thank you" comment at the end of the lengthy 911 call showed gratitude.

CASE STUDY #3   SUMMARY

All but one of the indicators were on the innocent side of the COPS Scale.

The victim was a 55-year-old alcoholic female. She had dated a man who lived next door in Eric's basement and who had committed suicide there. While walking a month prior to the 911 call, the victim was struck by a bicyclist, causing a floating rib fracture, which was untreated.

The caller met Rick in a local bar four days before the 911 call. Rick had been released from prison on that day after serving 10 years for murder. He was issued $50, one pair of jeans, and one shirt from the prison commissary. It took him only 30 minutes to drink $50 worth of alcohol, and he found himself penniless with no place to live. He met the victim at the bar and explained his dilemma, and the victim agreed to let Rick stay at her home temporarily.

On the one-year anniversary of her boyfriend's suicide, the victim carried a case of beer to Eric's house and headed to the basement to visit a shrine she had created in her boyfriend's memory. Eric heard a series of loud thuds and breaking glass and found the intoxicated victim lying awkwardly face down at the bottom of the stairs. Eric ran to the victim's home to get Rick, and the men carried the victim home by her arms and legs. On the way, the victim lost bladder control. Once inside the victim's residence, Eric began CPR and Rick called 911. The paramedics pronounced the victim dead at the scene.

When the police arrived, they discovered that Rick had a prior murder conviction and had only been out of prison for four days. Although Rick professed innocence, the police did not believe his truthful version of events, and he was arrested for the murder.

An autopsy revealed that the victim's floating rib fracture punctured her lung during the fall, and her awkward landing caused positional asphyxiation, thus creating additional oxygen depletion and resulting in her death. Rick, however, remained in jail pending the toxicology report. After three months, the toxicology report revealed that the victim's blood alcohol content was .29, with no evidence of drugs or poisons. The death was ruled accidental and Rick was finally released from jail. He subsequently filed a successful lawsuit against the police department and city.

After the full investigation, it became clear why Rick used the generic word "girl" to describe the victim. He had only known her for four days; she was not his girlfriend but simply a girl who offered him a place to stay.

It is noteworthy that Rick immediately provided both his first and last names to the dispatcher. He had just been released from prison after a negative law enforcement experience, yet this innocent caller did not hesitate to provide his full identity.

The following COPS Scale reflects the indicators that are present in this call:

911 COPS Scale ©

Considering Offender Probability in Statements

Place a check mark for any indicator that applies or circle n/a for not applicable

Innocent Indicators   ### Guilty Indicators

WHO is the call about?

Innocent Indicator			Guilty Indicator
Immediate Plea for Help for Victim	✓	n/a	___ No Immediate Plea for Help for Victim
Immediate Assessment of Victim	___	n/a	___ No Immediate Assessment of Victim
Focus on Victim	✓	n/a	___ Focus on Caller
No Acceptance of Victim's Death	✓	n/a	___ Acceptance of Victim's Death
Aid Provided to Victim	✓	n/a	___ No Aid Provided to Victim

WHAT is the call about?

Innocent Indicator			Guilty Indicator
Relevant Information	✓	n/a	___ Extraneous Information
Sensory Details	✓	n/a	___ Lack of Sensory Details
Prioritized Order	✓	n/a	___ Inappropriate Order
Bleeding Comments	✓	n/a	___ Blood/Brains Comments

HOW is the call made?

Innocent Indicator			Guilty Indicator
Urgency	✓	n/a	___ No Urgency
Fear for Caller's Safety	___	(n/a)	___ No Fear for Caller's Safety
Proximity to Victim	✓	n/a	___ No Proximity to Victim
Initial Sounds or Comments	___	n/a	___ Initial Delays

Aggressive Demands   ✓   n/a   Passive Defenses:

____ Defendant Mentality   ____ Ingratiating Remarks
____ Insults or Blames Victim ____ Mental Miscues
____ Minimizes

Cooperation with Dispatcher   ✓   n/a   Resistance to Dispatcher:

____ Dispatcher Confusion   ____ Diversion ____ Equivocation
____ Evasion ____ Hangs Up ____ Only Answers What's Asked
____ Pauses ____ Repetition ____ Self-Interruption
____ Short Answers   ____ Unintelligible Comments

Additional Guilty Indicators:

____ Attempts to Convince ____ Awkward Phrases ____ Conflicting Facts ____ "Huh?" Factor ____ I Don't Know
____ Isolated "Please" ____ Lack of Contractions ____ No Modulation ____ Unexplained Knowledge

Deputy Chief Tracy Harpster (Tracy.Harpster@gmail.com) and Susan H. Adams, Ph.D.

CASE STUDY #4   ANALYSIS

1. Dispatcher: *"911, what is the emergency?"*
2. Caller: <u>*"He's dead!"*</u>

The caller opened the call by expressing Acceptance of Death without providing an Immediate Assessment of the Victim to explain why the caller so quickly accepted the death. This is the beginning of a pattern of Short Answers.

3. Dispatcher: *"Hello."*
4. Caller: *"<u>I came home</u>."*

The caller added another short answer.

5. Dispatcher: *"Ma'am, where are you?"*
6. Caller: *"99 Center Road"* (crying).
7. Dispatcher: *"Ma'am, you need to calm down. What happened?"*
8. Caller: *"<u>I came home</u> my <u>husband is dead</u>"* (crying).

When asked "What happened?" for the first time, the caller used Inappropriate Order by immediately focusing on herself first instead of prioritizing what had happened to her husband. The caller used Acceptance of the Death for the second time and had a Lack of Contraction on line 8. The caller provided No Immediate Plea for Help for the Victim.

9. Dispatcher: *"You what?"*
10. Caller: *"My <u>husband is dead</u>"* (crying).

The caller again used the Lack of Contraction indicator and made no Immediate Plea for Help for the Victim and no Immediate Assessment of the Victim.

11. Dispatcher: *"OK. Ma'am. I'm going to have to ask you a couple questions, OK?"*
12. Caller: *"<u>OK</u>."*

Short Answers continue.

13. Dispatcher: *"What's the problem? Tell me exactly what happened."*

14. Caller: *"He's on the floor and <u>it looks like</u> somebody came in and robbed us. There's <u>stuff</u> everywhere. He has <u>blood under his head</u>" (crying).*

The caller inserted Equivocation twice more when she said "it looks like" and "stuff." She added the Blood/Brains Indicator at the end of the sentence instead of saying that he was "bleeding."

15. Dispatcher: *"OK. Are you with him right now? Ma'am?"*
16. Caller: *"<u>I'm in the hallway</u>."*

The caller used Evasion by not directly answering whether she was with the victim or not.

17. Dispatcher: *"OK. How old is he?"*
18. Caller: *"<u>He's 72</u>."*

The caller responded with another short answer.

19. Dispatcher: *"Is he conscious?"*
20. Caller: *"<u>No</u>" (sobbing).*

The caller's pattern of Short Answers continued throughout the call. These additional Short Answers will be underlined but not individually addressed.

21. Dispatcher: *"Is he breathing?"*
22. Caller: *"<u>No</u> (crying). God, <u>who would do this</u>?"*

The caller Only Answered What's Asked. By posing an unanswerable question to the dispatcher, the caller also used Diversion.

23. Dispatcher: *"Ma'am. We're gonna get you some help. Hold on, OK?"*
24. Caller: *"<u>OK</u>."*
25. Dispatcher: *"Did you see what happened?"*
26. Caller: *"No, I didn't. <u>I just got home from shopping</u>."*

The caller Minimized and ended with the Extraneous indicator by including the irrelevant information about her previous location.

27. Dispatcher: *"OK. Are you right by him now? Ma'am?"*
28. Caller: *"<u>I can go back</u>."*

The caller's own words indicate that she was not with the victim; therefore, the No Proximity to Victim indicator is present.

29. Dispatcher:	*"Let me know when you're by him."*	
30. Caller:	*"OK."*	
31. Dispatcher:	*"OK. Are you right by him now?"*	
32. Caller:	*"Yes."*	
33. Dispatcher:	*"OK, ma'am. Listen carefully. I need you to lay him flat on his back on the ground and remove any pillows."*	
34. Caller:	*"He's on his back."*	
35. Dispatcher:	*"OK. Is there anything in his mouth?"*	
36. Caller:	*"No. He..."*	
37. Dispatcher:	*"I need you to place your hand on his forehead and your other hand under his neck and then tilt his head back."*	
38. Caller:	*"He's all bloody."*	
39. Dispatcher:	*"He's all bloody?"*	
40. Caller:	*"Yeah."*	
41. Dispatcher:	*"Where is he bleeding from?"*	
42. Caller:	*"It looks like the back of his head."*	
43. Dispatcher:	*"He's bleeding from the back of his head. Ma'am, hold on, OK. Did you say everything is thrown around?"*	

Note that the caller said, "He's all bloody" but the dispatcher asked, "Where is he bleeding from?" The word "bleeding" reveals a focus on the victim's injuries, but "He's all bloody" may indicate resistance to performing CPR.

44. Caller:	*"Yeah, <u>it looks like</u> somebody's been through here"* (crying).
45. Dispatcher:	(over the radio) *"She said it looks like someone was in the house. Maybe a robbery."*

The caller used Equivocation by stating that "it looks like." If her husband had been assaulted and "stuff" was everywhere, an offender clearly had been there. The caller's comment that somebody's "been through here" is mild language to describe a homicide and robbery.

46. Dispatcher:	*"OK. Ma'am? We're gonna try to do CPR, OK?"*
47. Caller:	*"OK."*

Note: Short Answers are not counted when the caller is giving CPR because the caller's focus is on aiding the victim.

| 48. Dispatcher: | *"Can you feel or hear any breathing?"* |
| 49. Caller: | *"He's not, I checked, he's not breathing at all. He's gray."* |

If the caller had previously checked the victim's condition, this critical assessment should have been shared in line 2. However, if the caller only checked because of the dispatcher's prompting on line 48, her actions are not credible. Instead of taking time to check, she immediately responded with "I checked, he's not breathing at all." It would take several seconds to observe a victim to note whether the subject was breathing normally, breathing shallowly, or not breathing at all. The caller provided a Sensory Detail when she described the victim's color as "gray."

50. Dispatcher:	*"We're gonna try to help him, OK?"*
51. Caller:	*"OK."*
52. Dispatcher:	*"OK. We're gonna try to do compressions, all right?"*
53. Caller:	*"OK."*
54. Dispatcher:	*"If you need to put the phone down, it's OK. But just listen carefully. I'm gonna try to tell you how to do chest compressions."*
55. Caller:	*"OK"* (crying).
56. Dispatcher:	*"Place the heel of your hand on the breastbone in the center of his chest right between the nipples then put your other hand on top of that hand."*
57. Caller:	*"Uh-huh."*
58. Dispatcher:	*"OK. I need you to push down firmly two inches with only the heel of your lower hand touching the chest."*
59. Caller:	*"OK."*
60. Dispatcher:	*"Pump the chest hard and fast at least twice per second. You need to do this 400 times. That's only three and a half minutes."*
61. Caller:	*"OK"* (ten-second pause).
62. Caller:	(crying) *"It's not working."*
63. Dispatcher:	*"Ma'am, you just need to keep going, OK? They're on their way there, ma'am. Did you do this 400 times?"*
64. Caller:	*"I'm working on it. It isn't working"* (crying).

The caller advised that she was attempting CPR; therefore, the Aid Provided to the Victim is present.

| 65. Dispatcher: | *"The chest should rise with each breath."* |
| 66. Caller: | *"OK. I'm sorry. Hold on."* |

The caller used Ingratiating Remarks by informing the dispatcher "I'm sorry."

67.	Dispatcher:	*"Did you feel the air going in and out?"*
68.	Caller:	*"What?"*

Since the caller is attempting CPR and might be distracted, the "Huh?" Factor is not present on line 68.

69.	Dispatcher:	*"Did you feel any air going in and out?"*
70.	Caller:	*"He's cold."* (crying) The caller provided another Sensory Detail.
71.	Dispatcher:	*"OK. We've got to keep trying, ma'am."*
72.	Caller:	*"OK."*
73.	Dispatcher:	*"Is there anyone else there with you?"*
74.	Caller:	*"No. His mouth has—it's full of blood."*

The caller used another Self-interruption and a Blood Comment that may have been another way to resist performing CPR.

75.	Dispatcher:	*"His mouth is full of blood?"*
76.	Caller:	*"Yes."*
77.	Dispatcher:	*"We just need to continue to help him until they get there, ma'am."*
78.	Caller:	*"I'm working. I'm trying."*
79.	Dispatcher:	*"I know. You might have to blow through some of the blood, ma'am."*
80.	Caller:	*"Do what?"*

As noted previously, the caller said she was attempting CPR and she could have been distracted. The "Huh?" Factor therefore does not apply on line 80.

81.	Dispatcher:	*"You might have to, just clean out his mouth as best you can, but we might have to blow through some of the blood to get air into his body. Ma'am?"*
82.	Caller:	*"Yes."*
83.	Dispatcher:	*"OK, ma'am, what does it look like inside the house? You said there's stuff thrown around?"*
84.	Caller:	*"I haven't checked the other rooms, but in the kitchen, it looks like somebody's gone through the drawers and stuff and his wallet's on the floor (crying) and I haven't gone in any other rooms."*

The caller advised that she had not checked the residence; therefore, the offender could still be present in the home. The caller did not express any concern for her welfare, and thus No Fear for Caller's Safety is present. The caller Attempted to Convince the dispatcher that "it looks like" a burglary.

85.	Dispatcher:	*"Is he in the kitchen?"*
86.	Caller:	*"Yes."*
87.	Dispatcher:	*"OK. What's your name?"*
88.	Caller:	*"Isabelle."*

It is common for guilty callers to resist giving their full name when initially asked by the dispatcher.

89.	Dispatcher:	*"What's your last name, Isabelle?"*
90.	Caller:	*"Laird. L-A-I-R-D."*
91.	Dispatcher:	*"Ma'am. You want to try to keep doing CPR?"*
92.	Caller:	*"Yes."*
93.	Dispatcher:	*"OK. Keep going til they get there, ma'am. Don't give up."*
94.	Caller:	*(noises of CPR) (crying).*
95.	Caller:	*"Yes."*

The caller continued to cooperate with aid to the victim.

96.	Dispatcher:	*"Ma'am? What color is your house?"*
97.	Caller:	*"Um, there is (crying) ... They're here."*
98.	Dispatcher:	*"They're there?"*
99.	Caller:	*"They're here" (crying).*
100.	Dispatcher:	*"Somebody's there with her. Is it an officer?"*
101.	Caller:	*"Yes."*
102.	Dispatcher:	*"OK. I'm gonna let you go, ma'am. OK? Bye."*

The caller expressed No Urgency and she used the Short Answer indicator by answering questions with three words or less during more than 25% of the call.

CASE STUDY #4   SUMMARY

Most of the indicators noted in this call were guilty indicators.

One year after his wife died of cancer, the victim met the caller on a computer dating site. After a few dates, the caller learned that the victim was very wealthy, and she soon moved into the victim's house;

a short time later, the couple was married. The caller began to spend her new husband's money at a rapid rate. The victim's adult children were upset with the situation and confronted their father regarding their suspicions about the caller. Realizing their concerns and suffering from a depleting bank account, the victim promised his children that he would address the situation. One week later, he was dead on his kitchen floor.

The caller was initially cooperative with the police and advised that she had just come home from shopping to discover her husband "all bloody" on the floor. She quickly pulled a shopping receipt from her pocket to provide an alibi. She added that she was supposed to meet her husband for lunch and called him repeatedly; however, he never showed up at the restaurant. She directed the officers to the home answering machine and played nine messages to her husband to support her claim. All of the messages on the answering machine were similar in that they all expressed her "affection" for her husband ("Where are you Baby?" "I can't wait to see you at lunch, I love you so much!" and "I'm missing you baby, see you when you get here… love ya!").

Investigators began to focus on the caller after they analyzed her 911 call. They soon learned that someone had attempted to kill the victim a month earlier by setting his car on fire while he was inside. A financial analysis of the victim's bank accounts revealed that the caller had squandered most of his money and had assumed his deceased wife's identity to cash forged checks. The caller informed the investigators that suspicious cars were in the neighborhood, and the couple received threatening notes before her husband was murdered. She stated that the occurrences had not stopped and she was afraid for her safety. However, a surveillance video revealed that the caller had purchased the cards used to write the threatening notes and had placed them in her own mailbox.

The caller was eventually arrested and convicted of this husband's murder. She received the maximum punishment, life in prison for the offense.

As an interesting side note, the caller's first husband allegedly committed suicide eight months before she met her wealthy, new husband. In the first death, the caller claimed that her husband shot himself in the head as she lay beside him in bed.

The following COPS Scale reflects the indicators that are present in this call:

911 COPS Scale©

Considering Offender Probability in Statements

Place a check mark for any indicator that applies or circle n/a for not applicable

Innocent Indicators			Guilty Indicators

WHO is the call about?

Immediate Plea for Help for Victim	____	n/a	✓	No Immediate Plea for Help for Victim
Immediate Assessment of Victim	____	n/a	✓	No Immediate Assessment of Victim
Focus on Victim	____	n/a	____	Focus on Caller
No Acceptance of Victim's Death	____	n/a	✓	Acceptance of Victim's Death
Aid Provided to Victim	✓	n/a	____	No Aid Provided to Victim

WHAT is the call about?

Relevant Information	____	n/a	✓	Extraneous Information
Sensory Details	✓	n/a	____	Lack of Sensory Details
Prioritized Order	____	n/a	✓	Inappropriate Order
Bleeding Comments	____	n/a	✓	Blood/Brains Comments

HOW is the call made?

Urgency	____	n/a	✓	No Urgency
Fear for Caller's Safety	____	n/a	✓	No Fear for Caller's Safety
Proximity to Victim	____	n/a	✓	No Proximity to Victim
Initial Sounds or Comments	____	n/a	____	Initial Delays

Aggressive Demands ____   n/a   Passive Defenses:

____ Defendant Mentality   ✓ Ingratiating Remarks
____ Insults or Blames Victim ____ Mental Miscues
✓ Minimizes

Cooperation with Dispatcher ___   n/a   Resistance to Dispatcher:

____ Dispatcher Confusion   ✓ Diversion   ✓ Equivocation
✓ Evasion ____ Hangs Up ✓ Only Answers What's Asked
____ Pauses ____ Repetition ✓ Self-Interruption
✓ Short Answers   ____ Unintelligible Comments

Additional Guilty Indicators:

✓ Attempts to Convince ____ Awkward Phrases ____ Conflicting Facts ____ "Huh?" Factor ____ I Don't Know
____ Isolated "Please"   ✓ Lack of Contractions ____ No Modulation ____ Unexplained Knowledge

Deputy Chief Tracy Harpster (Tracy.Harpster@gmail.com) **and Susan H. Adams, Ph.D.**

CASE STUDY #5   ANALYSIS

1. Dispatcher: *"911?"*
2. Caller: (simultaneously yelling at another subject) *"I don't know what's happened, she's gone!"*

The caller did not delay or wait for the dispatcher to complete the first question. Instead, she exhibited the Initial Sounds or Comments Indicator.

3. Dispatcher: *"Can I help you?"*
4. Caller: *"Yes! We need, we need help at 3616 Sussex!"*

The caller gave an Immediate Plea for Help for the Victim.

5. Dispatcher: *"3616 what street?"*
6. Caller: *"SUSSEX!"*

The caller answered the dispatcher's question without delay. Note that the caller became angry because the dispatcher asked for the address to be repeated.

7. Dispatcher: *"What's the problem?"*
8. Caller: *"My, my daughter's gone! She's due in two weeks and my grandson's here alone and this whole house has been ransacked!"*

The caller immediately answered the dispatcher's question and then volunteered Relevant Information about the victim and the victim's home, which indicated that foul play was involved. The Prioritized Order resulted in the most serious problem listed first.

9. Dispatcher: *"How old is your-."*
10. Caller: *"My grandson is two."*
11. Dispatcher: *"...and he's gone?"*
12. Caller: *"He's here alone!"*

The caller answered the dispatcher even before the entire question was asked. The caller became agitated because the dispatcher was not tracking the problem.

13. Dispatcher: *"OK, you need to calm down so I can understand you!"*

14. Caller: *"I'm trying!"*
15. Dispatcher: *"OK."*
16. Caller: *"He's here alone and she's gone, her car's here..."*

The caller volunteered Relevant Information about the victim to again alert the dispatcher to the serious nature of the event.

17. Dispatcher: *"Who's gone?"*
18. Caller: *"MY DAUGHTER!"*

The caller was annoyed because the dispatcher was still not tracking who was the victim in the case.

19. Dispatcher: *"OK, how old is she?"*
20. Caller: *"She's twenty-seven years old."*
21. Dispatcher: *"OK, and how old is the child who was left alone?"*
22. Caller: *"She didn't leave him alone! My God! Something is wrong! She's due, she's due in two weeks! And she's just missing! Her car's here, her purse, and her house is trashed and she's not here!"*

The irate caller yelled at the dispatcher for not following the conversation and for insinuating that the victim was negligent for leaving a child alone. The caller Focused on the Victim and tried to make the dispatcher understand that a crime had occurred by providing Relevant Information about the victim and the condition of the scene. The caller did not accept the victim's death.

23. Dispatcher: *"OK, what's your name Ma'am?"*
24. Caller: *"My name is Tami Carter."*

The caller answered the dispatcher immediately, with her full name.

25. Dispatcher: *"Tami what?"*
26. Caller: *"CARTER! JUST GET SOMEBODY HERE NOW!."*
                    (sobbing)

The caller used an Aggressive Demand because the dispatcher was still not tracking vital information and not comprehending the serious nature of the event. The caller also expressed Urgency.

CASE STUDY #5   SUMMARY

All of the indicators in this call were on the innocent side of the COPS Scale.

The victim in this case was a 26-year-old female who had begun dating a police officer. The victim was unaware that the officer was already married with two children and had a third child with a different girlfriend. After dating for a few months, the victim became pregnant with the officer's child. She was shocked when he was not overjoyed with her news. Instead, he explained that someday they would have children, a house, and the picket fence, but now was not the right time. The officer asked the victim to consider an abortion so that they could be happy together down the road. The heartbroken victim refused his request.

Over the next few months, the officer continually pressed the victim to have an abortion with promises of marriage and a future together. In reality, the officer did not want a fourth child with additional child support deducted from his weekly paycheck. He increased the pressure on the victim and told her that he would break up with her unless she had the abortion. However, she was steadfast and refused. Finally, the officer told the victim "YOU WILL NOT HAVE THIS BABY!" The officer's words were prophetic because the victim was found stabbed to death in a ditch three hours after the victim's mother placed the 911 call.

The investigation revealed that the officer killed the victim and dumped her body. He was convicted of double murder: the murder of the victim and the victim's unborn child. The 911 caller in this case was innocent and had no knowledge of what had happened to her daughter when she placed the call.

The following COPS Scale reflects the indicators that are present in this call:

911 COPS Scale©

Considering Offender Probability in Statements

Place a check mark for any indicator that applies or circle n/a for not applicable

Innocent Indicators   **Guilty Indicators**

WHO is the call about?

Innocent Indicator	Check	n/a	Check	Guilty Indicator
Immediate Plea for Help for Victim	✓	n/a	___	No Immediate Plea for Help for Victim
Immediate Assessment of Victim	___	(n/a)	___	No Immediate Assessment of Victim
Focus on Victim	✓	n/a	___	Focus on Caller
No Acceptance of Victim's Death	✓	n/a	___	Acceptance of Victim's Death
Aid Provided to Victim	___	(n/a)	___	No Aid Provided to Victim

WHAT is the call about?

Innocent Indicator	Check	n/a	Check	Guilty Indicator
Relevant Information	✓	n/a	___	Extraneous Information
Sensory Details	___	(n/a)	___	Lack of Sensory Details
Prioritized Order	✓	n/a	___	Inappropriate Order
Bleeding Comments	___	(n/a)	___	Blood/Brains Comments

HOW is the call made?

Innocent Indicator	Check	n/a	Check	Guilty Indicator
Urgency	✓	n/a	___	No Urgency
Fear for Caller's Safety	___	n/a	___	No Fear for Caller's Safety
Proximity to Victim	___	(n/a)	___	No Proximity to Victim
Initial Sounds or Comments	✓	n/a	___	Initial Delays

Aggressive Demands   ✓   n/a   Passive Defenses:

____ Defendant Mentality   ____ Ingratiating Remarks
____ Insults or Blames Victim ____ Mental Miscues
____ Minimizes

Cooperation with Dispatcher   ____   n/a   Resistance to Dispatcher:

____ Dispatcher Confusion   ____ Diversion ____ Equivocation
____ Evasion ____ Hangs Up ____ Only Answers What's Asked
____ Pauses ____ Repetition ____ Self-Interruption
____ Short Answers   ____ Unintelligible Comments

Additional Guilty Indicators:

____ Attempts to Convince ____ Awkward Phrases ____ Conflicting Facts ____ "Huh?" Factor ____ I Don't Know
____ Isolated "Please" ____ Lack of Contractions ____ No Modulation ____ Unexplained Knowledge

Deputy Chief Tracy Harpster (Tracy.Harpster@gmail.com) **and Susan H. Adams, Ph.D.**

CASE STUDY #6   ANALYSIS

1. Dispatcher: *"911, what is your emergency?*
2. Caller: *"<u>Yes, ma'am, I've just been shot</u>, so have my parents."*

The caller began the call with an Initial Delay. He also used Inappropriate Order by focusing on himself first, although his injury was minor compared to that of his parents. Note: The word "just" is not considered to be an example of Minimizes because the comment is not regarding the caller's arrival on the scene.

3. Dispatcher: *"Where have you been shot at?"*
4. Caller: *"My leg..."*
5. Dispatcher: *"Who shot you?"*
6. Caller: *"I don't know."*
7. Dispatcher: *"You don't know who shot you? What kind of gun was it?"*
8. Caller: *"<u>Oh my God!" (moaning)</u>.*

The caller used the Evasion Indicator to avoid answering the question and gave No Immediate Plea for Help. Focus on the Caller continued and the caller provided No Immediate Assessment of his parents.

9. Dispatcher: *"Where were you shot at?"*
10. Caller: *"In my leg, in my groin."*
11. Dispatcher: *"Okay, where were your parents shot at?"*
12. Caller: *"<u>Possibly</u> in the head... <u>I don't know</u>. I'm sitting downstairs <u>trying—I don't know</u>, they're not moving, <u>I think they're dead</u>."*

The caller used the Equivocation word "possibly" to avoid the full commitment of knowing where his parents were shot. He then distanced himself further by denying this knowledge. After a Self-interruption, the second I Don't Know was a confusing phrase repeating his lack of knowledge about the location of the injuries that he maintained he had not witnessed, thus also revealing Unexplained Knowledge. The caller had No Proximity to his parents and No Aid was Provided to them. He ended the sentence with an Acceptance of Death of both parents. Although equivocal, the caller's last comment showed that his thoughts were on his parents' death, not their survival.

13. Dispatcher:	*"You have no idea who shot them?"*
14. Caller:	*"No, Ma'am"* (moaning).
15. Dispatcher:	*"How old <u>are you</u>?"*
16. Caller:	*"I'm 38!* Hurry.*"*

The caller finally expressed Urgency; however, it is unclear if it is intended for his critically injured parents or for himself.

17. Dispatcher:	*"They're hurrying. Is somebody inside your house? Where were they?"*
18. *Caller:*	*"Yes, they came in."*

The caller's description of the event "they came in" reveals there was no forced entry. The caller followed the dispatcher's lead by advising "they" came in, indicating that there was more than one offender.

19. Dispatcher:	*"You're at 1101 Cherokee Hill? Right?"*
20. Caller:	*"Yes, Ma'am"* (moaning).
21. Dispatcher:	*"What did they look like?"*
22. Caller:	*"<u>One person</u> with a gun, mask, <u>I don't know</u>. I didn't see him, I just heard shots and went upstairs and I got shot and I turned around and ran. Oh my god!"* (moaning).

The caller changed from "they" to "one person" which is the Conflicting Facts indicator. He also stated that the person had a gun and a mask but added the Conflicting Fact that he did not see the offender.

23. Dispatcher:	*"OK, is anybody else in the house?"*
24. Caller:	<u>*"No Ma'am."*</u>

The caller could not know for certain that the suspect(s) had left; therefore he possessed Unexplained Knowledge. He also had No Fear for His Own Safety although the offender(s) could still be present.

25. Dispatcher:	*"Have you been having any kind of problems with anybody?"*
26. Caller:	*"Not that I'm aware of…(moaning) Oh God! <u>Please</u>!"*

The caller continued using moaning sounds and followed with the Isolated Please indicator.

27. Dispatcher: *"Where is your mom and dad at?"*
28. Caller: *"My <u>mom was upstairs</u> and my dad's on the stairs."*

If the mom was upstairs and he turned and ran when he heard the shots, he would not know that she is not moving (line 12), where she had been shot, or if she was deceased, thus revealing Unexplained Knowledge.

29. Dispatcher: *"They're both on the stairs?"*
30. Caller: <u>*"Oh…God."*</u>

The caller used the Evasion indicator to evade the dispatcher's question.

31. Dispatcher: *"Your mom and dad were both shot in the head?"*
32. Caller: <u>*"I'm sorry, what?"*</u>

The caller expressed Ingratiating Remarks followed by the "Huh?" Factor.

33. Dispatcher: *"They're both shot in the head?"*
34. Caller: *"My dad was shot in the head, I don't know where my mom is."*

On line 12, the caller stated that both his parents may have been shot in the head. He now states clearly that his dad was shot in the head.

35. Dispatcher: *"OK."*
36. Caller: *"I can't walk."*
37. Dispatcher: *"What room are you in?"*
38. Caller: *"I'm downstairs in the den."*
39. Dispatcher: *"This just happened, right?"*
40. Caller: <u>*"I'm sorry, what?"*</u>

The caller used an Ingratiating Remark and the "Huh?" Factor for the second time.

41. Dispatcher: *"This just happened?"*
42. Caller: *"Yes, Ma'am."*
43. Dispatcher: *"And how did they get into the house?"*
44. Caller: *"All the doors are unlocked, <u>I guess</u>, I don't know."*

The caller used Equivocation.

45. Dispatcher:	"*When did you discover that they were shot? Did you hear it?*"
46. Caller:	"*I heard a shot upstairs, he and I both got up, I saw him go down and I got shot and I turned around and ran down here.*" *(moaning)*

The caller stated that he heard a shot upstairs (presumably his mother being shot) and he mentioned the third shot (his injury) but he did not mention the second shot (the father). The caller continued to use moaning sounds when asked specific questions about the event.

47. Dispatcher:	"*You have no description of what he looked like, if he was a male?*"
48. Caller:	"*I have no idea. I'm <u>guessing</u> it was a man....*" *(moaning)*

The caller used Equivocation and continued with the moaning sounds when asked specific questions about the suspect(s).

49. Dispatcher:	"*Was he wearing a mask or anything?*"
50. Caller:	"*Yes, Ma'am, all I saw was the back. It looked like a hat.*"
51. Dispatcher:	"*A mask or a hat?*"
52. Caller:	"*Like a mask.*" *(moaning)*
53. Dispatcher:	"*Was it black?*"
54. Caller:	"<u>*Yes, Ma'am. I don't know what color.*</u>"

If the caller possessed any knowledge about the offender(s)' description, he should have immediately volunteered that information at the beginning of the call. However, the dispatcher was forced to extract the information bit by bit during this section. The Conflicting Facts continued, because on line 24 the caller described an offender with a mask, but on line 50 he claimed to only see the back, with no explanation of why he thought it was a mask.

On line 52, the caller continued to use the "moaning strategy" when asked specific questions about the event. On line 54, the caller used the I Don't Know indicator when asked if the mask was black. Yet he had already agreed that the mask was black.

55. Dispatcher:	"*Was he a heavy build, thin build?*"
56. Caller:	"<u>*I'm sorry, what?*</u>"

The caller responded with an Ingratiating Remark and then used the "Huh?" Factor.

57. Dispatcher:	*"Heavy build?"*
58. Caller:	*"No, not fat."*
59. Dispatcher:	*"Was he like an average build?"*
60. Caller:	*"Ma'am, I don't know." (moaning)*

Once again, the caller began to moan when asked specific questions about the offender.

61. Dispatcher:	*"OK."*
62. Caller:	*(moaning)* "please hurry!"

The caller again expressed Urgency, although he did not specify if the urgency was for himself or his parents or both.

63. Dispatcher:	*"Are you sure no one else is in the house?"*
64. Caller:	*"There's no one that I know of."*

The dispatcher expressed concern for the caller's safety; however, the caller exhibited No Fear for the Caller's Safety.

65. Dispatcher:	*"Did he run back out the door?"*
66. Caller:	*"I don't know Ma'am...." (moaning)*

Once again, moaning resumed when asked about the offender(s).

67. Dispatcher:	*"Will there be any cars in the driveway?"*
68. Caller:	*"I'm sorry, what?"*

The caller added Ingratiating Remarks and used another "Huh?" Factor.

69. Dispatcher:	*Do you know if it was like a shotgun or handgun?"*
70. Caller:	*"I don't know, Ma'am, I ran..." (moaning)*

The caller continued his moaning response when asked about the weapon.

71. Dispatcher:	*"Have you checked your mom and dad or are you not able to get to them?"*
72. Caller:	*"Oh God,"*

The caller again used Evasion as a resistance technique.

73. Dispatcher:	*"We have an officer there. Is he inside?"*
74. Caller:	*"He is, I think."*
75. Dispatcher:	*"They are there, I'm going to let you go now."*
76. Caller:	*"OK, bye Ma'am."*

CASE STUDY #6   SUMMARY

All but one of the indicators were on the guilty side of the COPS Scale.

When officers arrived on scene they located the caller's father on the basement steps. He had been shot in the back of the head and was killed immediately. The 911 caller was lying on the basement floor crying, moaning, and holding his groin. The caller had been shot in the right thigh causing a grazing wound to the upper leg. However, the bullet passed through his thigh and struck the caller's right testicle, dissecting it from his body. Officers discovered the caller's mother deceased in her bedroom. She was seated at a computer with a gunshot wound to the back of her head. The 911 caller stated that an unknown intruder entered the home, shot his parents, and shot him as he struggled with the assailant. During the interview, the caller changed his story and stated that his parents were arguing and his father killed his mother and then shot him. He said he was able to get the gun away from his father and he shot him in self-defense. Later, he added to his story by asserting that after his father shot his mother and he shot his father in self-defense, he panicked and shot himself so he would not be a suspect.

The caller was convicted of the murder of both parents and sentenced to life in prison. It is interesting to note that on line 57, the dispatcher asked the caller if the suspect had a "heavy build" and the caller, without moaning, immediately replied "No, not fat." The slightly overweight caller was curiously supportive of the offender.

The following COPS Scale reflects the indicators that are present in this call:

911 COPS Scale ©

Considering Offender Probability in Statements

Place a check mark for any indicator that applies or circle n/a for not applicable

Innocent Indicators			Guilty Indicators

WHO is the call about?

Immediate Plea for Help for Victim	____	n/a	✓	No Immediate Plea for Help for Victim
Immediate Assessment of Victim	____	n/a	✓	No Immediate Assessment of Victim
Focus on Victim	____	n/a	✓	Focus on Caller
No Acceptance of Victim's Death	____	n/a	✓	Acceptance of Victim's Death
Aid Provided to Victim	____	n/a	✓	No Aid Provided to Victim

WHAT is the call about?

Relevant Information	____	n/a	____	Extraneous Information
Sensory Details	____	n/a	____	Lack of Sensory Details
Prioritized Order	____	n/a	✓	Inappropriate Order
Bleeding Comments	____	n/a	____	Blood/Brains Comments

HOW is the call made?

Urgency	✓	n/a	____	No Urgency
Fear for Caller's Safety	____	n/a	✓	No Fear for Caller's Safety
Proximity to Victim	____	n/a	✓	No Proximity to Victim
Initial Sounds or Comments	____	n/a	✓	Initial Delays

Aggressive Demands	____	n/a		Passive Defenses:

____ Defendant Mentality   ✓ Ingratiating Remarks
____ Insults or Blames Victim ____ Mental Miscues
____ Minimizes

Cooperation with Dispatcher	____	n/a		Resistance to Dispatcher:

____ Dispatcher Confusion   ____ Diversion ✓ Equivocation
✓ Evasion ____ Hangs Up ____ Only Answers What's Asked
____ Pauses ____ Repetition ✓ Self-Interruption
____ Short Answers   ____ Unintelligible Comments

Additional Guilty Indicators:

____ Attempts to Convince ____ Awkward Phrases ✓ Conflicting Facts ✓ "Huh?" Factor ✓ I Don't Know
✓ Isolated "Please" ____ Lack of Contractions ____ No Modulation ✓ Unexplained Knowledge

Deputy Chief Tracy Harpster (Tracy.Harpster@gmail.com) **and Susan H. Adams, Ph.D.**

CASE STUDY #7   ANALYSIS

1. Caller: *(heavy breathing)*
2. Dispatcher: *"9-1-1, What is-"*
3. Caller: *"PLEASE COME QUICK MY WIFE SHOT HERSELF!"*

The caller uttered Initial Sounds before the dispatcher even finished the opening question. He gave an Immediate Plea for Help for the Victim while quickly providing an Immediate Assessment of Victim. The caller also expressed Urgency.

4. Dispatcher: *"Where are you at?"*
5. Caller: *"41 CRAIN. SHE'S STILL BREATHING PLEASE HELP!"*

The caller Focused on the Victim, had No Acceptance of Death Indicator, and gave a second Plea for Help. The caller shared the most critical information first, in Prioritized Order.

6. Dispatcher: *"Okay, hold on hold on. It's your wife?"*
7. Caller: *"YES YES! (crying) She's still breathing, please help her" (sobbing)*

The caller expressed a third Plea for Help for the Victim. He shared Relevant Information with the dispatcher.

8. Dispatcher: *"Attention Ambulance Crew, please respond to 41 Crain, have a report of a female that has shot herself; she is still breathing."*
9. Caller: *"Please hurry, please, please help."*

The caller continued to use Urgency. Although he used the word "please," it was not Isolated; it was in conjunction with his urgent plea for help.

10. Dispatcher: *"Is she breathing fine?"*
11. Caller: *"Hardly, she's just gurgling. Please help!"*

The caller continued to Focus on the Victim and added a Sensory Detail referring to the sound of "gurgling."

12. Dispatcher:	*"Okay, as long as she is still breathing, then we won't need to do CPR."*
13. Caller:	*(crying)*
14. Dispatcher:	*"Where did she shoot herself at?"*
15. Caller:	*(crying) "In the head. (sobbing) Oh, God."*

The caller provided replies without resistance or equivocation.

16. Dispatcher:	*"Okay, okay, the officers should be there in just one moment, okay."*
17. Caller:	*(sobbing) "Oh, my God. Oh, my God."*
18. Dispatcher:	*"Okay, did she shoot herself like in the front of head or in the back of the head?"*
19. Caller:	*"I can't tell, it's not in the front, I can see her face."*

The caller is clearly near the victim; therefore, the Proximity Indicator is present. Regarding where the victim shot herself, even experienced officers cannot always determine entrance and exit wounds, and it would not be expected that the caller would know this information.

20. Dispatcher:	*"Okay. Do you maybe want to step out of the room?"*
21. Caller:	*"NOOO I can't leave her!"*
22. Dispatcher:	*"Okay, hold on."*
23. Caller:	*"I can't leave her. (crying) God, oh my God, Please get help."*

The caller refused to leave the victim, further displaying the Proximity indicator.

| 24. Dispatcher: | *"Attention Ambulance Crew, please respond to 41 Crain, report of a female who has shot herself. She is still breathing."* |
| 25. Caller: | *"HURRY!"* |

The caller expressed Urgency by yelling "HURRY!" while the dispatcher was alerting the medic crews. The caller used no pauses during this time period or at any other time during the 911 call.

| 26. Dispatcher: | *"Do you see an officer. Is your front door open?"* |
| 27. Caller: | *"No it's not, it's locked."* |

28. Dispatcher: *"Okay, can you go to the front door and unlock it."*
29. Caller: *"Yes. Yes.* IS SOMEBODY HERE?"

The caller showed Cooperation with Dispatcher by following the dispatcher's instructions in order to expedite aid for the victim.

30. Dispatcher: *"Do you got the front door unlocked?"*
31. Caller: *"Yes, the front door's unlocked."*
32. Dispatcher: *"Okay. What is your name?"*
33. Caller: *"Kevin Springer."*

The caller did not hesitate to provide his first and last name to the dispatcher.

34. Dispatcher: *"What?"*
35. Caller: *"SPRINGER!"*

The caller did not attempt to ingratiate himself with the dispatcher and instead became agitated when the dispatcher was not attentive.

36. Dispatcher: *"And they should be coming just shortly, okay. Do you see the officers outside the door?"*
37. Caller: (crying) *"Noooo. Nobody. There's nobody here!"*

The caller was upset that help had not arrived.

38. Dispatcher: *"Okay, I am going to set the phone down for one moment, okay?"*
39. Caller: *"All right. (sobbing) Please help!"*
40. Dispatcher: *"Kevin, Kevin, Kevin, do you see the officers at the front door?"*
41. Caller: (directed to dispatcher) *"YES! (sobbing). (directed toward first responder) Please help her, she's not moving, I came in here and grabbed her."*
42. Officer: *"Were you here?"*
43. Caller: *"No, she sent me to the store. Please help"* (crying).

The caller continued to Cooperate and answer questions by replying to the first responder without resistance.

CASE STUDY #7   SUMMARY

All of the callers' indicators were innocent indicators.

The husband in this case was innocent of his wife's death, and he cooperated fully with law enforcement. Officers found a handwritten suicide note from the victim apologizing for the act. The scene was "clean" and logical, and the coroner ruled the death a suicide after learning that the victim had gunshot residue on her sleeve, hand, and face. The victim had purchased the handgun one week earlier, and the gun store video revealed that she entered the store and purchased the gun alone. The toxicology analysis indicated no drugs or alcohol.

The following COPS Scale reflects the indicators that are present in this call:

911 COPS Scale©

Considering Offender Probability in Statements

Place a check mark for any indicator that applies or circle n/a for not applicable

Innocent Indicators			Guilty Indicators

WHO is the call about?

Innocent	Check	n/a	Guilty Check	Guilty
Immediate Plea for Help for Victim	✓	n/a	___	No Immediate Plea for Help for Victim
Immediate Assessment of Victim	✓	n/a	___	No Immediate Assessment of Victim
Focus on Victim	✓	n/a	___	Focus on Caller
No Acceptance of Victim's Death	✓	n/a	___	Acceptance of Victim's Death
Aid Provided to Victim	___	n/a	___	No Aid Provided to Victim

WHAT is the call about?

Innocent	Check	n/a	Guilty Check	Guilty
Relevant Information	✓	n/a	___	Extraneous Information
Sensory Details	✓	n/a	___	Lack of Sensory Details
Prioritized Order	✓	n/a	___	Inappropriate Order
Bleeding Comments	___	n/a	___	Blood/Brains Comments

HOW is the call made?

Innocent	Check	n/a	Guilty Check	Guilty
Urgency	✓	n/a	___	No Urgency
Fear for Caller's Safety	___	(n/a)	___	No Fear for Caller's Safety
Proximity to Victim	✓	n/a	___	No Proximity to Victim
Initial Sounds or Comments	✓	n/a	___	Initial Delays

Aggressive Demands	✓	n/a	Passive Defenses:

___ Defendant Mentality	___ Ingratiating Remarks
___ Insults or Blames Victim	___ Mental Miscues
___ Minimizes	

Cooperation with Dispatcher	✓	n/a	Resistance to Dispatcher:

___ Dispatcher Confusion	___ Diversion	___ Equivocation
___ Evasion ___ Hangs Up	___ Only Answers What's Asked	
___ Pauses ___ Repetition	___ Self-Interruption	
___ Short Answers	___ Unintelligible Comments	

Additional Guilty Indicators:

___ Attempts to Convince	___ Awkward Phrases	___ Conflicting Facts	___ "Huh?" Factor	___ I Don't Know
___ Isolated "Please"	___ Lack of Contractions	___ No Modulation	___ Unexplained Knowledge	

Deputy Chief Tracy Harpster (Tracy.Harpster@gmail.com) **and Susan H. Adams, Ph.D.**

Appendix B:
Glossary of Terms

Note: The CAPITALIZED terms were used more often by innocent callers in the 911 study and the **bolded** terms were used more often by guilty callers.

Acceptance of Death: Stating that victims were dead when their actual conditions would not necessarily be known.

AGGRESSIVE DEMANDS: Loud and forceful commands to expedite aid to the victims.

AID PROVIDED TO VICTIM: Helping the victims with medical or other aid.

Apology to Victim: Apologizing to the victims while on the phone with the dispatchers.

Asking Permission: Requesting consent to provide aid to victims.

Attempts to Convince: Statements repeated three or more times in an effort to persuade the dispatchers of themes such as "The house has been ransacked."

Awkward Phrases: Confusing and clumsy phrases used to respond to dispatchers' questions or to comment on the scene.

BLEEDING COMMENTS/CONDITION OF VICTIM: Describing the victims' injuries ("bleeding from his eye").

Blood and Brains Comments/Condition of Scene: Describing the scene ("blood on floor," "brains on couch").

Calling Another: Advising that previous phone calls were made before calling 911.

Condition of Scene/Blood and Brains Comments: Describing the scene ("blood on floor," "brains on couch").

CONDITION OF VICTIM/BLEEDING COMMENTS: Describing the victims' injuries ("bleeding from his eye").

Conflicting Facts: Information that conflicts with information previously provided.

COOPERATION WITH DISPATCHER: Following the dispatchers' instructions to provide information or take actions to aid the victims.

Defendant Mentality: Comments associated with guilty individuals, such as, "Am I going to jail?"

Dispatcher as Witness: Narration shared with the dispatchers as if the callers were discovering the victims for the first time.

Dispatcher Confusion: Callers' use of resistance techniques resulting in dispatchers' failure to comprehend the situations.

Diversion: A form of resistance that redirects dispatchers' questions.

Equivocation: Vague or ambiguous terms ("kind of," "something," "maybe").

Evasion: A form of resistance by repeating the dispatchers' question, answering a different question, providing a partial or confusing answer, screaming or crying instead of answering, or substituting distracting noises for answers.

Extraneous Information: Irrelevant information that does not assist the victims.

Eyes Comments: Spontaneous statements describing the victims' eyes ("He's staring at me.").

FEAR FOR CALLERS' SAFETY: Rational fear that offenders might still be present and might pose a threat.

Focus on Caller: Placing attention on the callers instead of the victims, accompanied by frequent use of the pronoun "I."

FOCUS ON THE VICTIM: Placing attention on the victims and their needs.

Freudian Slips: Accidentally using a word that reveals callers' subconscious thoughts.

Hangs Up: Disconnection by the callers, particularly during difficult questions; the ultimate resistance technique.

"Huh?" Factor: Confused response indicating that the callers found it difficult to track their own false narratives ("Huh?" "What?" "Eh?").

"I Don't Know": Initial claim of ignorance by using the phrase "I Don't Know" followed or preceded by information indicating that callers did "know."

IMMEDIATE ASSESSMENT OF VICTIM: Providing a description of the victims' injuries at the earliest logical opportunity.

IMMEDIATE PLEA FOR HELP FOR VICTIM: Demanding help for the victim at the earliest logical opportunity.

Inappropriate Order: Sharing information most important to the caller (alibi information, exculpatory information) before information most important to the victims.

Ingratiating Remarks: Overly polite language for emergency situations.

Initial Delays: Slow and unnecessary words at the beginning of the call that delay getting help to the victims.

INITIAL SOUNDS OR COMMENTS: Noises or words by the callers before the dispatchers completed their opening question.

Insults or Blames Victim: Verbally insulting or blaming critically injured victims.

Isolated "Please": Use of the word "please" without an accompanying plea.

Lack of Contractions: Wasting time by pronouncing full words instead of common contractions, as in "My wife is not breathing."

Lack of Sensory Details: Failure to spontaneously share sensory details with the dispatcher.

Mental Miscues: Verbal expressions of thoughts that callers did not intend to reveal, including Freudian Slips and Non Sequiturs.

Minimizes: Attempts to reduce one's culpability in the homicide by stating, "I <u>just</u> got out of work" or "I <u>only</u> just walked in."

Nervous Laughter: Weak, inappropriate laughter that reveals callers' anxiety.

NO ACCEPTANCE OF DEATH: Refusal to accept the deaths of the victims.

No Aid Provided to Victim: Failure to assist the victims with medical or other aid.

No Fear for Own Safety: Ignoring possible threats by offenders because the callers are the offenders.

No Immediate Assessment of Victim: Failure to provide a description of the victims' injuries at the earliest logical opportunity.

No Immediate Plea for Help for Victim: Failure to demand help for the victims at the earliest logical opportunity.

No Modulation: Speaking in flat, unemotional, or robotic tones.

No Proximity to Victim: Physical distance from the victims.

No Urgency: No demands by callers to speed up the medical response.

Non Sequiturs: Illogical statements that attempt to support callers' false claims.

Only Answers What's Asked: Resistance technique in which callers confine their answers strictly to the question asked, without volunteering information.

Passive Defenses: Comments revealing that callers are being guarded and defensive, including the following: Defendant Mentality, Ingratiating Remarks, Insults or Blames Victim, Mental Miscues, and Minimizes. (Note: Each subtopic is defined individually.)

Pauses: A form of resistance in which callers remain silent for three seconds or more while waiting for the dispatcher's next question.

Possession of a Problem: Taking ownership of a problem ("I have a...").

PRIORITIZED ORDER: Sharing important victim information before other noncritical information.

PROXIMITY TO VICTIM: Remaining physically near the victims to offer help.

Recounting Dialogue: Callers provide previous dialogues with victims on topics other than victim's health.

RELEVANT INFORMATION: Information that answers the questions Who? What? Where? When? and How? concerning the victims and the victims' injuries.

Repetition: A form of resistance in which callers repeat words or phrases three or more times in response to the dispatchers' questions.

Resistance to Dispatcher: Techniques to withhold the truth: Dispatcher Confusion, Diversion, Equivocation, Evasion, Hangs Up, Only Answers What's Asked, Pauses, Repetition, Self-interruption, Short Answers, or Unintelligible Comments. (Note: Each subtopic is defined individually.)

Self-interruption: Resistance technique of editing comments by stopping midword or midsentence to change the direction of the statement.

SENSORY DETAILS: Providing sensory details such as sight, sound, smell, touch, or taste without prompting by the dispatcher.

Short Answers: A form of resistance in which callers provide minimum information by answering with three words or less in at least 25% of the call.

Trending Indicators: Indicators that were trending toward guilt but were found in too few cases to use in predicting the likelihood of innocence or guilt. The Trending indicators include the following: Apology to Victim, Asking Permission, Calling Another, Dispatcher as Witness, Eyes Comments, Nervous Laughter, Possession of Problem, and Recounting Dialogue. (Note: Each subtopic is defined individually.)

Unexplained Knowledge: Revealing details about the victims or scenes that innocent callers would not have known.

Unintelligible Comments: A form of resistance in which callers speak with incoherent words or their voices trail off until their words are inaudible.

URGENCY: Demands by callers to speed up the medical response without prompting by the dispatcher.

Index

About the Authors

Deputy Chief Tracy Harpster and Dr. Susan H. Adams have assisted over 500 homicide detectives with their homicide cases, and they share their research at national and international conferences. They coauthored "911 Homicide Calls: Is the Caller the Killer?" published in the *Law Enforcement Bulletin* (2008); "Analyzing 911 Homicide Calls for Indicators of Guilt or Innocence: An Exploratory Analysis," with John Jarvis, published in *Homicide Studies* (2009); and "Is the Caller the Killer? Analyzing 911 Homicide Calls," published in the book *Behavior, Truth and Deception* by Michael Napier (2010). The authors also contributed to Vernon Geberth's *Practical Homicide Investigation* (fifth edition, 2015). Deputy Chief Harpster and Dr. Adams are members of the Vidocq Society, a nonprofit group of forensic professionals who offer their services to help solve cold case homicides.

Deputy Chief Tracy Harpster has served with the Moraine Police Department in Ohio since 1984. He has worked as a street officer, undercover narcotics officer, sergeant, detective sergeant, operations lieutenant, and deputy chief. He was a task force director in the Ohio Organized Crime Investigations Commission, investigating large-scale RICO, theft, money laundering, and gambling crimes. Deputy Chief Harpster was later assigned to the FBI Joint Terrorism Task Force in Dayton, Ohio and also served as the director of the Tactical Crime Suppression Unit Narcotics Task Force.

Deputy Chief Harpster received a BS degree in criminal justice from Bowling Green State University and is a graduate of the 216th Session of the Federal Bureau of Investigation National Academy, Quantico, Virginia. He received his MS degree from the University of Cincinnati. His thesis examined the indicators of innocence and guilt of 911 homicide callers, a topic that he teaches nationally.

Dr. Susan H. Adams, a retired FBI agent, is an international speaker and author in investigative interviewing
techniques. She has taught in Vienna, Prague, Edinburgh,
Ottawa, Toronto, and throughout the United States. Her
work appears in over a dozen international journals, books,
and law enforcement publications. As an instructor at the
FBI Academy, Dr. Adams taught investigative interviewing and statement analysis to National Academy police
officers and FBI agents. She currently teaches criminal justice at the Graduate School of the University of Maryland
University College.

Dr. Adams earned her PhD degree in human development from Virginia
Tech and received the University of Virginia's Jefferson Award for Excellence
in Research for her study examining indicators of veracity and deception in
written statements provided to law enforcement.